I0211280

Legacy of Faith
collection

Norvel Hayes

TEACHER OF
SUPERNATURAL LIVING

Harrison House
Tulsa, Oklahoma

Unless otherwise indicated, all Scripture quotations are taken from the *King James Version* of the Bible.

Scripture quotations marked AMP are taken from *The Amplified Bible, New Testament.* copyright © 1958, 1987 by the Lockman Foundation, La Habra, California. Used by permission.

Scripture quotations marked NKJV are taken from the *New King James Version,* copyright © 1979, 1980, 1982, Thomas Nelson, Inc. Publishers. Used by permission. All rights reserved.

Scripture quotations marked NIV are taken from the *Holy Bible, New International Version*®. NIV®. copyright © 1973, 1978, 1984 by International Bible Society. Used by permission of Zondervan Publishing House. All rights reserved.

Scripture quotations marked NLT are taken from the *Holy Bible, New Living Translation,* copyright © 1996, 2004. Used by permission of Tyndale House Publishers, Inc., Carol Stream, Illinois 60188. All rights reserved.

Scripture quotations marked TLB are taken from *The Living Bible Paraphrase* by Kenneth N. Taylor, copyright ©1974. Used by permission of Tyndale House Publishers, Inc., Carol Stream, Illinois 60188. All rights reserved.

Scripture quotations marked RSV are taken from the *Holy Bible, Revised Standard Version,* copyright © 1974 by Plume Publishers, a division of Penguin Group, Inc., New York, New York 10014-3657. All rights reserved.

Scripture quotations marked NASB are taken from the *Holy Bible, New American Standard Bible,* copyright © 1960, 1962, 1963, 1968, 1971, 1972, 1973, 1975, 1977, 1995 by The Lockman Foundation. All rights reserved.

Scripture quotations marked MSG are taken from *The Message,* copyright © by Eugene H. Peterson, 1993, 1994, 1995, 1996. Used by permission of NavPress Publishing Group.

The author has emphasized some words in Scripture quotations in italicized type.

Legacy of Faith Collection: Norvel Hayes
Teacher of Supernatural Living
ISBN Hardcover: 978-1-60683-016-1
ISBN Tradepaper: 978-1-68031-551-6
Copyright © 2011 by Norvel Hayes

Published by Harrison House Publishers
P.O. Box 35035
Tulsa, OK 74153
www.harrisonhouse.com

Printed in the United States of America. All rights reserved under International Copyright Law. Contents and/or cover may not be reproduced in whole or in part in any form without the express written consent of the Publisher.

Contents

Part 4: *Norvel's Present-Day Ministry*

Introduction

The Legacy Series offers a lifetime of priceless hindsight and godly foresight into some of the world's most influential Christian leaders of the last century. This volume is laden with a wealth of knowledge from a lifetime of healing and deliverance experience from a Word of Faith giant, Brother Norvel Hayes. The lessons that can be learned, if taken to heart, are invaluable in catapulting this present, emerging generation to greater spiritual heights while fulfilling the Great Commission. The hope is that all will find this series to be an unprecedented inspiration for those who are devoted to the full Gospel of God's faithfulness and devotion to a broken world.

Since the time of the Church's first expression of the Gospel message, there have been various seasons that featured different aspects of God's redemptive plan. These movements, or revivals, have often been accompanied by signs of the miraculous healing power of the Gospel. They include the ministry of the apostles, the church fathers and early missionaries in Europe, the doctors of the Reformation, the Holiness of the eighteenth century evangelists such as John Wesley and George Whitfield, and the Azusa Street revival and subsequent Pentecostal shifts. Finally, these movements are represented in the mergence of the healing and charismatic renewals of the later part of the twentieth century. All of these different developments were critical in laying the foundation that led to the birthing of the spiritual revolution that the global Christian community is experiencing today.

Each move has respectfully been unique in its rich insight, wisdom, and proclamation of the full gospel of Jesus Christ, and they have all been indispensable to the health and prosperity of today's church. First Corinthians 10:11 tells us that the things which happened to our ancestors are illustrations of the way in which God works. They are written for our benefit, who are the heirs of the ages which have gone before us or in whose lives the climax of the ages has been reached.

In each movement, God has always had pioneers who paved the way for the moving of His Spirit. These pioneers broke ground, challenged, confronted, incited, excited, and evoked God's people to growth and participation in how the Spirit was moving. They were radical, daring and willing to blaze a new path for God's absolute truth. They were passionate to the core and dedicated to the end — they were a force to be reckoned with.

These spiritual giants have been an unlikely group of men and women who have found themselves thrust into the spotlight and even world prominence. These men and women were bold and daring. They were pioneers who forged ahead, even when they were discouraged by their peers, and they traveled roads that few, if any, had traveled before. Norvel Hayes was no exception.

Norvel is known as a late twentieth and early twenty-first century Word of Faith giant. *The Message Bible* describes God's celestial bodies as "sky-jewelry, moon and stars mounted in their settings" (Psalm 8:4); therefore, Norvel Hayes can be described as, *"God's diamond in the rough."* This does not infer any lack of refinement on Norvel's character, but rather his unaffected soul that has been uncut by man. The apostle Peter has also been similarly viewed down through the ages.

Norvel is natural, real, and earthy. One of the mottos of his ministry is: "*Don't ever try to get popular. Don't ever get fancy. Just stay normal. God loves normal people, full of the Holy Ghost!*" His common sense, life experiences, and clear, grass roots understanding of God and His plan are demonstrated in his simple, down-to-earth teachings, illustrations, and stories. He has effortlessly capitalized on his country hills-of-Tennessee upbringing, and has successfully intertwined his corporate businessman's education and training in his teachings.

Over a span of forty years, Norvel has taught the Word of God across the nation and even overseas to crowds of multiplied thousands at a time. He has ministered to people where they are, while asserting his unique understanding, warm heart, and distinct communication skills. No one has ever shared the gospel message quite like Norvel Hayes. He has not been your typical Word of Faith Bible teacher. Unimpressed, unstirred, and unmoved by pressures or enticements that would cause others to conform to a certain mold, Norvel Hayes has come on the scene like no other in his era. His teaching style has successfully communicated to people that they are genuinely loved by both God and Norvel Hayes, as in, "For whom the Lord loveth he chasteneth" (Hebrews 12:6).

Norvel Hayes has been a commander and chief trainer in God's Boot Camp—enlisting, instructing, and equipping God's people for bombarding the gates of hell, for taking back what the enemy has stolen, and for possessing the land Jesus bought with His precious blood. He has taken on the assignment of putting the body of

Christ through God's Boot Camp and taking them on a journey of transformation where they will be conditioned and prepared to fight the enemy.

A great Christian mind and science fiction writer, C. S. Lewis, stated in his book, *The Screwtape Letters*, "There are two equal and opposite errors into which our race can fall about the devils. One is to disbelieve in their existence. The other is to believe and to feel an excessive and unhealthy interest in them. They themselves are equally pleased by both errors…"[1]

Norvel Hayes addresses both of these extremes as he teaches the body of Christ about the first sign that Jesus said would follow them who believe, "In my name shall they cast out devils" (Mark 16: 17).

Norvel founded New Life Bible College, in Cleveland, Tennessee, in 1977. He shares: "I have the students watch me cast out demons. That is how they learn. Also, we have counseling sessions that they sit in on." Dealing with the enemy has not been confined to back rooms in this ministry. Norvel has ministered along these lines in seminars, conferences, prisons, churches, homes, businesses, prisons, mental institutions, bar rooms, high school and college campuses, as well as other places as the Spirit leads him. *He is not ashamed of the Gospel of Jesus Christ!*

---

[1] C. S. Lewis, *The Screwtape Letters*, (New York: Harper Collins, 2001), ix.

Part One

The Early Years

Chapter 1

Movements of God

The Voice of Healing Revival was birthed primarily in small Pentecostal churches. These churches were predominantly made up of people who were economically poor and they usually gathered in gospel tents with sawdust floors or other places of worship that were old and rundown. During the Voice of Healing Movement, the office of the evangelist and the particular power gifts of the Spirit: faith, healing, and the working of miracles helped validate and solidify the salvation message.

Then the healing revival led to something even stronger and more expansive—the Charismatic Movement. The Charismatic Movement was stronger and more expansive, in the sense that an even fuller and more-encompassing revelation of God and His plan and purposes, *or a fuller gospel,* was being brought forth. During this movement, emphasis was placed on the baptism of the Holy Spirit, speaking in tongues and all nine gifts of the Spirit, instead of only the power gifts that were tools for the evangelist, in particular. The day of the evangelist was not over, but rather another dimension was being added to it.

During this movement, the scene and locale changed. Mass healing campaigns were no longer being assembled in buildings with sawdust floors. Instead, banquets, conferences, and seminars were being hosted in big hotels. Huge auditoriums and more elaborately adorned churches were also being utilized during this time. During this time, the focus also shifted from a single personality and his evangelistic association. Thousands upon thousands of members of traditional churches had become powerfully drawn to the great healing revival, its revivalists, and its charismatic message by the end of 1950.

During the early 1960's, the Pentecostal message of speaking with other tongues, along with healing and miracles, expanded outside the confines of organized, traditional, old-line Pentecostalism. Some of the old-time Pentecostals were perplexed by this and even viewed it as a false revival of compromise, as multitudes that did not adhere to their strict way of living were now speaking in tongues. Hundreds of thousands of Americans became discontent with their own particular denomination's dull and apathetic spiritual stance. They were in quest of a more active and effective experience. Among those who were being drawn to what was then called the neo-Pentecostal movement, were the wealthier middle class, the more-educated, the younger generation who were wise in the world's ways, and university students and professors.

Gifted teachers began to take the place of fiery preachers. This became even more prevalent as the Charismatic Movement fed into the ensuing Word of Faith Movement. During the Word of Faith Movement, emphasis was placed on the importance of the teaching ministry. The teaching ministry has helped establish God's people in their faith. It has also helped in explaining more clearly the truths and corresponding experiences that had been restored during the Charismatic Movement, especially in the non-Pentecostal denominational churches.

Both the Charismatic and Word of Faith Movements took a sharp turn away from the days-gone-by premium placed on ignorance, as had been displayed by the "kiss your brains goodbye, so as not to get in the flesh" or "get out of the way so that the Holy Ghost could take over and have His way," mentality. Fanatics for God were coming to find out that they could be intelligent fanatics—*fanatical and intelligent at the same time*—unlike those the apostle Paul referred to in Romans 10:2, "For…they have a zeal of God, but not according to knowledge."

Unlike the Voice of Healing Revival that was focused on the doctrine of divine healing, the Charismatic and Word of Faith Movements included healing, as well as other areas of emphasis, such as speaking in tongues, prosperity, prophecy, dreams and visions, the ministry of angels, and demonology. The Full Gospel Business Men's Fellowship International (FGBMFI) was founded in the 1960's during this time, by a successful dairyman from California, Demos Shakarian. The FGBMFI was a non-denominational organization of businessmen that established local chapters around the world. Their meetings usually highlighted the testimony of an individual, ranging from a common laborer to a corporate executive, or a high-ranking military official, movie star or another Christian figure who accomplished something or had gone through some life-changing ordeal. The FGBMFI was a strong, organizing force that continued to maintain a strong presence during the Word of Faith Movement. Against this backdrop, we find the ministry of Norvel L. Hayes— who describes himself as a "nice, rich, First Baptist businessman, before God got hold of me and got me delivered from myself."

Chapter 2

From the Hills of Tennessee

Norvel Hayes was born and raised in the rural hills of Tennessee. He was the youngest of three children, two boys and one girl. His mother and father were honest, down-to-earth, old-fashioned Southern Baptists. They were good Christian people and Norvel was indelibly influenced by his praying mother, who loved Jesus with all of her heart. His mother was involved in the church, told people about Jesus, and won many souls for the kingdom. However, when she was thirty-seven years old, she died of cancer.

At the time of her death, Norvel was ten years old. When his mother was ill, people would pray, "Lord, heal Mrs. Hayes—if it be Thy will." What they were actually saying was, "Lord, if it's not Your will to heal her, just go ahead and kill her." Some said that it was God's will for his mother to be sick and die and leave her family at a time when they needed her so much. But, as a boy, that made God seem cruel to Norvel.

Norvel's brother died at the early age of nineteen of Bright's Disease. His church prayed the same way for his brother, "Lord, heal Glen Hayes—if it be Thy will." So Norvel thought that it must have been God's will for his brother to die, too. At that time, he did not know that this way of praying for the sick was unscriptural and a result of doubt and unbelief.

Norvel recalls standing by his mother's coffin when he was ten years old, not wanting to say goodbye and trying not to cry. He makes the following statement years later, "That is why I am so bold and ruthless against the devil, and particularly against cancer. Cancer is a work of hell. All diseases come from the devil. All heartaches come from the devil. But Jesus came down from heaven to bring us eternal life and life more abundantly here on earth."

Rich, Successful Businessman

Several years later when Norvel was older, he married a beautiful woman named Noreen, while living in New York. Noreen was raised in a socialite family in Boston and New York. Norvel came from a Baptist background, while Noreen came from a Catholic one. When they got married, however, they agreed to never let religion wreck their home. For several years they attended separate churches, but over the years, Noreen got tired of going to mass and started to attend the Baptist church with Norvel.

Norvel thought Noreen was crazy for marrying him, since he only had twenty dollars to his name at that time. Later when Norvel was in his late twenties, he became successful in business. He thought that if he had money he would be happy, so he asked God to make him rich. He started out working for a sharecropper for twenty-five cents a day and in about two and a half years, he was making $100 a day. Then he began to make $1,000 a week, then $5,000 a week.

When you make that much money, it doesn't take you very long to get what you think you want. To Norvel's surprise, when he got to where he thought he wanted to be, he was even more miserable than when he was a penniless teenager. He *finally* realized that money did not bring happiness. Norvel owned a manufacturing company and earned four to five thousand dollars a week. He had a nice home that sat on five acres, that was surrounded by a big fence and had a long driveway with large shrubs on each side that wound toward the house through an acre of his perfectly manicured grounds. He had four Cadillacs parked in his garage and on his property.

Norvel had a wonderful family. His wife, Noreen treated him like a king. She met him at the door every day when he came home from work, looking like she just stepped out of *Vogue* magazine. Norvel and Noreen had one daughter named Zona. Zona thought her dad was great, too. She thought that he was better than any other daddy and she wanted to go with him everywhere he went. Part of Norvel felt good about them doting on him so much, but he really thought it was too much. At the time though, he didn't care, because he liked the attention.

Norvel attended the First Baptist Church in Indianapolis, Indiana, with the rest of the rich men in town. He became friends with doctors, lawyers, and older businessmen. Men who were even twenty-five years older than him, started asking him for advice. It amazed him. They respected him, because he was a successful young man and made more money than most of them.

The First Baptist Church in Indianapolis was different from the Southern Baptist church that he grew up in. In his church in Tennessee, everybody got down on the floor and prayed until God showed up, and then they shouted all over the building. However, in the First Baptist Church in Indianapolis, nobody got down on the floor and prayed, because rich people usually liked to attend a church where nothing spiritually was happening. At this time in his life, Norvel felt the same way. He wanted to be sincere, but he had built a kingdom around himself and was trapped in it.

Norvel was a rich and powerful businessman, but when he looked in the mirror, he didn't like what he saw. He liked himself while he was driving in the busy traffic in Indianapolis where he lived, but when he thought back to his life in Tennessee where he was raised, he did not like who he had become. While living in the big city, Norvel did not care if the whole world went to hell. He did not pass out any tracts, knock on any doors, or do anything else for God. If his neighbor's house had burned down, he probably would not have visited them. His attitude was, *Leave me alone. I've got it made. Just let me go to church on Sunday morning and be a nice business executive.*

Norvel just wanted to be a nice First Baptist businessman and put on his tailor-made suit, drive up in his Cadillac, and sit on the pew in the most beautiful church in town. Then when church was over, he would run to his car and drive home so no one would bother him. He sat behind the fence on his estate and watched the squirrels and birds, and checked on his fruit trees. That was about the only thing he enjoyed doing. He was locked in his big estate with squirrels, birds, trees, and Cadillacs, but his heart was empty and his mind was confused. He was not happy. He caught himself living in a false world that was worthless and empty. He went to church on Sunday mornings, but his attention was more on material than spiritual things. Norvel was a successful businessman and he had a good marriage and a lovely daughter, but he was still not happy.

One day while Norvel was on a business trip in Georgia, he fell on his knees and prayed, *God, I'm tired of this empty life. Use me! Take me!* Then he added, *God, you go ahead and mold me and use me. My life is yours. I am tired of trying to find happiness in money, clubs and social life.* He stood up and went about his business and did not feel any different, but a week later, God manifested Himself to Norvel for the first time.

As Norvel was driving home from Columbus, Ohio, he was just praying and thanking Jesus for the day. Then all of a sudden, it was as if a whirlwind came down from heaven and surrounded his car and Jesus was sitting in the front passenger seat! Norvel started to weep. He couldn't help himself. Jesus stayed in his car for an hour and a half, and Norvel wept the whole time.

As he pulled into the Richmond, Indiana, city limits, that whirlwind of power began to lift off of him. It left his car, and he began to come to himself. In a few minutes, he found himself sitting in the driver's seat just as he was before Jesus appeared. God's glorious presence was gone, but Norvel felt different. Everything about him—his mind, body, and heart—felt like they had just been washed with four bars of soap. He felt cleaner than anyone could ever imagine. The whole time Jesus was with him he cried, and business executives do not cry—that is—*unless Jesus rides in the car with you!*

Norvel reflects:

> At least I had enough sense not to mouth off something stupid like, "Now listen, Jesus, I'm an important business executive." I was sitting with the One who made worlds! Can you imagine how stupid it would have been for me to tell Him how important I was? I thought I was important

until Jesus showed up. Then I found out that He was the important one, and I didn't have any higher position than His executive suite janitor. Glory to God!

When Jesus appeared to me, He changed me. I didn't know He was a killer. He murdered all the darkness! He slaughtered all the confusion and He killed everything in me that wasn't joy!

The only message I heard from Jesus during that visit was that He wanted me to follow Him the way His disciples in the New Testament did. (See Matthew 4:18-22; 9:9; John 1:43.) I wanted to answer Him, but I couldn't because I was crying so hard that I was gasping for breath!

I wanted to say, "What do You want me to follow You for, Lord? I don't have any sense! I thought You called preachers, not businessmen! Why would You want a business executive, Lord? I'm not a preacher. I'm not anything!" Of course, Jesus already knew all that. That's why He came to me—to straighten out my thinking and make me into something.

After Jesus left, peace and joy possessed every ounce of me for the first time, since I was a teenager. I even had peace in my eyes! It seemed as if the whole world stopped still before me. I'm glad nobody saw me crying. I would have been embarrassed. But Jesus had mercy on me and appeared to me while I was alone. If you want to know the truth about the matter, I thought Jesus must have been pretty hard up. I couldn't figure out what He wanted with me. I had business sense, but I knew I didn't have any spiritual sense. All I knew was that heaven was a good place and God was good. But when Jesus left, I knew two more things: *He loved me and He wanted me to follow Him.* All I had ever done for Him was to give a little money to help build the church in my town, and now He wanted me to work for Him!

As Norvel drove home that day after Jesus appeared to him, he thought his family would be excited when he told them, but he was wrong. When he told Noreen about his visitation with Jesus and how God wanted him to do something for Him, she was not happy at all. She was afraid that she would have to move to Africa or live in a tent or something like that. She told Norvel that she did not want to be around church people all her life, because she was raised in a social world and did not want to give up her social world to be a missionary.

Norvel assured her that they were not going to Africa to live in a tent as missionaries, but he also told her that he would do whatever the Lord wanted him to do, and if He wanted him to go to Africa then he would go. So she told him that she wanted a divorce. She said that if she couldn't have all of him then she didn't want any part of him, and Norvel said that she wouldn't have any then. So after eleven years of marriage, Norvel and Noreen got a divorce.

Eventually Noreen moved to San Francisco. After she left, Norvel tried to shake off her memory, but he couldn't. He was still in love with her. He began to seek the Lord. He was so hungry for God that he went to every church he could find. If he saw a revival listed in the newspaper, he went to it. He attended one every night if possible. Sometimes he asked someone to watch Zona for him, and other times he just took her with him.

Zona was eight years old and would cry half the night because her family was breaking up. She had nightmares and would wake up in the middle of the night screaming, "No! No! No! Not my mommy and daddy! No! No! No! Not our home! No!" When Noreen remarried, Norvel thought about that all the time. For a year, he couldn't get to sleep until he finally wore out his body at four or five o'clock in the morning. He just wanted to close his eyes and never wake up. He even prayed that he would die. Then one day, as he was praying in his office, the Holy Spirit reached deep down inside of him, and took hold of all his love for his ex-wife, and in one moment pulled it out of him. He felt like a sock turned inside out, as every emotional attachment to his ex-wife was suddenly gone. He was as free as a flying bird. *That burden was lifted off of him.*

Later, when Norvel had to meet with Noreen one day to settle the ownership of a small piece of property, they decided to have dinner together. Noreen told him that she was not happy with her new marriage and would come back to him if he wanted her to, but Norvel told her that he no longer loved her. So they settled their business and she went back to California to her new family and Norvel stayed in Tennessee and tried to find his ministry.

Norvel had no earthly idea what his ministry was. The only thing that he knew to do at that time was to pray, because that's what the old-fashioned Baptists did when he was a kid. The Bible says, "And a little child shall lead them" (Isaiah 11:6), and that's exactly how God led Norvel, even though he didn't know it at that time. Zona began to beg him to move to Cleveland, Tennessee, where he was raised. Some of her cousins lived there, so Norvel finally agreed. He was not going to be guilty of breaking her heart more than it already was.

After Jesus showed up in his car and Noreen left him, Zona could have anything she wanted as far as he was concerned.

When Norvel gave his life to Jesus, he wasn't ready for Him to call him into the ministry. Some things had to change before he could begin to walk in God's divine destiny for him. When they moved back to Cleveland, Tennessee, Norvel bought a restaurant and God began to deal with him. The Lord God himself started visiting Norvel two or three times a week. He did not think that there was any way that God would ever use a man who was divorced, so he could not figure out why He was visiting him so often and so strong. He was so ignorant of the things of God that he didn't know what to do next. So, step by step, God began to train him.

Part Two

God's Boot Camp

Chapter 3

Inducted Into God's Boot Camp

*Y*ou *must be willing to go into God's Boot Camp and let Him train you. Let God himself do it for you. You must let the Holy Ghost, who is fire, burn the denominational doctrines—every doctrine that is not scriptural—and everything else out of you that is not of Him. Let Him burn out every doctrine and everything else that is not in the Bible.*

Norvel often refers to this time of finding his ministry and training for his ministry as "God's Boot Camp." He asserts that every believer needs to be subjected to this special kind of spiritual preparation in certain areas of his or her life. What is boot camp? Boot camp is a training camp where you are trained to be useful in God's army. Do you think it would do any good for God to send you to a place where you have to cast out devils and set people free if you didn't know how to cast out devils? NO! You have to be trained to do that!

You have to know your authority as a believer. Luke 9:1 says, "Then he called his twelve disciples together, and gave them power and authority over all devils, and to cure diseases." You have power and authority in Jesus' name. When you received the baptism in the Holy Spirit, you received power from the Holy Spirit inside of you to get the job done.

Norvel's boot camp training began when God sent a full gospel pastor to him in order to get him to believe the Bible. The first thing he noticed about this pastor was that he would say things like "hallelujah" or "glooooooory!" His byword was always "hallelujah!" and the "glory" was so long and drawn out that it really made Norvel nervous. Whenever the pastor would say it, his jowls would shake and tremble and he would close his eyes very seriously.

When Jesus told Norvel that He wanted him to follow Him, he thought that meant he should go to church on Sunday. He really didn't know what it meant, but the Lord knew his heart. So one day, as he was working in his restaurant, this full gospel pastor named Brother Littlefield walked in and asked him if he was the new owner. He told him that the previous owner had sponsored a radio broadcast for their church and asked Norvel if he wanted to do this also. As Norvel opened his mouth to answer Brother Littlefield, the Spirit of God spoke to his heart, "You need to talk to him."

So Norvel took him to his office and poured his heart out to Brother Littlefield. Norvel told him that the call of God was on him and he didn't know what to do about it. He told him that he didn't know what his ministry was or what God wanted him to do. The only thing he knew was that Jesus loved him and wanted him to follow Him. So he asked the pastor if he could help him.

Brother Littlefield told him to be faithful to the church and start doing the little things, like helping people and feeding the poor. He told him that God finds great favor with people who feed the poor. He also told him to start working in the ministry of helps in any way that he could, as well as helping other businessmen find God. Later Brother Littlefield even asked Norvel to come to his church and teach a Sunday school class. So he did.

One day after class, Norvel walked upstairs and sat in the sanctuary and listened to the sermon. This was the first time he heard Brother Littlefield preach. During the sermon, a woman suddenly started speaking in tongues. It really grabbed his attention, but nobody else seemed to notice. At the time, Norvel did not know that she was speaking in tongues, because he had never heard anything like that before. He thought that she was a mental case.

The woman didn't say anything else, so Norvel started listening to the sermon again. Suddenly he heard her again. He did not know what she was saying. Then she started jerking. He thought something had to be wrong with her, but he could not figure out what it was. Then just as suddenly as she started jerking, she stopped and sat there as nice as could be. Then, sure enough, in a few minutes she started speaking in tongues again.

Norvel was just an ordinary First Baptist business executive, so he did what any good Baptist would do and bowed his head and prayed. Norvel recalls, *Oh, God,* I prayed, *have mercy upon this poor soul who has come here today from the mental institution. Help her, Lord, if it be Thy will. Help her out of those goofy spells.* Norvel has thought about that prayer many times since then. He was as sincere as he could be at the time, but he didn't know that the woman was talking in tongues. If God would have told him that night that she's not from the mental institution and that she was speaking with other tongues, he would have said, "What? Leave me, Satan!"

Norvel made up his mind that when the service was over, he was going to act like a nice Baptist and just ease on out the door. He did not want to shake hands with anybody, *especially that woman!* He decided that he would never bother those people again. So when the service ended, he left. However, a few days later, that pastor came to see him again. He was as nice as ever and he acted like nothing had happened that Sunday in his church. Norvel thought he would apologize to him for that woman's behavior, but he didn't even mention it. It didn't seem to bother him, but it made Norvel a nervous wreck!

Brother Littlefield continued to keep in touch with Norvel. Once he called and invited him to go to a Full Gospel Business Men's Fellowship meeting with him. He told him that a lot of businessmen got together at this meeting and would talk about the Lord. But Norvel would not go. One day the pastor told him that a rich man who owned a certain chain of department stores, was going to be the speaker and tell his life story. This seemed interesting to Norvel, so he finally decided to go.

When he walked into the hotel where the meeting was being held that night, a man walked up to him and introduced himself. Norvel stretched forth his hand to shake hands with him, when all of a sudden, the man grabbed his hand and threw his arms around him and gave him a big, crushing bear-hug. When the man finally let him loose, he slapped him on the back and just stood there grinning from ear to ear. Norvel was so embarrassed.

As Norvel stood there and tried to figure out why that man had hugged him, all of a sudden it happened again. Another man came up and did the same thing. Norvel just stood there in a daze. Then he started looking around and realized that everyone was hugging everyone. The devil told him to get out of there and run for his life. He told him to run as fast as he could, because all those people were crazy. In his mind, he wanted to agree with the devil, but instead he decided to stay.

Nervously, he went into the dining room where the meeting was going to be held and sat down. Then a guy got up to lead some choruses. The first line of the first song began, "I don't care what church you belong to…." That was enough for Norvel. He wanted to say, "Well, I do; I'm First Baptist—and First Baptist care! What do you mean, 'I don't care what church you belong to'? I do care what church I belong to. I'm either Baptist or Baptist, you understand that? And if you don't know that, the Baptists will let you know it. To a Baptist, brother, you're either Baptist or you're just trying to get there! That's the way it is!"

The next thing Norvel heard was, "Just as long as you're for Jesus you stand!" He thought that part was good, since he believed in standing for Jesus. Finally it was time for the rich business executive to give his testimony. He started out by saying, "In my department store, I have a special chair in my office that I pray for people in. From my office, I can look out over the shoppers. Sometimes God shows me someone who's dying of cancer."

Immediately, Norvel came alive. He said to himself, *Yeah, is that right? I wonder if he's telling the truth. My mother died with cancer. I wish God would have shown her to him.*

The speaker continued, "I go out to that person and tap them on the shoulder and say to them, 'I need to talk to you, please. The Lord shows me that you have cancer.' I invite them to my office. I ask them to sit in that special chair and I lay my hands on them, in Jesus' name. And I pray for them, and Jesus heals them while they're sitting right there."

Norvel thought, *Oh, my God. I've never seen Jesus heal anybody in church, much less in a department store or in the office.* He was still wondering if the speaker was telling the truth.

The speaker continued to say that sometimes as he looked out over his store, the Lord would show him somebody who was an alcoholic. "And I'll go out and say, 'I need to talk to you in my office.' And I slowly lead that person to my special chair—the deliverance chair. I set them down in my office, in my chair and I take authority over the devil. I pray for them, and they get saved and get delivered."

At this point, Norvel was still wondering if this man was telling the truth, because he had never heard anything like this before. "But, you know," the speaker went on, "I couldn't do things like that until after I was baptized in the Holy Ghost and spoke with other tongues." Once again, the Baptist in Norvel rose up! As he watched the speaker, he looked on one side of his mouth and then the other. He also looked at the inside of his mouth as he talked. Norvel finally concluded that the speaker didn't know what he was talking about, because he did not have any other tongues. He only had one, so Norvel decided he was either a con or just flaky.

Norvel recaps, "I know you're probably thinking that nobody in the world is that dumb! Let me tell you, I was. And the First Baptists that I knew were that dumb, as well. Dummy 'me' had never heard anyone talk about speaking in other tongues. I didn't know anything about it. I didn't know anything about tongues. I had no earthly idea what this man was talking about. I had no earthly idea of anything he was talking about. It was all a foreign language to me. He might as well have been speaking in Japanese. I heard every word he said, but I had no earthly idea what he was talking about."

Norvel thought about leaving the meeting right then, but since the Pentecostal preacher had brought him, he wanted to be respectful and stay. But he decided that when he got out of there, he wouldn't bother these people any more. As far as he was concerned, it was over before he got out of there. So after the Full Gospel Business Men's meeting that night, he left his pastor friend and went his own way.

A little while later, the pastor came to his restaurant again and sat down and invited him back to another meeting. Norvel had already decided that he wouldn't bother with those people any more, but God kept reminding him, for thirty days, of those two songs he heard at that Full Gospel Business Men's meeting: *"I don't care what church you belong to,"* and, *"Just as long as for Jesus you stand."* So for some reason, Norvel started going back to the Full Gospel Business Men's service the next month. To hear those old songs—like, *"I don't care what church you belong to"*—drove him up the wall, especially since he had heard that particular song for a month. He would wake up in the morning, and hear it. He would go to bed at night and try to sleep and he would hear that song, *"I don't care what church you belong to...I don't care what church you belong to."*

Besides that other song, "Just as long as for Jesus you stand," there was another little chorus that they sang, "There's a river of life flowing down through me." Me! "It makes the lame to walk and the blind to see." Norvel said to himself, *There's nothing that flows through me that makes the lame to walk and the blind to see. Must be something new flowing through people; it doesn't flow through me. It doesn't flow through our church. It doesn't even flow through the pastor to make the lame to walk and the blind to see.*

Norvel had never seen a lame man walk or a blind man receive his sight. He had only read about it in the Bible. When you are born a certain way and raised a certain way, you can end up reading the Bible through denominational glasses. The only thing that means anything is what you've been taught. So those songs continued to ring in his ears, *"I don't care what church you belong to,"* and *"Just as long as for Jesus you stand,"* and *"There's a river of life flowing down through me. It makes the lame to walk and the blind to see."*

Norvel went back the second month and they sang the same songs. In this particular meeting though, the speaker was a small fellow with black, wavy hair parted in the center and slicked back. He was wearing a pinstriped suit and looked like a gangster, a hit man from Detroit, or the head of the Chicago Mafia. When he got up to speak, he started telling about things that had happened to him, and how his wife kept putting salvation tracts out for him all the time. He said that she kept on doing this, until finally one day he got saved and baptized in the Holy Spirit and spoke with other tongues.

When he said this, Norvel said to himself, *What? You mean there are two of them on earth?* He couldn't imagine that there were two people on earth who spoke in tongues. As he sat there and continued to listen to the speaker, he also thought, *Well, dear Lord in heaven, this guy is as screwy as the other one.* And the devil said to him, "That's right! And you're in a cult outfit—get out of here! This is a cult—didn't you know that? They believe their own thing." The devil continued. "This is not the way you were raised; this is not the way you were raised. And you know you were always told all your life, 'Don't get above your raising.'"

When the meeting ended, Norvel left and went back to his restaurant and sat in a booth in the back, just minding his own business. When he looked up, he saw three guys. They were all Italians and they looked like they were from the Mafia. One of them was the Full Gospel Business Men speaker. Norvel thought, *Oh, no, that's that guy that's got a bunch of tongues!*

When the speaker got close to him, he pointed his finger at Norvel and said, "When I walked in the door, the Lord spoke to me and said, 'One of these days, you're going to be one of us.'" *No! No! No!* Norvel said to himself. *You can't be; you only have one tongue. You can't be; you only have one tongue. You can't be; you only have one tongue.*

Conned by the Pastor

Norvel continued to attend these meetings, and one day his Pentecostal preacher friend called him and said, "Norvel, would you do a pastor a favor? They are having a convention in Nashville, Tennessee and I would like you to drive me up there on Thursday. We'll come back on Saturday afternoon, because I need to preach on Sunday morning. Would you do a pastor a favor?" Norvel thought, *Oh God, how can I turn him down? He works with little poor children. There he is, you know, asking me to do him a favor.* So Norvel said he would and went with him.

When they arrived at their hotel in Nashville and checked into their room, his friend told him to get ready to go down to the meeting. To Norvel's surprise, they had meetings all day: *morning, noon and night.* They usually had five, six, or even seven meetings a day at the Full Gospel Business Men's Convention. During one of the meetings, they called on Methodist pastors, who said they had been filled with the Spirit, to testify. They also called on the Southern Baptists, so a Southern Baptist pastor got up and said, "I'm Baptist; I'm Southern Baptist." Then he started preaching about what happened to him and how he got baptized in the Holy Ghost and spoke with other tongues. He also told how the power of God came upon him and that now he prays for the sick.

Since Norvel was Baptist, this got his attention and he thought, *Whoo! Now I can believe him a little bit 'cause he's Baptist. Oh, yeah, I have respect for him because he is Baptist.* After the Southern Baptist pastor spoke, a Presbyterian minister from Pennsylvania gave his testimony. When he got through with his testimony, he began to pray for people. The Spirit of the Lord began to bless people as this man began to pray for them. Then he began to dance like a turkey, taking high steps when he danced.

As Norvel stood there, the minister danced over to him and grabbed him around the waist and shook him, and said, "Oh, Brother Hayes, there is no other kind except this kind." Then he turned him loose and danced off. By this time Norvel was thinking, *God, this is too heavy for me, man. I can't, I mean, this is just too heavy for me. I don't understand this. Dear Lord, help me!* He began to pray, "Oh, God, I think You need to help my mind. Lord, help my mind. I have no earthly idea what is going on; help my mind Jesus. Help my mind." He shook the Baptist right out of Norvel!

After a few months, Norvel finally got to the point where he could see and believe that this was real for *some* people, but not for *him.* Despite this, he kept going to the meetings and conventions. Finally one day, after about a year, he made up his mind that this was real, and he believed and it was for everybody, *including him.* Since he was such a hard case, he thought that God would be pleased, thrilled and overjoyed to finally get him. He boldly went down to the front, got on his knees, and said, "Okay, God, I believe. And I believe it's for everybody. And I believe it's for me. Here I am; just feel free. Since I believe it, just feel free and give it to me." But he didn't feel a thing.

Norvel even had people pray for him, but he still could not receive the baptism of the Holy Spirit. Finally, Norvel realized that God was not as proud to get him as he thought He would be. He began to study the Bible on the subject of faith. "Now faith is the substance of things hoped for, the evidence of things not seen" (Hebrews 11:1). Jesus said, "What things soever ye desire when ye pray, believe that ye receive them, and ye shall have them" (Mark 11:24). Norvel finally saw it! You believe it and you receive when you pray. But you don't really believe that you receive it when you pray, unless you act like you've already got it and talk like you've already got it. If you're waiting for it, you haven't believed you received when you prayed. *Norvel finally believed that he received—not would receive.*

Norvel began to walk around every day and thank God for the baptism of the Holy Spirit. He would say, "Oh, it was so sad, all those months that I wrestled with You and didn't get baptized in the Holy Spirit, but now that I've got it, now that I've got it, now that I've got it, now that I've got it—I believe I receive, I believe I receive, I believe I receive. I accept it by faith. I believe I receive."

About thirty days later, while Norvel was attending a meeting in an old theatre building, a guy came up and began to preach. When he gave the invitation, something got into Norvel's feet. He had never experienced anything like this before. He tried to stop it, but when he tried to stop his right foot, it wouldn't stop. Then the left one started and neither one would stop. *It was something that was alive and real.*

His feet felt so good that he could hardly stand it—they were jumping and Norvel couldn't keep them from jumping. He tried to make them stop, but he couldn't. He was concerned, *Oh, God, I might disturb the service.* When he saw that his feet weren't going to stop, he thought, *I've got to get out of here!* So he got up and went out of the building. He got in his car and said, "Oh, my God, how can I drive the car?" He could hardly drive and the gas pedal was going *whoo, whoo.*

Then, whatever he was feeling got all over his body and the devil said, "You're having a heart attack!" Norvel decided, *Well, if I am, it feels better than anything I've ever felt in my life. If this is a heart attack, give me two of them. I mean, something is going all through my body and my hands. Oh, God, what is this? It's alive in me, and it won't stop. It's alive; and it's in me—and it won't stop. What is this?*

Norvel drove all the way to Chattanooga, back towards Cleveland. As he made a turn toward Cleveland, all of a sudden something alive was in his belly. It just began to rise up on the inside of him. It was alive and really warm. It rose up slowly, slowly, slowly, slowly—all the way to his mouth. When it got up there, it got hold of his tongue—which started going, *Da-da-da-da-da-da-da-da.* Somehow, he got hold of that by faith and just spoke out, and a language began to flow out of him.

Chapter 4

Boot Camp Training

When Jesus was talking with His disciples, He said, "Take heed and beware of the leaven of the Pharisees and of the Sadducees" (Matthew 16:6). This leaven refers to the doctrines of men.

Jesus wants you to recognize Him as what He says He is in His Word, not what your church or anyone else says He is *if it is contrary to the Word.* He wants you to talk and act like He is what He says He is without shame or embarrassment.

You need to be delivered from shame, from *anything* within you that is ashamed of God or ashamed of the gospel. God said that if you are not ashamed of Him, He won't be ashamed of you. Any part of the Bible you're not ashamed of, that's the part God will give you. Any part of the Bible that you are ashamed of, that's the part that God will make sure that you don't get. "Whosoever therefore shall be ashamed of me and of my words…of him shall the Son of man be ashamed" (Mark 8:38). "Whosoever believeth on him *shall not* be ashamed" (Romans 10:11, emphasis added).

One day after Norvel had attended the Full Gospel Business Men meetings for almost two years, he heard about an overseas trip they were planning. His Pentecostal pastor friend urged him to go, so he did. They met in New York and flew to England for two weeks to witness in London's hospitals, schools, and on the streets. They worked on the streets until after midnight, standing in the rain, trying to get kids saved and off of drugs. This was Norvel's first effort to do anything of this nature for God.

Norvel had some interesting experiences on this trip. One of these experiences occurred one day after they were in London for about a week. Norvel was visiting with one of the Pentecostal businessman in the hotel lobby. As they stood there talking, a little red-haired hippie fellow walked by. He was wearing thick glasses and his eyes were crossed. Norvel didn't know it, but the Holy Spirit was preparing him for his ministry. He was at the right place at the right time.

The businessman who he was talking to said to him, "The Lord just told me that if we'll go over and pray for that hippie, He will heal his eyes right now. Do you believe that?"

"Sure," Norvel said. "Why not!" *(He really wasn't sure what he believed, but he knew he was trying to believe.)*

The businessman walked over to the hippie and said, "Take your glasses off, son. God told me that if we prayed for you, He would heal your eyes right now." So the young man took off his glasses and the businessman said, "Come on, Brother Hayes. Let's lay hands on him." Norvel agreed, and they laid hands on him and began to pray. The businessman told the devil what to do, and started claiming a miracle for the young man. When they finished praying, Norvel's friend picked up a paper with print on it, and told the hippie to read it without his glasses. The young man took the paper and started reading aloud, word-for-word.

At that time, a fellow with a camera slung over his shoulder walked up. "Wait a minute!" he said. "I'm a reporter for the *London Herald*." He turned to the hippie, "Before they prayed for you, young man," he asked, "could you read that?"

"No," said the young fellow. "I couldn't read anything."

Then they tried an experiment. They found that the hippie could read the paper without his glasses, but when he put his glasses on, he couldn't read anything. So, the reporter turned to Norvel and his friend and asked. "What are your names and who are you all?"

"We're businessmen from America," his friend said. "There are three jet-loads of us here. We've come to invade London!"

The reporter started writing in his little book. The next morning the newspaper headline read in big letters, "U. S. BUSINESSMEN COME TO LONDON, BEATNIKS GETTING DELIVERED." Within two days, that hotel was packed. You couldn't get a room. People poured in from all over Europe, and they started holding meetings every day. They had a full gospel convention!

Another Encounter with the Lord

One day while in London, Norvel decided to stay in his room and pray instead of ministering on the street. During this time the Lord spoke to him for the first time in an audible voice. As he walked out of the bathroom in his hotel room, God's power hit him and knocked him down and God began to speak to him. He said to him in a loud voice, "You can't live your life over again! Go get the Bible!"

Norvel started weeping, staggered across the room, and picked up his Bible—it was like picking up an electric wire. He fell to the floor and started sobbing, crying for mercy. The room was so full of God's holy presence that he could not stand up. His flesh couldn't stand it. God's presence was so clean, so holy. The Holy Ghost inside of him—the Spirit of God—*was jumping!*

Nobody was in the room except God and Norvel, so Norvel buried his face in the carpet and sobbed, "What do You want, God? What do You want with me? Help me, Jesus! Have mercy on me!"

"You have been raging against Me," God said. Then He quoted the following Scripture to him: "Because thy rage against me and thy tumult is come up into mine ears, therefore I will put my hook in thy nose, and my bridle in thy lips, and I will turn thee back by the way by which thou camest" (2 Kings 19:28, see also Isaiah 37:29). If you don't believe the Bible, you're raging against God. At the time God spoke to Norvel in England, he was wondering about whether casting out devils was for today, and if it was God's will to heal everyone. He was allowing his thoughts to go against God's Word in those areas, so in essence he was raging against God. Norvel's mind was so messed up with manmade doctrines that God could hardly do anything with him. He didn't even understand basic biblical doctrines about baptisms, laying on of hands, faith, and the gifts of the Spirit.

God started waking Norvel up with an audible voice. Next God quoted the following verse to him: "And this shall be a sign unto thee, ye shall eat this year such things as grow of themselves, and in the second year that which springeth of the same; and in the third year sow ye, and reap, and plant vineyards, and eat the fruits thereof" (2 Kings 19:29, see also Isaiah 37:30). God was talking to him about *his* ministry. "This tonight is a sign unto you," He said. "During the first year from now, I want you to let things happen as they will. And during the second year, I want you to let things spring up in your life, even as during the first year. But during the third year from now, I want you to sow seed for Me and plant vineyards for Me; and you, Son, are going to eat the fruit thereof."

That day, God gave Norvel the first glimpse of his ministry. He didn't show him all of it at once. When God said to him, "You can't live your life over again," He meant, you can't let past experiences keep you from stepping into God's divine plan for your life. If you do, Satan can use those experiences to steal your destiny. You have to leave the past behind and go on with God.

Hungry for More

When Norvel returned to the United States, a pastor friend invited him to come to his church. After the service, he asked him to help him pray for the sick. As Norvel prayed that night, his hands began to feel strange, as if the bones would pop right through his flesh. His hands had never felt like that before, so he asked his friend what was happening to him. He told him that he was experiencing God's healing power flowing through his hands.

Norvel walked over to the sick people at the altar and began to lay his hands on them. One by one, they fell under the power of God. This was new to Norvel, but he knew it was God and thought it was wonderful. Shortly thereafter, God taught him how to be a channel for His healing power.

Norvel was at his house one day and his friend, a full gospel pastor, showed up. He said, "Brother Norvel, God told me to come and get you to go with me to pray for a Methodist woman. She is in bed and can't get up."

Norvel asked, "Why can't you just go pray for her?"

He said, "I don't know. The Lord told me to come and get you."

Norvel agreed to meet him thirty minutes later at the church. They met there, along with the song leader and drove out to the Methodist woman's house. They decided that, since she was all alone, they would stop and get her some food. She was just a young woman about thirty years old with three small children, and her husband was out of town on business.

When they arrived, the pastor spoke up and said, "God told me to bring Brother Hayes and pray for you." He told the song leader to stand by the foot of the bed, while he knelt by the side of the bed, and he told Norvel to lay his hands on the woman and pray for her. Norvel touched her forehead lightly with his fingertips and said, "Satan, I take authority over you, in Jesus' name and I command you to take your hands off of her. Now, Lord, I thank You for healing her." At that moment his right hand and arm felt warm. The power of God surged through his right arm and into her. Although he only touched her lightly with his fingertips, her whole body began to quiver. At first he thought maybe she was chilled or something. Then she began to shake. She shook so much that the whole bed vibrated with God's power. His right arm was so hot. He said, "Lady, the Lord Jesus Christ is healing you!"

She sat up and exclaimed, "I have never felt so good in my life."

Norvel stood there with the ends of his fingers still on the woman's forehead, and she was still literally shaking. In a matter of five minutes, she was completely restored to normal and all signs of illness had completely disappeared. She just sat there rejoicing and praising God. Tears ran down her face as she basked in the presence of Jesus. As they started out of the bedroom, Norvel turned to her and said, "Well people are supposed to be up and out of bed. Get up."

The woman got up, still rejoicing and singing unto the Lord, and began to do the chores which had been left undone for several days. She was singing and rejoicing so much that they couldn't even talk to her, so they said, "Good-bye," and left her singing and healed. A few nights later she came to a Full Gospel Business Men's Fellowship meeting and gave a glorious testimony of how Jesus had healed her.

That was how Jesus trained Norvel to pray for the sick. Mark 16:18 says, "They shall lay hands on the sick, and they shall recover." You have to go where there are sick people in order to lay hands on them, and see them healed by the power of God. Jesus said, "I was sick, and ye visited me" (Matthew 25:36). "Inasmuch as ye have done it unto one of the least of these my brethren, ye have done it unto me" (Matthew 25:40). As you visit sick people and bring healing to them, you visit Jesus. As you try to help people who are sick and broken-hearted or beaten down by life itself, you do it as unto Jesus. This is how you are trained when you are in "God's Boot Camp". Until you are willing to go through God's Boot Camp, you will never be able to appropriate the promises of God in your own life or help others effectively.

Norvel had never visited any poor homes in his life. He lived in a nice home and had four Cadillacs. He didn't want to go to a poor person's house. He also didn't have any desire to help high school kids get off of drugs or help guys in jail and penitentiaries. He had no desire to knock on doors in his hometown or pass out tracts. He just wanted to go to church, love the Lord, make money, and be nice. He had a selfish, self-satisfying heart.

When Norvel received that vision from God, he finally got delivered from himself. He realized that *"he"* was his main problem. He got to the place where he began to take orders from God. His heart was turned from a heart of stone into a heart of flesh. Norvel began to care about people, regardless of their status in life. He also began to have a desire to help high school kids and to visit poor people.

He started going to various high schools and talking to the principals. God gave him supernatural favor with these principals. He told the principals, "I want to help these high school kids get off dope, and I want to bring different high school speakers into town to minister to these kids." He also began to work with a dedicated group of Lee College (now Lee University) students known as the "Pioneers for Christ." Norvel had never seen such dedication among young people and he loved every one of them and will never forget them. These "Pioneers for Christ" would work in an area that was like a city dump. After Norvel worked together with them for two years, they finally raised enough money to build a church for the poor families in that area.

One time they found a woman with three little children there, who had been sleeping under a tree for several nights, because they didn't have a home to go to. The Pioneers for Christ built them a little home around that tree, with a couple of little rooms made out of slabs that they picked up at the sawmill. After they built that house, Norvel went there one day to pray for that woman. When he walked into that little place, flies were everywhere. A little girl walked up to him, dirty and stinky, with a milk bottle in her hand.

It looked like she hadn't changed clothes in six months. "Mister, we don't have any food. Our little baby only has this much milk," the little girl said as she held up that bottle to show him.

When Norvel looked down at her, as she looked up at him and said that, the Holy Spirit inside his belly began to rise up and half choke him. He broke down and began to weep. He looked up to heaven and said, "Oh God, is this my ministry? Is this what You are giving me? God is this what You have for me?"

When Norvel cried out to God that day, he heard a voice come down from heaven to him. God said, "Son, be thankful to Me here, and I'll promote you. I only promote people I can trust." Some people live in a world of wondering. They say, *I wonder what my ministry is.* People say, "Brother Norvel, can you tell me what my ministry is?" or, "Brother Norvel, can we pray and see where I should go and what I should do for God? I need to know what my ministry is. Can you tell me?" Norvel boldly says, "Oh, yes, I can tell you what your ministry is. It is knocking on doors and passing out tracts, feeding the poor, and helping the needy." And that's exactly what Norvel did for the next seven years.

Norvel led high school assemblies, worked with kids to get them off of drugs, fed the poor, raised money to build churches, and prayed for everything that moved. He brought in speakers, like Nicky Cruz, and turned them loose in front of a thousand high school students. Then he would sit in the back of the auditorium or behind the stage curtains, and the Spirit of God would come on him. He sometimes just wept the whole time that Nicky or one of the other speakers he brought in, were ministering to the students.

Jesus: My Business Partner

Little by little, as he went through God's boot camp, he began to make Jesus his business partner. When he first gave his heart to God, Norvel probably wasn't worth over $200,000. After he got into the Bible himself and began to read it—giving his life and not just his heart to God—he began to pray and to confess, "Jesus, You're the best businessman I ever met. Jesus, I'm making You my business partner. Jesus! I choose to be successful rather than unsuccessful."

God says in 3 John 2, to His beloved son or daughter, that above all things in the world He wants you to be rich. And above all things in the world besides that, He wants you to live in health and not be sick. Sickness will destroy you. And God says, "Hey, I'll give you these two things—all you want. I'll give you both of them if you'll let your soul prosper—morning, noon, and night. Let your soul prosper first."

Money is one of the greatest blessings in the world if you know how to use it. The *love* of money is the root of all evil, not *money*. Norvel made Jesus his business partner and started reading financial Scriptures. Then he would say, "God, I believe these and claim them for myself. Thank you, Lord, for the finances coming in." He confessed this all the time. That's the reason it came his way all the time. He didn't become a multi-millionaire because he was smart. He became a multi-millionaire, *because he obeyed the Word*.

Norvel confessed, "The gift of the Spirit called the word of knowledge will come unto me supernaturally. And through that gift, Jesus, You will give me ideas and show me what to do to make hundreds of thousands of dollars with which to pay all of my bills and to then have thousands of dollars left over to spread the gospel and thousands of dollars left over to buy whatever I want!"

If you've been calling Jesus your miracle worker for ten years and now you need a miracle, it's easy to call upon Him for your miracle. But if you let those things that God's promised you lie dormant and you just deal with them nonchalantly, putting no emphasis on them at all, then when it comes time for a miracle or a healing or a financial breakthrough, it's hard to get. Smith Wigglesworth said, "If you wait until you get sick or have a deadly disease to start believing God and start building your faith, then you've waited too long. And it's hard to get healed."

If you'll do what you're supposed to do as far as your finances are concerned, you can be just as wealthy as you can handle. God wants to make you just as wealthy as you can stand. It all depends on what kind of desires you have in your life and what kind of emphasis you put on money. It also depends on what kind of emphasis you place on things and how you control them and money.

As Norvel began to believe and confess, "Jesus, You're the best businessman I have ever met," he began to get blessed more and more. He went from owning one restaurant to opening up six restaurants. He also built a subdivision in Florida. Then he bought two hundred acres of raw property and brought in bulldozers to knock down the trees. Then he built five miles of streets and roads through it and developed five hundred and forty-four lots. He sold about three hundred of these over a short period of time. He also owned his own manufacturing company at this time.

Divine Destiny

Dr. Kenneth Hagin was speaking one night in California and a respected lady in the ministry got up and just walked up to him and said, "The Lord has a prophecy for you, Brother Hagin." She started giving it out to him. She said, "The Lord wants you to go to Washington D.C. next week to the Full Gospel Business Men's convention. The Lord says there is a man that's going to be there that He wants you to meet. It's a divine destiny that you meet him. And God has put you together. And He will show you who he is when you get there."

Brother Hagin came to the convention, but he wasn't the main speaker, so he was given fifteen minutes to give a testimony. As he opened his mouth, the Spirit of God came on Norvel and showed him the anointing that was on Brother Hagin's life. After the meeting was over, Norvel walked into the dining room to get something to eat and saw Brother Hagin sitting at the table. So he walked over there and said, "Brother Hagin, my name is Norvel Hayes. I'm a businessman from Cleveland, Tennessee. When you opened up your mouth and began to speak today, the Spirit of the Lord came upon me, and it was like God drew me up in His presence and began to show you to me. And the Lord said to me that He wanted you to come to Cleveland, Tennessee. I'm just telling you what the Lord told me."

He said, "I know it. I'll come. I saw you."

Norvel thought about that for a long time. He wondered what Brother Hagin meant when he said, *"I saw you."* He was sitting in the middle of three thousand people.

So Brother Hagin came to Cleveland, Tennessee. One night when he was speaking, all of a sudden the spirit of prophecy came upon him and in the middle of the prophecy he called out Norvel's name. The moment he said his name, God hit Norvel and he broke and began to cry.

The prophecy said, "Son, the devil is going to attack your finances. But I am telling you tonight, if you will keep praying and stay faithful to Me and keep working for Me and keep on praying and praying and praying and praying, you will come through the attack, and then you'll be more successful financially than you've ever been in all of your life."

Norvel had never had a problem with anybody attacking his finances, so he thought to himself: *Well, what does he mean - the devil's going to attack my finances? I don't care anything about the devil. I know how to run a manufacturing company. I know how to build subdivisions. I know how to plot out land. I know how to have land surveyed. I know how to build streets. I know the kind of people to contact. I know the deals I need to make. I know how to buy raw land and develop it. I know how to run a restaurant. I know about food costs. I know exactly what I'm doing. What does He mean?*

At the time, Norvel had six restaurants, a Florida subdivision, and salesmen all over the country. Everything was going well for him. Then suddenly, one of his restaurant managers began to steal money, and it took him a while to catch him. Then another one went bad. The secretary at his manufacturing company in Columbus, Ohio—the best secretary he ever had in his life—stole thousands and thousands of dollars from him. During this time his real estate agent also contacted him and said, "I haven't sold a lot in three months. I can't sell one lot. Mr. Hayes, I've tried to sell your lots in your subdivision down in Florida, but I can't sell a lot." It went from bad to worse.

Thank God for the Holy Spirit. Thank God for the gift of prophecy. Thank God for people standing up and giving out prophecy. Thank the Lord that the One who lives in you can tell you what the devil's going to do before he ever does it, and also tells you how to get out of it. Norvel remembers, like bells ringing in his ears, *"But if you will pray and pray and pray and pray and work for Me and stay faithful to Me, Son…work for Me, keep on working for Me, and pray and pray and pray and pray…don't lose your ministry, Son…pray and pray and pray, I'll bring you out of it."*

Don't let the devil steal your ministry. It doesn't matter what you go through, don't ever lose your ministry. Whatever you go through with your family, finances, friends, relatives, or people, has nothing to do with God and your relationship with Jesus. Don't lose your ministry just because the devil comes by. A lot of things in your life may be the work of the devil, but don't lose your ministry in the midst of it all.

The Bible says that all the bad things that come to you come from the father of darkness—who wants to rob, kill, and steal from you, your family and your business (John 10:10). He wants to steal your business away from you. Always remember that God had nothing to do with all those bad things that happen to you. It's always the work of the devil and hell. *Always.*

Norvel told the devil, "You can't have my businesses, in Jesus' name. I claim success upon them, in Jesus' name." He just kept on, kept on, kept on praying, kept on working, kept on praying, and kept on working. If you don't make very much money, or even if you lose money during it all, take some money and go feed the poor. Find someone somewhere and do something good with your money. If, in the midst of the storm, it looks like you have no profits, get a few dollars somewhere and buy some tracts, help a church, or just keep on doing something for God. *And keep on praying and keep on praying and keep on praying.*

One day Norvel asked his main secretary, "Marilyn, how much money do I have in the main account to run all these businesses? After you write your check, how much money is in the main account?"

She said, "$85.00."

He said, "I won't accept that, I see thousands and thousands and thousands and thousands and thousands and thousands of dollars in there."

Norvel wouldn't give up praying, and he wouldn't give up working. He passed out tracts and helped poor little kids. Then he went down about 10 o'clock at night to his office and opened up the main checkbook and it maybe had $150, $300, or possibly even $400 in it. He would walk the floor in his office and pray and laugh. He didn't feel like laughing. He felt like crying. But you don't go by your feelings. You go by faith.

Norvel was in his office one night and he said, "Satan, you just might as well get this straight, flako, once and for all: I don't have to have any businesses to work for God. I don't have to have any money to work for the Lord. The only things I have to have are the Bible and the Holy Ghost—and I've still got both of them. Hey, flako, attack something else I own—go ahead. Every time you attack something, I'm going to go and pass out tracts. Every time you attack something, I'm going to find somebody and cast the devil out of them. Every time you attack one of my businesses, I'm going to go work hospitals and pray for everybody there. Every time you attack one of my businesses, every time you do anything to me, it means more victory! Go ahead, Satan, attack everything, you flaky thing, you. If you attack something of mine next week, I'm going to bring four sinners to church—not just one!"

Then he would tell Jesus, "I'm claiming my rights in Christ Jesus! Jesus, You're the best businessman I ever met!" He just kept doing this for five years.

Pray in the Spirit

The Lord says that if you get somewhere and you don't know what to do, do this: "Likewise the Spirit also helpeth our infirmities: for we know not what we should pray for as we ought: but the Spirit itself maketh intercession for us with groaning which cannot be uttered" (Romans 8:26). The Spirit of God knows you. It doesn't matter what condition you're in—He knows you. "And he that searcheth the hearts knoweth what is the mind of the Spirit, because he maketh intercession for the saints according to the will of God" (Romans 8:27).

Well, what is the will of God? The will of God is this: "Beloved, I wish above all things that thou mayest prosper and be in health, even as thy soul prospereth" (3 John 2). God is saying, "My little beloved children, I'll just go ahead and give you these things if you'll let your soul prosper. Don't lose your ministry if the devil comes and attacks you." Norvel interceded and prayed for five years. There is power in intercession—*power*. What kind of power does it bring you? It brings the knowledge of God to you.

You must also have determined faith that believes God for the impossible. Determined faith just absolutely will not let go, even if it takes five years. Always remember: *If you can learn how to make intercession and have determined faith, then when it comes to believing God for the impossible, regardless of how high the mountain looks—it's called the last crucial test of dedication—God will bless you mightily.*

Be Obedient

Norvel was teaching at a meeting in San Antonio, Texas. After the meeting, while he was sitting in his hotel room, the Spirit of God came upon him and said, "Go to Tulsa, Oklahoma, for Me. I'll show you two things after you get there."

Norvel called Brother Hagin and said, "Brother Hagin, the Lord said if I come to Tulsa, He'd show me two things after I got there."

Norvel had no earthly idea why he was going to Tulsa. But he didn't have to know. If God says do something, just go ahead and do it. As he was sitting in Kenneth Hagin's home, the Spirit of the Lord came upon him and said, "Pray." So he started praying. After he prayed for a while, the Lord said, "You can go home now."

On the way to the airport, Brother Hagin said, "Brother Norvel, the Lord showed me the two reasons why He sent you here to Tulsa. I started praying back there and making intercession as the Lord wanted me to. The first reason He sent you here was the duty of the calling that's on you. The second reason is, the Lord told me to tell you Norvel, the time has come now. You've passed His test. He said to tell you that He's going to open up the windows of heaven wide, and He is going to allow the light of God to shine upon your finances. And they will come to you by flood, by flood, by flood."

The Breakthrough

So Norvel didn't change. He just kept on working for the Lord. About two weeks went by. He had previously bought a little piece of property down in Florida for $13,000. The real estate company called him and said, "You know that little piece of property you just bought down here in Florida? I have a buyer that wants to give you $28,000 for it? Would you sell it?"

Norvel thought, *$13,000...$28,000—I'd double my money and make $15,000 off of that. Why not?* So he said, *I believe I'll sell it. Go ahead and sell it to him for $28,000.*

Norvel had also previously purchased a piece of property off a dirt road down in Florida for $15,000. He noticed that a black top county road had been put in front of that property. A few days later, he received another call from the real estate company, saying "Mr. Hayes, you have a piece of property down here and I have some people that want it. They said they will give $87,500 for it." So he sold it, too.

Another property in which he had invested $55,000 turned into a quarter of a million. Then one day Norvel was driving up Highway 19 and said, "God, what do You want me to do with all this money?"

God said, "You better use it for Me."

As he was driving early one morning and had planned to go fishing, the Lord said, "Don't go fishing. Buy a piece of property for Me today." God showed him the piece of property He wanted him to buy. He said, "There are five acres on a seven-lane highway there in Crystal River, Florida. I want you to buy that for Me, and I want you to put a mission on it. I want you to have workers go from door to door, and I want you to win some of these old people to Me."

So Norvel obeyed the Lord and bought the five acres of property for $90,000. He paid $10,000 down on it. Then he began to have little missionary-type meetings, sending out cars—eight to ten to twelve a day—and sending people two by two, working from door to door. The Lord said, "Fix this place up. You've been faithful to Me in this mission ministry. I have great things in store for this place.'

So Norvel said, "Yes, Sir, yes Sir, I will." He began to fix the place up. He put in a brand new auditorium. He never took up one single offering for it. He didn't have the money in his account to build the auditorium when he started, but when it was finished, it was paid for. The parking lot was paid for. The new sound system was paid for. The new seats were paid for—and he never took up one offering. God just sent people. Then one day, the real estate company called him and said, "I have a buyer for that property. He will give you $1,500,000 for it." So Norvel made a million dollars with a $10,000 investment. Remember the Lord had said to him, "My light's going to shine upon your finances."

Chapter 5

God's Boot Camp for Casting Out Devils

U sually God will put you with someone or in a place where there are those who know God better than you do so they can train you. And that's exactly what He did for Norvel. Just because you have the Holy Spirit in you and Jesus is your personal Savior, does not necessarily mean that you know God very well. If you know Him, and He is in you through Jesus Christ, then that will get you to heaven, but it may not help you to do His work here on earth. A lot of people have accepted Jesus and have been going to church a long time, but have never really gotten to know *Him* very well.

First John 4:4 says, "Greater is he that is in you, than he that is in the world." When you come upon a situation that you do not know how to handle, you need to remember that the One who is on the inside of you is greater than the one who has done the damage. But you can never be bold and speak with authority until you know who you are in God. Luke 9:2 says, "And he sent them to preach the kingdom of God, and to heal the sick." The only way you will ever see sick people healed is when you learn how to let the power of God flow through you to touch and heal them.

Norvel didn't know anyone who really knew God and obeyed the Bible. Then one day, he heard about a man named Lester Sumrall. He had never heard him speak, but he heard that he prayed for hours before his meetings and God wrought many miracles through him.

He heard of one miracle in particular that took place in one of Lester's meetings. One of his Full Gospel Business Men friends, who worked at a dealership as a car salesman in Columbus, Ohio, told him about a man in his church who had an operation in which all the ligaments in his hand were removed, and his hand became withered. Doctors told the man that he would never use that hand again.

He told him that the visiting minister, Lester Sumrall, had asked to stay in a back room and pray until the service started. He didn't come out until it was time for him to be introduced. When he did, the salesman explained said that he just walked up to the pulpit, looked out over the congregation, and said, "Will the man with the withered hand stand up." Then he told the man to stretch out his hand to him.

As the man stretched out his hand, Lester said, "In Jesus' name, hand, be made whole!" All of a sudden, right in front of the church, you could see his fingers that were sticking out of the end of the cast, begin to move. *This was impossible!* The man got so excited that he took a knife and cut the cast off and his hand had been made whole just like the other one. The church went wild.

As the salesman related this to Norvel, he said, "That's in the Bible! That's in the Bible!" I've have wanted to see something like that all of my life. I have never seen anything like that in my life. I want to see something like that so bad I can hardly stand it. I mean, I've got a burning desire in me to see something like that. That's in the Bible!"

Searching for a Man of God

When Norvel returned to Cleveland, he desired to learn more about this minister. He found out that Lester Sumrall was from South Bend, Indiana. He asked his pastor friend if he had ever heard of Lester Sumrall. He said that he had heard of him for years, ever since he was a kid. As Norvel related the story of the man with the withered hand, his pastor told him that those things happened a lot in Lester's ministry.

Norvel was so hungry to see these types of miracles that he asked his pastor to contact Lester Sumrall and get him to come to minister at his church. His pastor told him that Lester had a large ministry and would not come to a small church like his. So Norvel said, "Well, maybe he'll come. If I call him, would you let him use your church and come?" Finally, after Norvel's pleading, the pastor agreed that if Lester said that he would come, he could come anytime he wanted to.

Norvel went to his office, called information, and got Lester Sumrall's telephone number. He called his ministry and asked to speak to him. "Whom should I say is calling?" his receptionist asked.

Norvel said, "Norvel Hayes, a businessman from Cleveland, Tennessee."

She said, "Just a minute please, let me see."

In a few seconds a man came on the phone and said, "Hello."

Norvel said, "Is this Rev. Lester Sumrall?"

He said, "Yes, it is."

Norvel then said, "Rev. Sumrall, my name is Norvel Hayes and I was in the First Baptist Church. I got baptized in the Holy Spirit and I've never seen God heal anybody or give them eyesight or the lame walk and those kinds of things. I was in Columbus, Ohio, at a used car lot, and a man told me that you came to Columbus, Ohio, to a church." He went on to share all that the car salesman had shared with him about the healing of the man with the withered hand. And then he said, "Brother Sumrall, Rev. Sumrall, I want to see that so bad I can't hardly stand it. I'm hungry; I'm hungry to see it."

Lester said, "I believe you are."

Norvel then proceeded to say, "A certain minister here would let you come to his church. Can you come hold us a meeting? Please, Brother Sumrall, please Rev. Sumrall, come! I want to see this; I've never seen it in my life. I was raised in the First Baptist Church—raised Baptist, you know; and I helped build the First Baptist Church in Indianapolis. I've never seen it and I want to see it. Please come, Brother Sumrall, please come when you can."

Lester agreed to come on a certain day and minister for three nights. Norvel got back with that Pentecostal pastor in Cleveland, Tennessee, and told him that Lester was coming and when he would be there. The pastor was shocked! He couldn't believe that Lester Sumrall was actually going to come to his small church.

Norvel and the pastor planned the meetings with great anticipation. When Dr. Sumrall came, he prayed for everything that didn't move! He cast out devils and prayed for everyone. This was part of God's divine holy plan to bring reality to Norvel about Him. God had shown Norvel such favor with Lester Sumrall and they became friends instantly. Soon Norvel realized that God had sent someone else to help train him in his boot camp, and this time it was Lester Sumrall.

As Norvel and Lester were eating dinner during the last night of his meeting, Lester asked Norvel to come to the Full Gospel Business Men's Annual Convention in Phoenix, Arizona. He also told him that he was booked on a television show around that time and wanted him to come and help him with it. So Norvel agreed to go.

After they finished the television and radio broadcast, Lester said, "Norvel, I'm going to go to San Bernardino, California, today after the radio broadcast. It's the home of the Hell's Angels (an outlaw motorcycle gang and organized crime syndicate whose members typically ride Harley-Davidson motorcycles). I'm going to go to the Orange Dome Auditorium and put on a crusade there for several days—five or six days." He asked, "Why don't you go down there with me and speak for me the first night?"

Norvel said, "Speak for you in a big crusade and auditorium? Not me. I just give testimonies."

Lester said, "Well, that's what I mean—give a testimony from a businessman's perspective."

Norvel agreed to do that, and found himself in the meeting in San Bernardino, California, with Lester Sumrall. After the singing that first night, Norvel was introduced, and he spoke for fifteen minutes on what Jesus meant to him as a businessman. He turned around, walked off the stage and behind a curtain, and at that moment the Spirit of the Lord came upon him. He broke and began to weep and weep and weep and weep, and the word of the Lord came to him saying in no uncertain terms, "Don't leave this meeting, Son."

The Lord told him not to leave because He had a reason for wanting him to stay at that meeting. It's so important for you to obey God. When God tells you to do something, He usually won't tell you the reason why He's telling you to do it. You first have to obey Him, and then He will explain why. What Norvel was finding out is that every Christian who wants to do something for God needs to be trained by someone already in the ministry. That is why the Apostle Paul would take different young men with him on missionary journeys. He was training them. You have to learn from someone who knows.

Norvel told Dr. Sumrall that the Lord had dealt with him to stay in these meetings, and that he would assist him in anything he wanted him to do. He said, "I'll help your sister sell books. I'll help you at the altar—anything." Lester told him to stay and enjoy himself and to help his sister and her husband with the book table. So, Norvel went to every service and enjoyed each one of them. After each service, the Lord would tell him not to leave yet.

The third day of the meetings arrived and Norvel was in the morning service. At the end of Brother Sumrall's message, it happened again —the Spirit of God came upon Norvel. God was just blessing him and blessing him and blessing him. Lester gave an invitation and when he did, Norvel stepped up from his seat to receive the people who came for prayer. There was one woman who came forward real quick and walked up to him.

She said, "I believe that you men are men of God."

Norvel said, "Well, that's nice to believe that. If you're going to come to church, you better believe that the men in charge are men of God."

She said, "Well, something strange happens to me and I want you fellas to pray for me, because I believe that you really know God." She continued, "Every time I go to town, something jumps on my back. I park my car, get out, and walk down the sidewalk; and all of a sudden, my back is wracked with pain—totally wracked with pain. And it hurts so bad I can't stand it. And so I work my way back to my car and I drive home.

"I lie on my bed and pray, pray, pray—sometimes as much as eight hours. And then, all of a sudden, all of the pain in my back will just leave. I'm just as normal as anybody else. I'll wait a day and then need to go to town for some things. I'll get in my car, go to town again, park my car, walk down the sidewalk, and aaahhhh—there's that pain again. I head back towards my car, get in, and go home. Every time I go to town that happens to me. Please, pray for me. Pray for me. I need prayer."

Novel was from the First Baptist Church. He didn't know anything about something jumping on somebody downtown. He had never heard of anything like that before, but he said, "Well, alright, we'll pray for you. Give me your hand, and we'll just pray right now." He was going to say a little prayer for her. She reached out and the moment he touched her hand, she jumped and recoiled, clenching her fists violently and growling like a mad animal. Then she yelled, "*Ahhhoooaaaahhh*!"—in church, in the altar! It stunned him completely. Norvel had never seen anyone act like that before, especially in a church service. He didn't know what to do!

He said to himself, *What's wrong with her? Is she nuts?* And he sort of growled back at her—"*Grrr,* yourself"—thinking, *I don't even know what you're doing!*

The woman looked at Norvel like she wanted to fight. He didn't even know her. He thought, *Surely a woman wouldn't attack a man in church. I mean, I've got more sense than that.* But she kept standing there, staring at him. Demons are bold and stubborn. They want to destroy people and do them harm. They don't want to leave. So Norvel did something that he wished that he hadn't—he happened to look toward the congregation, and several hundred eyes were looking at him to see what he was going to do.

Norvel muttered, "Oh, God, no!"

Norvel didn't know what to do, because all he had been taught to do was to say nice prayers for the people who came to the altar. That's good to be taught to say nice prayers, *until you start dealing with the devil.* He doesn't listen to nice prayers. That lady kept on standing there, and he still couldn't believe that she was going to attack him. She looked like she wanted to fight, and she would look at him, and then she would growl. Then, all of a sudden and to his utter amazement, she tore into him, and began clawing at him. He couldn't believe it. He couldn't believe that a crazy woman attacked him in church.

Norvel had already made up his mind, just in case she did attack him, that he wasn't going to let her beat him up in church! He had decided that if she started hitting him, he was going to throw her on the floor! So, when she tore into him, he grabbed her by one of her arms and held her off of him. He thought, *I'm not going to let this goo-goo woman beat me up in church. I can't slug her; I'm afraid they'll put me in jail. Besides that, I'm a nice fella.* So he just held her off of him, and when he did, she started whimpering and fell to the floor. The congregation was still looking at him to see what he was going to do.

He didn't know what was wrong with her, and thought this was the strangest church service he had ever been in! He was new in the Charismatic Movement, and he was trying to be a nice Full Gospel Business Man who just prayed nice prayers for people. But here this woman was, lying on the floor, whimpering; and all of a sudden, Norvel heard this voice that sounded like it was from another world and it said, "Cast that thing out of her!"

Norvel jumped, because the voice was so loud. As he looked up, he saw Lester Sumrall on the stage, standing there, relaxed and leaning on the pulpit, full of the peace of God. He was standing up there, telling him to "cast that thing out of her."

Immediately, Norvel began to get hot flashes. He was embarrassed because he didn't know what to do. He thought to himself, *What thing? What thing am I supposed to cast out of her? Does she have a THING in her?* Meanwhile, this woman was still lying on the floor groaning and moaning. So Norvel said, "Yeah, ah, yeah, sure. Okay. Alright, Rev. Sumrall," still thinking, *Cast that thing out of her—what thing?* He kept thinking, *Yeah cast that thing out of her. Cast that thing out of her. Cast that thing out of her.* All of a sudden, that voice that sounded like it was from another world—came over the microphone again; and Lester Sumrall said, "And don't let her talk either!"

Norvel jumped, looked at Lester, looked at the congregation staring at him waiting to see what he was going to do, and looked at her, and said, "Yeah, okay. Sure. Sure. Don't let her talk! Cast that thing out of her, and don't let her talk!" And all the while he was wondering, *What am I supposed to do?* His great knowledge of God just got exposed.

When you don't know what to do, just stand still and be steadfast. *Cast that thing out of her, and don't let her talk. Yeah, sure. Cast that thing out of her, and don't let her talk. Yeah, that's right,* he thought to himself, *Yeah, okay, sure.* He looked at that lady, and he couldn't stop her. She was gasping for breath and whimpering. He wondered, *Should I just raise her up, slap her in the face, and say, "Be gone"? It's not nice to slap a woman, period, and especially in church! But she's not going to stop—she's crazy. The woman's gone nuts, I'm telling you. Oh, God, what am I doing here? Lord, deliver me to the First Baptist Church. Lord, what am I doing with these goofed-up people? Lord, if you'll let me get out of here, I'll never bother these people anymore.*

Thank God for Rev. Murphy who was married to Lester Sumrall's sister. He was sitting on the front row watching all this, when all of a sudden, he just flipped out of his seat and was on his knees right beside this lady. He knelt down next to her and said, "In Jesus name, you come out of her!"

Norvel didn't want the congregation to think he was stupid, so he just said, "Yeah!" acting like he knew what he was doing. He learned a long time ago that if you act like you know what you are doing, nobody will know that you're ignorant. So he said, "Yeah! Come out of her!" That's the first time he ever said that. He had no earthly idea what he was talking to. He was just copying Rev. Murphy, because he acted as if he knew what he was doing. Then Rev. Murphy said, "I said, 'Obey me and come out of her!'" He said it strongly!

So Norvel said, "Yeah, and I said it too! Come out of her! Whatever you are, come out of her!" Every time Rev. Murphy said it, Norvel would say it, too.

Rev. Murphy told Norvel, "Talk with authority, like you mean it."

He said, "I command you, come out of her!"

And Norvel said, "Yeah, and I command it, too."

It's a wonder that devil didn't say, "Oh, shut up!" Norvel continued to copy Rev. Murphy. He had no earthly idea what he was doing. He didn't know anything about any "thing" being in her. He was just doing whatever Rev. Murphy did. Whatever he did, Norvel did. Rev. Murphy would say, "You obey me; come out of her." And Norvel would say, so the audience could hear him, "I say it, too; now, you obey me, too."

The woman was still whimpering; and Rev. Murphy continued, "Come out of her, in Jesus' name; come out of her."

And Norvel said, "Yeah, yeah, in His name, you do it."

Norvel didn't know anything about anything. He had no earthly idea what he was talking to. He was just copying Rev. Murphy. And all of a sudden, as he said, "Come out of her, in Jesus' name," the woman stopped whimpering and "fell out"—went limp. Norvel concluded, *Oh, God, we've killed her.* He decided, *Oh, God, I've got to get out of here. I've got to get out of here. We've killed her, and I'll go to the penitentiary forever. I've got to get out of this crazy place; this is the wildest place I've ever seen in my life. Let me out of here, God. Let me out of here!*

Two or three minutes passed. Then, all of a sudden, this lady's face changed, and tears began to flow. When she came to be prayed for, she looked like a nice lady. And then she started to look like a living devil, like she had changed into another creature. When she fell out like she was dead, a glow came on her face and a calmness came over her, as tears came streaming down. *She looked like an angel.*

She began to say, "Thank You, Jesus. Oh, thank You, Jesus. Thank You, Jesus. Thank You, Jesus. Oh, thank You, Jesus." That astounded Norvel, and he could hardly believe what he was seeing. Somebody who looked like a devil had within just two or three minutes, turned into somebody who looked like an angel, and was thanking Jesus. Just a few minutes before, she wanted to fight him in church and now she was thanking Jesus. Rev. Murphy reached down, got the lady by the hand and the arm, and helped her up. And Norvel did, too—whatever Rev. Murphy did, Norvel did. They helped her onto one of the seats. By the time they got her set down, the Spirit of God just overshadowed her and she wept and laughed—all at the same time, and God blessed her and blessed her and blessed her and blessed her.

Norvel pondered this, *That's amazing; she looks like an angel. She's the most beautiful woman I've ever seen in my life. Look at her; look at her face and clothes—she looks like an angel, thanking Jesus and with tears streaming down her face. And the glow of freedom and peace that was on her!* He said, "Oh, God!" While he was standing there, the Lord said, "You can go now. You can leave. You can go home now."

Norvel said, "Oh, ah, okay. Alright, Jesus, I'll go home."

He told Rev. Sumrall at lunch, "Brother Sumrall, the Lord spoke to me after the service this morning and told me I could go home now."

What did that mean, 'You can go home now?' Well, Norvel had been through school, had taken his course. It doesn't take but one, you know. He had made up his mind to do what Jesus was doing. You have to make up your mind to do what Jesus does, and it doesn't take but one course. You see, the Lord wanted Norvel to see all that had happened in that meeting there. Norvel thought that Rev. Sumrall's ministry was real nice, but he didn't identify himself with it. He never thought that God would want him to get involved with anything like that—*He was First Baptist!*

Chapter 6

Sixteenth Chapter of Mark?

When Norvel returned from San Bernardino, California, he was driving around to each of his six restaurants one afternoon conducting business. While he was driving, all of a sudden the Spirit of the Lord moved upon him in his car, saying, "Go study the sixteenth chapter of the Book of St. Mark. Go study it, Son; study it. You must study it." Norvel didn't know what was in the sixteenth chapter of St. Mark, but he could hardly wait to read it and find out. So, he wheeled his car around and took off toward his house.

When he got to his house, he grabbed his Bible and opened it up to the sixteenth chapter of the Book of St. Mark. He had no earthly idea what was in there, since he was a member of the Baptist Church. But the Lord told him to study it. He wanted him to *study* all of it. Now there's a difference in *reading* the Bible and *studying* the Bible.

In Mark 16:1, it says, "And when the Sabbath was past, Mary Magdalene, and Mary the mother of James, and Salome, had bought sweet spices, that they might come and anoint him." This was after Jesus had been put in the tomb. He had only been dead for about three days. Verses two through five say, "And very early in the morning the first day of the week, they came unto the sepulchre at the rising of the sun. And they said among themselves, Who shall roll us away the stone from the door of the sepulchre? And when they looked, they saw that the stone was rolled away: for it was very great. And entering into the sepulchre, they saw a young man sitting on the right side, clothed in a long white garment; and they were affrighted."

Of course that "young man" was an angel. Norvel's eyes were opened up to the reality of angels. He learned that angels took orders from God, would talk to him, and had ministries on the earth. Verses six through eight of Mark 16 read, "And he [the angel] saith unto them, Be not affrighted: Ye seek Jesus of Nazareth, which was crucified: he is risen; he is not here: behold the place where they laid him. But go your way, tell his disciples and Peter that he goeth before you into Galilee: there shall ye see him, as he said unto you. And they went out quickly, and fled from the sepulchre; for they trembled and were amazed: neither said they any thing to any man; for they were afraid."

As soon as Norvel read that eighth verse where it said, "they were afraid," the Holy Ghost came upon him and he began to weep and weep. The love of God overshadowed him and went down through him, and began to come out of him this way and that way—he got saturated with the love of the Lord. He felt it so strongly. He could hardly stand it. On this earth we have some great preachers, Bible scholars, churches, and crusades, but the strongest tool in the world is the pure love of God.

Norvel was caught up in the glory of the Lord and when it finally lifted, he looked back at the Bible to read the ninth verse: "Now when Jesus was risen early the first day of the week, he appeared first to Mary Magdalene, out of whom he had cast seven devils." Then Norvel saw something he had never seen before, and shares what he believes, in his personal opinion, about the ninth verse of Mark 16:

> I believe that Jesus appeared first to Mary Magdalene—a woman *"out of whom he had cast seven devils"*—because she loved Him the most. You see, Mary Magdalene was looking for Him. She wasn't sitting at her house with hardness of heart and unbelief. She believed what He said, and she was looking for Him. God responds to faith. When you're looking for God, you can find Him. Those who diligently seek God shall find Him. Hunger and thirst after righteousness and you shall be filled. (Matthew 5:6.)
>
> I never knew that before—that when Jesus appeared on earth following His resurrection, the first human being He appeared to was a woman, and especially a woman out of whom He had cast seven devils. Right there, the Lord let me see in the spirit world the importance of casting out devils. I immediately thought of that woman in California. That had been my first and only experience of this sort, so naturally I would think of her—having a devil in her, you know, trying to fight me in church. That thing had left her; I could see that it had. And, because of that, I could see why Mary Magdalene was looking for Jesus that day at the tomb—because if you're possessed with seven devils and somebody comes along and casts them out of you and you're free from them, you want to follow up on that person. Because of that person, you're free from devils that tormented your life.

If someone is being buffeted or possessed or oppressed with a devil, and you break its power and make it leave, that person will love you—and they will love God. When that woman in San Bernardino revived again after falling to the floor, she looked like she had received the same thing I was receiving right then as I read Mark 16, verse 9—*the love of God.* I was now realizing that she received that love because a devil was cast out of her. I repeat: I believe that Jesus appeared first to Mary Magdalene because she loved Him most...because she had been set free from seven devils.

I kept on reading. Verse ten was next: "And she went and told them..." I mean, she was willing to tell them—just like it was. Continuing with verses 10 through 11: "And she went and told them that had been with him, as they mourned and wept. And they, when they had heard that he was alive, and had been seen of her [Mary Magdalene], they believed not." They did not believe that Jesus appeared first to a woman out of whom He had cast seven devils. They didn't believe that. Always remember people: *It doesn't make any difference what people believe; it's what the Bible says—that's what counts.*

Verses twelve through fourteen of Mark 16 say, "After that he appeared in another form unto two of them, as they walked, and went into the country. And they went and told it unto the residue: neither believed they them. Afterward he appeared unto the eleven [the disciples] as they sat at meat, and upbraided them with their unbelief and hardness of heart, because they believed not them which had seen him after he was risen."

When I got to the next part of Mark 16, starting with verse 15, the Lord spoke to me again that day. "Now, Son, these are the most important words that ever came out of my mouth: 'And he said unto them, Go ye into all the world, and preach the gospel to every creature.'"

Get this straight: *The gospel is the most important words that ever came out of the mouth of Jesus.* **The gospel.** Do you preach to anybody? Do you ever run up on any creatures and preach?

Someone might say, "Brother Norvel, I'm not called to preach. That's not my calling." My answer to that is: "Oh yes, it is." Now you may be thinking about preaching in a church or a crusade or upon stage. But that's not what that means. Everybody in the world who is born again can preach the greatest sermon in the world by opening up their mouth and telling what Jesus has done for them. There isn't a person who can't do that.

That verse doesn't specifically mean you have to be called to a public ministry—just open up your mouth. Paul said that if you'll open your mouth, the Holy Ghost will put words in your mouth. You know what the Lord has done for you; just give your testimony. Tell about what you used to be, and what you are now that the Lord has saved you. You don't have to go into all the gory details—just tell them that you were a scuzz ball, and now since the Lord saved you and touched you, you are sweet and precious."

The Kind of Gospel that Fits Your Case

The woman in California had a right to receive the gospel of the Lord Jesus Christ. The woman who attacked Norvel in church was bound, but she had a right to receive the gospel. By the "gospel", we mean "the kind of gospel that fits your case." There are all different kinds of gospels, and they are all true: *salvation*—if you're lost; *healing*—if you're sick; a *miracle*—if you need one; *peace*—if you're confused. There are all kinds of freedoms through the gospel, but you have to know what kind—what part—of the gospel that will help that particular situation.

A person who is dying of cancer but is already saved does not need John 3:16. Understand that! If you are saved and dying of cancer, you already have John 3:16. You need James 5:14 and James 5:15, "Is any sick among you? Let him call for the elders of the church; and let them pray over him, anointing him with oil in the name of the Lord: And the prayer of faith shall save the sick, and the Lord shall raise him up..."

You need to know about the power of faith. You also need to know that it is God's will to heal. In order for you to be able to help yourself and others, you've got to know what kind of gospel to present to each person. That's the reason it's important for you to study the Bible and know what's in there. When you study the Bible and get the Word of God on the inside of you, the Holy Spirit will bring to your remembrance the verse of Scripture that you need for whatever case you're dealing with...*to fit the need at hand.* You need to study the gospel, the entire spectrum of God's Word or you will never do what God wants you to do, and you will never have what

God wants you to have. You will live and die and never see God manifest Himself.

Continuing in Mark, chapter 16, Jesus said in verses 15 *and* 16, "Go ye into all the world, and preach the gospel to every creature. He that believeth and is baptized shall be saved; but he that believeth not shall be damned." It was when Norvel came to the next verse— verse 17—that the word of the Lord came to him again, saying, "Son, hardly anybody on earth believes this verse and very few people ever obey it." Norvel had never even read the verse, so he didn't know what it said. But the word of God came to him like lightning and told him that.

He looked down at verse 17 and read: "And these signs shall follow them that believe; In my name shall they cast out devils…" He thought to himself, *I've believed the Lord ever since I was a little Baptist kid, but I don't cast out devils.* Norvel had never obeyed Mark 16:17, except for the one time when he was in Lester Sumrall's meeting and didn't know what he was doing. But in this verse Jesus is saying, "I have a command for you: If you're saved, I want you to use My name and cast out devils."

Then Norvel thought about what had happened in California with that woman. He said, "Lord, I think You're trying to show me something." Think about what Jesus said: "If you believe in Me, I want you to cast out devils." This was the first commission from the Lord Jesus Christ, the Head of the Church. Someone might say, "Well, I believe in Jesus." Then Jesus says, "Oh, you do? Well, if you believe in Me, I want you to use My name. I'm going to give it to you for free. And I want you to cast out devils. I want you to resist devils."

Now why would the Lord want you to deal with the devil first of all? Why was that His first commission? Because the devil is the one that can kill you and steal from you and destroy you, that's why. God also loves you so much that He doesn't want you to be destroyed by the devil. He doesn't want you to be deceived by the devil. He wants you to deal with the devil head on.

You better start resisting devils, because devils are what get you into trouble. Always know that you can trust the Bible all the time. Because Jesus said, "In my name shall they cast out devils," just believe that you can say, "In Jesus' name, come out! I cast you out!"—and the demons will go. You may say, "But, Brother Norvel, I'm just a sweet little lady. I want to be a lady." Well, be a sweet lady in public. In your private life, when people need help, be a tiger and cast out devils! You have a voice. Just because you are a sweet little lady, you can still get mad at the devil when he is doing evil to people. Say, "Come out, in Jesus' name!"

Just because you are a real sweet lady and you are a Christian, don't just sit around and let the devil do anything he wants to do to you. Let the Lord do anything He wants to do to you, but don't let the devil do *anything* to you! You have to learn to resist the devil. If your teenagers won't serve the Lord, the devil has come to your house to steal your children. Don't let him have them! Bind him up and throw him out of the house! Say, "In Jesus' Name, turn my son loose. I bind you! In Jesus' Name, I resist you. Go from my children! And I confess, in Jesus' name, that the Holy Spirit will create a desire in my children to go to church, and that they will love me and their father and show respect. I bind you, you disrespecting devil! Thank You, Lord, for the desire coming into my children to go to church and serve the Lord!"

Keep on resisting. If you resist the devil, you can break his power over anything! Bind that thing in Jesus' name, and resist it! The words *resist*, *bind* and *rebuke* are some of the best words in the Bible. They will keep your enemy away from you. They will make your enemy flee!

Let's read from verses 17 and 18 of Mark 16: "And these signs shall follow them that believe; In my name shall they cast out devils... They shall take up serpents; and if they drink any deadly thing, it shall not hurt them..." The word "serpent" is a name for the devil or for a demon. "Satan" is a name for the devil. "Devil" is a name for the devil. "The prince of darkness" is a name for the devil. He has a lot of names. The Bible says to take up serpents and throw them out! Don't wait for them to leave or they will hang around—they are like leeches!

As Norvel continued to study the rest of Mark 16, he was utterly amazed at what he read. But first the Spirit of the Lord said to him in regard to the rest of verse 18: "Notice, Son, the last eleven words that came out of My mouth—'they shall lay hands on the sick, and they shall recover.'"

Every time you open up your mouth and speak the words of the Lord to hurting people, He wants to confirm your words with signs following. He will confirm your words with signs following, just as much as He will do so for any big-time preacher. "So then after the Lord had spoken unto them, he was received up into heaven, and sat on the right hand of God. And they went forth, and preached everywhere, the Lord working with them, and confirming the word with signs following" (Mark 16:19,20).

God wants you to be a witness unto Him. One of the main ministries in the world is for you and me to be a witness for Jesus to somebody who needs help. Just keep it that way for the rest of your life. Don't ever try to get popular; don't ever get fancy. Just stay normal. God loves normal people, full of the Holy Ghost! And especially remember: Learn to resist the devil, in the name of Jesus, whenever and wherever he rears his head.

God didn't waste any time giving Norvel an opportunity to obey Mark 16:17. It was the very next week, after he had the experience in California in Lester Sumrall's meeting, that he encountered a girl who was completely demon possessed. This time was different because Norvel was equipped with Mark Chapter 16, and had been trained to obey God. He recaps the following incident:

I felt led of the Lord to attend a prayer meeting on Wednesday night in my town. I said, "Okay, okay, Lord, alright, if that's where You want me to go." On the Sunday before that, I had a little encounter with this demon-possessed girl that didn't amount to much and I had, for the most part, put it out of my mind. I had gone to the full gospel church in my town that day and was by the side door on my way out, when the full gospel pastor said to me, "Hey, Brother Norvel, can I talk to you for a minute? Hey, Brother Norvel, Brother Norvel, come here. Can I talk to you for a minute?"

I said, "Well, okay."

"Brother Norvel, I have got the worst case of a young girl with problems that I've ever had in my life, and I've been in the ministry for years. She is the worst case I have ever had in my lifetime. They have thrown her out of the college dormitory here in town, she can't go to school, and she's roaming the streets. She has come to me for help. She has gone to other pastors for help. She's gone to this one for help and that one for help. And I've talked to her and counseled with her and prayed with her, and I can't do anything with her. I'm telling you, I can't do anything with her. She's the wildest thing I've ever seen."

I asked, "What did she get thrown out of the dormitory for? What did they throw her out of college for?"

"Well, because she goes to be with all the boys."

"Oh," I said, "Dear God, really?" I asked, "All of them?"

"Well, I mean, the ones that want to. She's seeking help, but she's can't find any. And I know you deal with college kids sometimes on college campuses. Would you be willing to talk to her?"

I said, "Sure, I'll talk to her." She was still sitting in the church pew, so I went up and sat down, and talked to her. I told her that Jesus loved her. She was looking down; she wouldn't even look at me. I looked around the church as people were leaving that day and when I looked back, the girl was gone—disappeared, just gone. I said to myself, *I don't believe this. I'm talking to myself.*

I got up and said, "Pastor, did you see that girl?"

He said, "Yes, she went out."

I said, "Man, she left awful quick. I didn't even see her get up."

He said, "Norvel, she is the worst case I've ever dealt with in my entire ministry. I'm telling you, she's the worse case I've ever dealt with in my life."

I didn't really know much about this young lady, so I expressed to the pastor, "Oh, well, I was going to counsel with her, but you know how those cases are, oh, well." So I went about my own business, making plans to attend an upcoming convention. And the Lord said, "Don't go to the convention; stay here and go to prayer meeting." That's when I said, "Okay, okay, Lord, alright, if that's where You want me to go."

So I went to prayer meeting at the same church I had attended on Sunday. Forty or fifty people were there. The preacher preached and I was sitting back in the congregation minding my own business. The preacher gave an invitation and one person got up out of her seat, went in front and knelt down. I looked at her and thought, *that looks like that girl I was going to talk to Sunday. Maybe I can talk to her now.* So I just got up out of my seat—nobody else in church did, but I did. I went up and knelt down beside her, and I began to pray for her.

I could hear the girl saying, "God, help me. Somebody, help me. Help me, Jesus; help me, Jesus. I don't want to be this way, Jesus. Help me, Jesus; help me, God. Help me; help me."

As I knelt beside her, I prayed for her. I mean, I prayed and I prayed and I prayed—I got to praying *strong*. I prayed an old-fashioned Baptist prayer, blessed be God, trying to reach heaven for this girl. And I prayed and prayed and prayed—for about fifteen minutes, I guess. And by that time, there must've been five or six other people around her praying for her. So I just got up and went back to where I had been sitting.

All of a sudden, the Spirit of the Lord came upon me and I began to see a vision. I saw myself in California. I saw myself get up and walk up to the altar. I saw the woman come over to me and I could hear her say, "I believe that you men are men of God. Would you pray for me? Something jumps on me when I go downtown." I saw myself take the woman's hand. I saw her jump back and growl. I saw her tear into me, and then I grabbed her by the arm. I saw her fall on the floor and heard her whimpering. I heard Lester Sumrall say, "Cast that thing out of her!" And I heard myself saying, "Sure, ah, yeah!"

God let me see this whole thing in a vision. Sitting right there on that church pew, I saw the whole thing. I saw Rev. Murphy come up and I heard him say "In Jesus' name, come out of her!" And I heard myself say, "Yeah, I said it, too." And after awhile, I saw that woman go limp, like she was dead. Then I saw the glory of God come upon her as she was set free. And then the scene changed from California, to Cleveland, Tennessee; and I saw myself in my Cadillac riding around to my different businesses. I saw myself. And I heard the voice say, "Go study the sixteenth chapter of the Book of St. Mark, right now!"

I saw myself turn my car around and head straight to my house, get the Bible and open it up as fast as I could and I saw myself reading it, every verse from the first. I saw myself come to the end of the eighth verse and right before the ninth verse. And the Spirit of the Lord came upon me, sitting there in that church pew that Wednesday prayer meeting night and tears came streaming down my face as I was saturated with the love of God—just like I had been that day in my house.

I heard the Lord say in my spirit, "I appeared first to Mary Magdalene out of whom I had cast seven devils. Are you ashamed of that, Son?"

"No, no!"

I came on down to the most important words that ever came out of Jesus' mouth: **"Go ye into all the world, and preach the gospel to every creature."** And then I heard the Lord say in regard to the seventeenth verse, "Son, hardly anybody believes this, neither do they obey it—"In my name shall they cast out devils"…if you believe in me."

By this time, I got what Jesus was saying to me loud and clear. I started to beg and plead with Him, just like a whipped puppy, "No, no, God; please, God! Oh, God, no, please! No, don't make me do this, God. I'm from the First Baptist Church, Jesus. You understand— First Baptist, First Baptist, First Baptist, First Baptist Church. I'm from the First Baptist Church. I don't know how to do this. I don't know how to do this."

"Yes, you do!" He said to me.

Again, I said, "No, no, no, no, oh, God, don't make me do it. Oh, don't make me do it. Don't make me do this, Jesus. Please, don't make me do it. I've got friends in here. I've got friends in here."

"You're ashamed of this?" He asked.

"Well no, but I don't know how. I don't know how, Lord. I've had no experience, no training."

"Yes, you have!" He responded.

"No, I haven't; I haven't."

"California!" He reminded me.

"Just one time, Jesus. Just one time."

"That's all you need!" He stated.

I asked, "What do I do? What do I do?"

He said, "Do what they did [referring to Lester Sumrall and Rev. Murphy]. They said, 'In Jesus' name, come out of her.'"

"Do what they did?"

I just flat told God that I didn't want to do it—wasn't going to do it. "I don't want to do it, Jesus. I don't want to do it." And, you know, He wouldn't let me go.

I said, "I don't want to do it, Jesus. I don't want to do this. I've got friends in this place. I've never done this in public, Jesus; I don't want to do it. I want to be a nice Christian businessman. I don't want to get involved in things like this. My relatives might hear about it. My old friends might hear about it, and I don't want to be involved in things like this."

"If you believe in Me, in My name you shall cast out devils!"

"No, no, no Lord Jesus! Jesus, that girl came from a full gospel college. They know You there. Believe me, Jesus; they know You a lot better than I do. Please get them to do to it; get them to do it, Jesus."

"I can't get them to do it; they've quit!"

Quit! It's amazing that when someone gets to be a doctor—a theologian—he stops casting out devils. When he was a fiery evangelist, he got used to being set free and he went out and fought the devil and did whatever God wanted him to do. But when he became a professor or a teacher, he stopped casting out devils in public on Sunday morning in front of the church. Some men in this situation—most of them—no longer want to get involved in that kind of stuff. They're half backslid. They probably know God as well as they ever knew Him, but they've stopped obeying Him.

I didn't want to get involved in stuff like casting out devils. I knew exactly how these men felt. I had big shot friends and I didn't want to get involved in stuff like that. I'd have to be out of my mind to want to! I said, "Jesus, I don't do things like that."

He said, "The sixteenth chapter of the Book of St. Mark does."

I said, "Lord, they don't do it where I went to church and where I grew up. Jesus, they don't do it. And think about that good pastor that pastored that church back when I grew up as a kid. Lord, You remember him. And think about this pastor over here where I go to church now. Lord, You visit this church and these people love You. These people love You, and they don't do it. And this pastor over here at this other church I've been to, he doesn't do it."

Every time I would say, "They don't do it," the Lord would say to me, "The sixteenth chapter of the Book of the St. Mark does it! And you read it!"

I said, "Yes, Sir, I know it, Jesus; I know it. I know it, Lord; but Jesus, Jesus, please don't make me do that. Please don't make me do that."

Then He said, "You've been going around the country standing in front of these fancy banquets telling people that you love Me. 'Oh, I love Jesus. I love Jesus. I love Jesus. Look what Jesus has done for me. Jesus has done a lot for me. Look what Jesus has done for me. I love Jesus.'"

He said, "Tonight I demand that you show Me you love Me. Remember, Son," He said to me, "Words are cheap. Just because you go around the country and stand in front of fancy banquets, telling people that you love Me, that doesn't mean you do. If you love Me, you love My Word and you love My gospel. I demand that you show Me tonight that you love Me!"

"But," I said, "Jesus, I don't want to do that; I don't want to. Jesus, I don't want to do that; I don't want to."

Then this is where Jesus got to me. He said, "Look at her; look at her! They've been praying for her for twenty-five minutes, and you prayed for her for a long time yourself. And nothing happened, and nothing is going to happen. Devils don't listen to prayers."

I said, "I'm looking at her, Jesus; I'm looking at her. I see her. I see her, Jesus."

"Look at her again! You heard her moans and her cries for help—'Jesus, please help me; Jesus, please!' Those are the cries of a lonely heart, and they have come up before the throne of God. Son, she's totally possessed with a demon—the spirit of lust. I didn't put that demon in her, the devil did. And look at her straight."

What Jesus said to me next is one of the reasons why I have such mercy and compassion today, for people no matter what they've done. Jesus told me that night, "It doesn't make any difference to Me if she's been to bed with a hundred men. I didn't make her do it; the devil did. I still love her, and I will always love her. And I love all the ones like her. And if you're going to work for Me, you better understand that tonight."

I knew the call of God was on me heavy and strong. I wrestled with God, I guess for thirty minutes, but I couldn't win. So I said, "Okay, Lord, I'll do it; I'll do it. Just give me power, and I will do it, because I don't have enough power to do it." I said, "I promise you, God, if You'll give me power right now to do it—to make that evil thing leave her—I'll do it. I know she's begging for help, and there is nobody to help her."

Then, all of a sudden, power came into me. I didn't know what it was at the time, but now I know that it was the gift of faith. I mean, every ounce of me got possessed with power. My fingers had supernatural power. My hands had supernatural power. My tongue had supernatural power. My bones had supernatural power. My eyes had supernatural power. I couldn't see anything except victory for that girl. I could feel it in my feet.

I got up out of my seat and walked down front; and I said, "Have her stand up! God's going to set her free!" And the people next to the girl had her stand up. I said, "You foul spirit that's wrecked this girl's life, in Jesus' name, you come out of her!" I said it only one time, and it was like something passed by me in the air—*wheshewww!* The young girl's body flew back and hit the floor, and she landed flat on her back. The moment she hit the floor, her hands went up in the air and she began speaking in other tongues, as tears began to stream down her face. She was totally free and the Holy Ghost came back into her—she had come from a full gospel family.

Her dad was there that night. He was a professional man, and he and his wife had been through hell with their daughter. They saw what happened that night. God's power was all over that place and the people began to shout throughout the congregation. Her father came over and laid his hand on my shoulder, and he wept like a baby. He wept and wept and wept, as he told me that his daughter had been prayed for and prayed for. She had been prayed for, but she never received any help. And now he could see that she was totally free—*she was totally free.*

He started thanking me, and the Spirit of God was on him so strong that he got weak and had to hold onto me. He cried and wept as he continued to thank God and pray for his daughter.

After service, the pastor's wife thanked me for helping this girl get set free. "Norvel, I want to thank you for doing what you did." The devil had told me, "They'll throw you out of this church." But God wanted to use me to get this girl totally free. *And He did!*

Jesus Thanked Me for Obeying Mark 16:17

This young lady began to come to church every week with her parents. Her relationship with them and God was restored. Something like five or six months went by, and I got a phone call one day from the pastor. He said, "Brother Norvel, do you remember that girl that God used you to set free in my church a few months ago?"

I said, "Oh, yeah! Do I remember? I'll never forget it as long as I live."

"Well, the family has called and the girl is going to get married. She's been dating a boy, and he wants to marry her! She requested that you come and read the Bible at her wedding. She asked me to perform the wedding ceremony and she wants you to read the Bible right before I do that—because you're the one that God used to get her free."

I had that date open, so I went. That girl's wedding day will be a day I'll never forget as long as I live. That was the first time Jesus spoke to me *and thanked me*. Did you ever have Jesus speak to you and thank you for doing something? I could hardly stand it—to think that Jesus would speak to me and thank me for obeying a verse of Scripture for somebody else.

I was standing at the wedding. Just the pastor and I were standing there, and there were flowers everywhere. Then the music began for *"Here Comes the Bride."* This young lady came walking around the corner and then straight and slowly down the aisle to receive her groom in marriage. I was standing there with my Bible, ready to read the Scripture. The bride-to-be was going to walk up and look at me and then I was going to read the Bible to her—any Scripture that I chose. Then she was going to step over in front of the pastor and he was going to perform the marriage ceremony.

As she was walking towards me, all of a sudden the Holy Spirit on the inside of me began to rise up. He said to my spirit, "Thank you, Son, for praying for her. Thank you for obeying the sixteenth chapter of the Book of St. Mark. Thank you for casting the devil out of her. I want to thank you. Your standing in the gap and obeying that chapter is the reason that she's not dead and not living in sin. It is the reason she is walking down the aisle to receive her mate. And now she's as clean and white as snow."

Chapter 7

Have You Been Through God's Boot Camp?

od will not send you to a place where you are not equipped to do the job for Him. If you are asking God why He doesn't use you more, ask yourself, "Am I equipped?" Have you been trained? Have you ever prayed for a sick person and actually seen him or her get healed? Have you ever used the name of Jesus to cast out devils? What is it that you know how to do for God? Have you been through God's Boot Camp?

God wants to train you to *do* the gospel. You will never learn how to pray for the sick until you go with someone and watch them pray for sick people, and then come to the place where you can believe it and do it yourself. Then you will be able to put your hands on sick people and see them healed. That is the way Jesus trains you to pray for the sick. You either know what you are doing or you don't. It doesn't take very long to learn, but you have to submit yourself to the training.

Are you willing? If you are not willing to go through God's Boot Camp, God cannot help you. If you are willing, God will train you.

You have to come to a place where you know that in Christ Jesus there is no defeat. You must learn to use God's Word and to mean what you say. I remember something Lester Sumrall said to me one night after praying for a demon-possessed girl who had been set free. Dr. Sumrall and I were at our hotel. He turned to me and said quietly, "I guess you know that God will hold you and me responsible for teaching others."

That is the reason for this message. I want to stir your heart by the Holy Ghost to have you boldly commit yourself to be willing to be trained in God's Boot Camp. Maybe some of you once started and it became too hard. It isn't easy, but God will see you through. You need it. You cannot serve God effectively without it. But, you see, I had to be willing to be trained. God will not take you and train you unless you are willing.

I had to get with other men and women who knew God better than I did, and study their ministries. I had to get into the Bible and learn who I was in Christ Jesus and the authority I had in God's Word. I had to come to realize that I had the Greater One dwelling in me. Until then, I could not *really* help people.

Now God sends people to me for help. I can't just pat them on the back and tell them to go merrily on their way—and *maybe someday* God will help them. Unless the power of God can be imparted to them, they will remain helpless. God wants you to help others, and if you won't submit yourself to His training, God won't use you.

You *Have Power and Authority*

"Then he (Jesus) called his twelve disciples together, and gave them power and authority over all devils, and to cure diseases. And he sent them to preach the kingdom of God, and to heal the sick" (Luke 9:1,2). This is the power and authority that God has given you to equip you for His work. You have power and authority over all devils and to cure diseases. But you must make the effort to be trained in how to exercise this power and authority. Go before God and dedicate yourself to His training. Let the Holy Ghost teach you how to use the Word of God. It does not fall on you like the rain.

You must be willing to obey Him—even if it means laying aside your education, your social status, your financial situation. It is not easy. Doing what the Word says sometimes seems embarrassing to some people. It shouldn't be. It seems embarrassing because many people are not used to being a doer of the Word. There are not many people who are really willing to minister to the unlovely.

It is a wonderful thing to be humble and to love Jesus, but you need even more from God. You need your spirit to be bold before God. You need to be bold in front of your friends. Take your stand like a soldier! As you turn to God, He will do a work in your heart to bring you out of the valley of decision. He will put you in a place and with people who know more about God than you do and who are able to train you.

The Decision Is Yours

Make yourself available and ask Jesus to put you through God's Boot Camp regardless of the cost, to burn out the pride and embarrassment in you. Desire and be willing to see people healed and set free by the authority you have in Jesus' name, and believe in your heart that He will perform His works through you. Claim that you will be made a warrior for God. And go forth with holy boldness to obey the gospel. Do not play games or play church. Work for God.

During those first seven years of ministry, God manifested Himself to me. He talked to me and sent people to train me. At the end of those seven years, the Lord told me, "I want you to teach people the Scriptures and what I have taught you."

God never called me to preach, so I don't. He called me and anointed me to sit in the office of the teacher. There is a *drive* in me to do it. I *have* to teach. I don't want to disobey Him. That's why I send such a strong message to you to have total victory over the devil and to help others have the same.

As God has led me over the years, He has changed my whole life. I'm a different person from the man Jesus first visited in that car in Indianapolis. I have said it over and over down through the years: I found out that *"I"* was my main problem. The greatest deliverance you will ever have is to let God deliver you from *yourself*. Once you do that, the devil can't steal your destiny.

God had a destiny for me, and Satan wanted to steal it. But God was ever-present to help keep Satan from doing that. I had to take time to learn God's ways, give my talents to Him, learn to resist the devil, and choose to stay humble; and God led me into my ministry and His destiny for my life.

God has a destiny for you, and the devil wants to steal it. God is ever-present to help you keep Satan from doing that. Just like I did, you must take time to learn God's ways, give your talents to God, learn to resist the devil, and choose to stay humble—and God will lead you into your ministry and destiny forever. God woke me up one morning and said, "You tell the people that I have a job for each of them to do if they will let me mold them and train them. Tell them I have never made two faces alike. I have never made two mouths alike. I've never made two snowflakes alike. I have never made two personalities alike." No one looks like you, no one says things the way you do, and no one else can do the job that God created you to do! God never made two people the same, and He has a specific commission for you and your life, if you will let Him train you in His boot camp.

God wants you to put you where you can learn to be the kind of soldier He can train. Most people will never allow God to do this, because it isn't easy. They won't pay the price. They won't allow themselves to be taken out of their comfortable, intellectual, social, or financial world. You must approach God with an open mind and spirit and ask Him to mold you into the person He wants you to be and to train you how to do what He says.

Have you ever heard of an American soldier who enjoyed going through boot camp training? No. It's not easy. It's hard and disciplined, but you have to go through it. If you are not real nice about it, you can get into trouble. In God's Boot Camp, you can get into trouble with the Holy Spirit, because if you don't obey, you won't get any orders from Him. God won't trust you. If He can't trust you—*if you are not willing to be trained*—He won't tell you the things that you need to know to be trained. So you need to cooperate with the Holy Spirit. You have to be willing to do whatever God wants you to do. You need to decide if you will enlist in God's army and go to His boot camp. *The decision is yours.*

Training Others to Cast out Devils

Jesus said to Norvel, "Son, I'm going to ask you to do something for Me and I will bless you if you do it. When I promote My servants with position or money, nearly all of them stop casting out devils in My name. I'm asking you, Son, as long as you are on the earth, to cast out devils. They must obey you as long as you live your life according to My Word."

Then He added, "Son, I don't want you to ever stop casting out devils as long as you live. Never stop. Never stop. Don't ever stop casting out devils."

The Lord spoke further to him that night, saying, "Son, you know, there is a whole world out there that is like you used to be. How did you get to this place where you cast out devils in My name? Teach people this—how you got this way—step by step by step by step."

Norvel relates the following:

I began to cast out devils and I won't ever stop, because I can see the freedom in it. Since that time, I learned more and more about devils—some of them are weak; some of them are strong. When they've been in somebody for a long time, they're strong. Like that girl—maybe a year before that, she was a strong Christian girl, but she got with the wrong boys and headed in the wrong direction. And lust came into her, and she went with it. But the Lord set her totally free from that. So that demon came out of her the first time I said, "You foul spirit that's wrecked this girl's life, in Jesus' name, come out of her!" The first time I ever addressed a demon, it had to obey.

It's all in obedience to the sixteenth chapter of the Book of St. Mark. A lot of pastors don't even know it—Jesus' command to cast out devils—is in there. They don't know about Mark 16:17, or they just don't obey it. You say, "I wish my pastor did." Now, right there your thinking is messed up already! I wish your pastor did, too; I wish all pastors did. But that's not what Mark 16:17 says. That's not what Jesus says. In the sixteenth chapter of the Book of St. Mark, Jesus said, "These signs shall follow *them that believe.*" He didn't say that these signs shall follow *"somebody else"* or *"just pastors."* If you're a believer, you're not going to be free from Jesus' commission in verse 17 to cast out devils in His name.

Jesus said, "Those that believe in Me, in My name, they shall cast out devils." Do *you* do it? God doesn't like it when you throw the responsibility of the gospel over on somebody else. When God says "believers," He means *you*. And why does He want you to do this? Because He doesn't want the devil messing you up. "Submit yourselves therefore to God," according to James 5:7; "resist the devil, and he will flee from you." God wants *you* to learn to resist the devil, in Jesus' name, and to do it *for yourself* first of all. If you get to the point that you can keep yourself free, then you can go out and help other people. Don't ever be afraid or ashamed or back away from this like I did. Don't be afraid to say, "In Jesus' name, come out, you devil; leave this person alone. In Jesus' name, I said, 'Obey me!'"

I've had God send me places to get a person set free, and sometimes it takes me hours before that person is delivered. You may find it easy to live a Christian life—to testify, pray, sing, and so on. So you shrug your shoulders and say, "Oh, well, I don't need Mark 16:17." Oh, yes, you do! And besides that, if you don't need it very much, there's a whole world that does and *they* need *you*—a believer who has been given power and authority to cast out devils in Jesus' name.

Sometime you might be in some city and God will try to get you to help somebody—like He has had me or Lester Sumrall do. You might tell God, "Well, God, I'm busy and I don't have time. And, besides that, You can get somebody else to do it. You have a lot of pastors and maybe evangelists in this town—get somebody else to do it. Get somebody else to take authority and cast that devil out. Get somebody else to deal with that case—get somebody else."

If this is where you're coming from, what I have to say next will get a hold of you, way down to the bottom of your toes. Suppose you're sitting in the middle of some full gospel church and you hear someone whimpering or even growling; and you think, *Oh, well, they're so bad off, God can't help them. Just bless them Jesus.* I've got news for you: Jesus is going to tell you like He told me, "No! Bind that devil—you bind that devil—in My name. You tell it to come out of that person."

It won't make any difference what you see right then—just bind that devil up. God says, "You joined My church; you're a believer—whatever you bind on earth shall be bound in heaven." (Matthew 16:19.) "Shall be"—not "maybe it will be." God will say, "You bind that devil up!"

If You Don't Do It, They Will Die!

When you start shoving off your God-given responsibility that is yours, because you're a believer, and you tell God to get somebody else to do it, get ready for Jesus to move upon you with compassion and for hot, warm tears to commence flooding your eyes. Get ready for the Lord to speak to you and say, "Son (or Daughter), I don't have anybody else. I don't have anybody else. I can't talk anybody else into it. You're it; you do it for Me. If you don't do it, they'll die. I don't have anybody else in this city that'll do it. I've been trying to get them to do it for a long time, but they won't. They all pray for these oppressed or possessed individuals—which is unscriptural. It's always Scriptural to pray for what you are supposed to pray; but for a demon- possessed person, that alone is not what I said to do."

Jesus didn't say, "In my name, pray a nice prayer for them." No! He said, "In my name shall they cast out devils." "They"—who? Believers. Not special people. Not special-called people. "Well, Brother Norvel, I've had people tell me that the Lord really uses you like that and that is your ministry." Do you know what God thinks about that? That's a bunch of phony junk. Casting out devils is your ministry, too. It is the ministry of *every* believer. Get this straight, my brother and sister; get this straight once and for all: The gospel and the freedom of the gospel is *for everybody*. Anything I can get Jesus to do, you can get Him to do, too. God doesn't have any big people and little people.

Start Confessing Your Freedom

The Lord told me one time, that over fifty percent of getting someone delivered after you have prayed for him and bound the devil up is getting them to start confessing, "In Jesus' name, I am free." Get the person himself to start saying, "In Jesus' name, I am free; in Jesus' name, I am free. In Jesus' name, I am free; in Jesus' name, I am free." Tell him, "Listen closely to me—when you say you're free, you're free!"

Jesus said in Mark 11:23 that you can HAVE—you can possess— whatever you SAY. You start confessing your freedom, and you'll be free from devils. You start confessing your healing, and you'll be free from diseases—you'll be healed. You start praying for and confessing salvation for your relatives and thank God, He will visit them. But you've got to *say* it. You can't just go around being silent. The Word of God doesn't automatically work for you just because you're a Christian. The power of God does not automatically tell work for you just because you're a Christian.

You say, "Well, I think God should do this...or I feel like God should do that..." Nooo! God doesn't go by how you think or how you feel. He goes by His Word. And His Word says for *you*—the believer—to cast out devils. His Word says for you to speak to the mountains...and they will be removed. Yes, the gospel is nice alright, but there is a certain way for it to work. It's not enough to just think that it is nice. You have to speak it and do it—just like God says. God will tell you, "I don't have anybody else to get this person free. Either you do it for Me, or they'll die." That'll get your thinking straightened out.

I hope there will be several people in your town that will do it. There are a lot of good Christians all over the country, but I'm not talking about just being a good Christian. I'm talking about a duty—a duty that the Lord has put upon you and me as believers to set the captives free, in the name of Jesus. That's what I'm talking about. Who can do it? Anybody can do it—*any believer.*

I'm not talking about getting involved in some goofed up doctrine where people try to make devils talk to them or try to make people cough up demons—which is all false doctrine, get that straight! Just stick to the doctrine of Jesus, and you'll be alright. What do I mean by that? Just speak with authority. Just say two things—what Jesus said to all devils—"Come out!" and "GO!" In Jesus' name, tell those demons to "come out, and go" from that person. It's so easy!

If you've got cancer and the doctor says you're dying, there's so much power involved in Jesus' name and the devil is so weak. Just stand in the middle of the floor in your living room, and say, "In Jesus' name, I command you, cancer, go from me! In Jesus name, cancer, I command you, go from me! In Jesus' name, cancer, I command you, go from me, In Jesus name, cancer, I command you, go from me!"

Do it about fifty times in the morning and about fifty times in the afternoon. Do it *every day*—"In Jesus name, cancer, come out! I command you to go from me!" Don't give cancer any choice, and don't wait around to see if you're going to be healed by some evangelist that comes to town. You can stand in your own living room and say, "In Jesus' name, cancer, GO from me! In Jesus' name, cancer, go from me! In Jesus' name, cancer, go from me!"

I don't doubt that after you do this about a couple thousand times, the cancer will totally turn loose of you and fly off in the air like a bird, and you'll be left standing there feeling like you're sixteen years old.

You mean, that's the way you make devils leave you?

Honey, that's the only way. There aren't five or six ways to make devils leave you—just one; and that's in Jesus' name, speaking with authority, "GOOOOO from me!" If you're praying for somebody else, you say with authority, "In Jesus' name, come out of him. GOOOOO from him!"

You *command*; you never *ask* the devil anything—learn that. You never ask the devil anything! You treat him exactly like you would treat a mad dog that has come into your house and grabbed your child by the leg! "Cancer, I'm going to kill you; I'm going to kill you!" If it was a mad dog, you would get something and knock it in the head to get it away from your child. That's exactly the way you treat any devil. I don't care what kind; I don't care what kind.

If any part of your body just acts like it wants to be sick, just acts like it doesn't want to function normally…if you have one kidney, and it just acts like it doesn't want to function normally…if your blood just acts like it doesn't want to flow normally—say, "No, you don't, in Jesus' name; no, you don't. I command you, Satan, take your hand off of my blood. I claim pure blood, in Jesus' name, Satan; go from me, in Jesus' name. Go from me." Many times, Christians just go along and accept something that's not normal—something that's harming them, that's damaging them, that's causing them pain, that's causing them heartache, that's causing them unrest—and they don't even know it's the devil. They just go along and say, "Oh, well, I'm Spirit-filled; and I love the Lord. And, ah, I think I'll go to such-and-such city and get Brother So-and-So, some well-known minister, to pray for me."

I'm not saying that God can't use others who are anointed to help you. I'm not knocking that. But why do you want to wear the tires off your car when you can get something yourself? Why don't you tell the devil to take his hands off of you? Why don't you tell the devil that your body is God's property, and that he has no right to your body? He has no right to your mind. He has no right to your children. None! Know that every devil that tries to mess you up in any little, teeny way is a total invader. Don't put up with invaders! Throw invaders out!

You don't play around with the devil. Never play around with the devil; never talk softly to him. You can talk softly to God, and you can talk softly to human beings. A soft answer to a human being will sometimes turn away wrath. (Proverbs 15:1.) But to a devil—you don't talk softly to a devil. To a devil, you say what you mean, and you mean what you say. You have to throw devils out, and you have to throw them out ruthlessly. And the bolder and the more ruthless you get, the more God likes it—the more God likes it, the quicker He'll move for you. But you can only get that way with devils. Don't get that way with God, and not with Christians, either. You deal gently with God and gently with Christians. Don't get so bold in your Christian life that you're scary to others. Some Christians scare me, and I'm not easily scared.

Some Christians say, "Well, I'm believing a verse of Scripture, and God doesn't have any choice—He'll have to give it to me."

That scares me, man. You're not ever going to make God do anything. Don't talk like that.

You say, "Well, I'm just standing and believing on a verse of Scripture and the Lord Jesus has to give it to me."

I mean, He'll give you any verse of Scripture you ask Him—if the right conditions are met. But you've got to approach the gospel and approach Jesus reverently—and humbly. I can show you in the Bible, that God bestows great favor on people who have a humble heart. "But he giveth more grace. Wherefore he saith, God resisteth the proud, but giveth grace unto the humble," (James 5:6). "Whosoever therefore shall humble himself as this little child, the same is greatest in the kingdom of heaven," (Matthew 18:4). "And whosoever shall exalt himself shall be abased; and he that shall humble himself shall be exalted," (Matthew 23:12).

This is talking about humility toward God—not toward the devil. When it comes to God, approach Him with reverence; approach

Him with a humble heart. And approach Him with faith, and not the kind of faith that's only in your head.

One very well-known minister gave away a plane, and God blessed him with a new one. That doesn't mean that you can rightfully decide: *I'm going to go out tomorrow and give away my van and God will give me a new van—He'll have to.* I've got news for your dumb head: You're totally out of God's will. You're so far out of God's will, that it will be a miracle if God can help you. You might give away your van if you just want to be generous or if God tells you to give it away. If God tells you to give your van away to some missionary or some good cause of the gospel, then do it. But don't go around doing something because Brother So-and-So did it; don't do that. Don't do that!

Let God lead you. God may lead you to Washington, D.C., to pass out tracts. He may lead you to the Philippines to teach little children and take care of the office work for some orphanage. But you have to careful telling God that you won't do something or you won't go somewhere for Him, or that He has to do a certain something for you. You have to watch yourself—you can't *tell* God to do anything.

You and I have to be very reverent when we deal with God. We have to do so with respect, with *great* respect. If we don't respect the sixteenth chapter of the Book of St. Mark, we're not going to ever cast out devils. We have to respect it, my brother and sister. Respect it! If you respect it, you'll see freedom come. Blessed be the name of Jesus forever!

Part Three

Inspirational Teachings by Norvel

Chapter 8

Know Your Enemy

The following teaching was taken from Norvel's book entitled, *Know Your Enemy*.

"And he said unto them, Go ye into all the world, and preach the gospel to every creature.

He that believeth and is baptized shall be saved; but he that believeth not shall be damned.

And these signs shall follow them that believe; In my name shall they cast out devils; they shall speak with new tongues; they shall take up serpents; and if they drink any deadly thing, it shall not hurt them; they shall lay hands on the sick, and they shall recover."

Mark 16:15-18

The most important subject in the world is Jesus and after that, the next most important is your enemy. You need to know where the devil comes from, where demons come from, how they operate, and who they attack. *Demons are personalities without bodies.* A demon is desperate for a body, and the number one target is a human body. They will operate through animals to a certain degree, but they prefer to use the bodies of men and women. Satan and thousands times thousands of demons are moving through the air. Many thousands of them do not have bodies in which to live. A third of the angels in heaven were thrown out when Satan fell. (Revelation 12:4,7-9.) We do not know how many that was, but we do know it was a multitude.

Deceived Churches and Christians

In this teaching I want to deal with a particular kind of demon, or particular assignment of many demons, which is the primary way Satan deceives the Church. I have taught in many churches around the country—*and this may surprise many people*—but there is more room for demons in full gospel churches than in denominational churches! Most churches do not know very much about the devil at all. All they know is that he is mean.

Satan has so many ministers and so many Christians deceived! He is the number one deceiver on earth. He does not want you to see him as the devil. He wants you to think that whatever happens to you or whatever way you are is God's fault or your own fault. He does not want to be recognized. He wants to stay in the background and have you not talk about him or know that he is anywhere around.

Have you ever heard someone get behind the pulpit and say, "I just want to talk about Jesus all the time; I don't want to talk about the devil"? That is exactly what the devil wants to hear you say. He does not ever want you to know he is operating in you or in your church. If you do not expose him from the Word of God and do not know what God says about him, you will never know your enemy.

How would you parents like it if the United States Army drafted your son at eighteen years of age and then immediately took him overseas and dropped him by parachute into some war zone? If the army did not put him through basic training, he would not know how to protect himself, how to fire a gun, or even how to dig a foxhole. He would not know how to do anything. If he was fortunate, he might live about three minutes.

Exactly the same thing will happen to you in different phases of your life if you do not know your enemy. You must know how to deal with him. Some people do not recognize their enemy when it comes to sickness and disease. They think those things are *"God's will,"* or that *God allowed* those things to afflict them, or that He even put sickness and disease on them—*"to teach them a lesson."* God does not do that.

The Bible teaches that all *good* things that ever come to you come down from heaven, from the Father of Light. All good things come from God, and all things that come to destroy you, to cause you harm or confusion, or to bring heartaches and trouble into your life come from the devil and his workers. Demons and foul spirits will oppress you if you allow it. They will possess you if they can. However, a devil can *never* possess you unless you participate with him, or yield to his temptations. If you begin to participate in some sin then he will have a foothold in you.

Deceived by Religion

Satan deceives churches and the Church with religion: doing their own thing in their own time and by their own will, through their own way. God wants us to do His thing in His time and in His way. "I.... I.... me.... me. This is the way we do it. This is the way I do it." Who cares how you do it? Let God set up the church the way He wants to set it up. He wants you, a born-again believer, to respond to Him the way He says. He wants you to put first things first.

You will never build a church for God that will be successful until you come to the place where you will spend adequate time praying in front of Almighty God. Also, you must learn how to worship and praise the Lord then teach your congregation this. If you will do this, I will guarantee that the Spirit of God will begin to draw people into your work. No man can come to Jesus, the Bible says, unless the Father draws him. (John 6:44.) If you pray, praise, and worship Him, I promise you that the Spirit of God will draw people to your church.

The devil also deceives churches with doctrines and interpretations of God's Word that range from having a little error to being almost entirely in error. Entire movements and denominations, down through the last two hundred years, have been deceived by false doctrines. If the doctrine of your church is that God does not heal today then a sick person asking for prayer is laughed at and told, "We don't do that here!" They are treated as if they are in error and into something weird, when actually those who do not believe in laying hands on the sick are into something weird, something unscriptural.

A friend of mine went to a denominational church in my hometown after hearing Kenneth Hagin and me preach a few times. He knew the church did not have any anointing oil, so he bought some and took it over. He said, "Pastor, here is some oil. According to James 5:14 and 15, if you will anoint me with oil and pray for me, I will be healed."

The pastor said, "Ah, Mr. Green, you know we are not supposed to do that now. That was back in Bible days. If we were supposed to do that now, there would be no need for doctors, hospitals, and nurses." This is the reason so many Christians die before their time. God will let you do your own thing, if you want to. He does not like it, but He will let you. Paul wrote Timothy about these times: "Now the Spirit speaketh expressly, that in the latter times some shall depart from the faith, giving heed to seducing spirits, and doctrines of devils," (1 Timothy 4:1).

When those seducing spirits get into your mind, they will make you think all sorts of things. You will dream up all types of church services and think that God is pleased with them. You will hardly do anything the Bible says, but you will come up with all sorts of programs and activities of men. Now you have gotten completely away from the doctrines of Christ and gone with the doctrines of men. The one thing the Head of the Church does not want you to get involved in is doctrines of men.

That church that I attended as a child might have had the aisles full of people wanting to give their lives to Jesus. However, if they were sick, it was too bad. "We don't do that anymore!" was the answer they got. "Cast out devils? Are you kidding? We would not get involved in that stuff. That's weird!" We called our Sunday morning service "the eleven o'clock worship hour," but we never worshipped anything.

What is the doctrine of God? Matthew 15:8 states, "This people draweth nigh unto me with their mouth, and honoureth me with their lips; but their heart is far from me." The doctrine of God states: *Put Him first. If you will put first things first, you can walk in the peace of God.* If you want to know God better, find some friends who know Him better than you do and hang around them. Watch the company you keep. You may have some friends you need to move away from.

The devil works heavily with doctrines of men throughout the human race. It seems as if the "colder" the church, the more people they have! Forget the doctrines of men and come to God as yourself, as an *individual*.

Where Did Satan Come From?

First of all, you need to know where the devil came from. God created everything; therefore, He created Satan. Originally, the devil was a very beautiful being. As far as I can find out, he probably was created before anything else. Certainly, he was created before the earth and man. We do not have as much information as we might like to have on the devil, but God gave us all that we need to know.

There are a lot of things about heaven and hell that we would like to know a little more about. We would like for God to come down to earth and write us a third-grade-level book and just spell out everything for us. Well, God *has* written us a book called the Bible, and it has in it everything we really *need* to know—not everything we might *like* to know. Therefore, everything we *need* to know about the devil is in the Bible.

If God created the devil, and God can never create anything that is not good and perfect, what caused Satan to fall? He fell on account of his beauty. He developed pride, and that led to self-will, lustful desires, and greed for power. Then he moved into rebellion against his Creator. That process is the same when it comes to human beings. Look at Ezekiel 28:13-19:

Thou hast been in Eden the garden of God; every precious stone was thy covering, the sardius, topaz, and the diamond, the beryl, the onyx, and the jasper, the sapphire, the emerald, and the carbuncle, and gold: the workmanship of thy tabrets and of thy pipes was prepared in thee in the day that thou wast created.

Thou art the anointed cherub that covereth; and I have set thee so: thou wast upon the holy mountain of God; thou hast walked up and down in the midst of the stones of fire.

Thou wast perfect in thy ways from the day that thou wast created, till iniquity was found in thee. By the multitude of thy merchandise they have filled the midst of thee with violence, and thou hast sinned: therefore I will cast thee as profane out of the mountain of God: and I will destroy thee, O covering cherub, from the midst of the stones of fire. Thine heart was lifted up because of thy beauty, thou hast corrupted thy wisdom by reason of thy brightness: I will cast thee to the ground, I will lay thee before kings, that they may behold thee. Thou hast defiled thy sanctuaries by the multitude of thine iniquities, by the iniquity of thy traffick; therefore will I bring forth a fire from the midst of thee, it shall devour thee, and I will bring thee to ashes upon the earth in the sight of all them that behold thee. All they that know thee among the people shall be astonished at thee: thou shalt be a terror, and never shalt thou be any more.

Ezekiel 28:13-19

The supernatural being who is our adversary and whom we call Satan or the devil, was created with a talent for music. That is the reason some Bible scholars believe that, at one time, Satan was an angel of light, who sang praises and led the other angels in singing praises to God Almighty. Even today, you will notice that demons have the same kind of musical talent. Satan still has that talent, although he has fallen from heaven. Running back and forth through the atmosphere, their music and type of dancing permeates various kinds of modern music: rock, heavy metal, punk, and so forth.

Pride Comes Before a Fall

Iniquity was found in the "anointed cherub." Iniquity is defined as greed, lust, possessiveness, pride, selfishness, and all the other carnal and soulish sins. Those iniquities, which have been found in mankind since Adam and Eve chose Satan's way instead of God's way, abounded in the being of light until he started a revolution, a rebellion.

The devil and his demons try to get every human being to become like them. *The Lord has told me to warn Christians that the devil works in us and around us, to cause pride to rise up, so that all of the multitude of iniquities might be developed within us.* If you find yourself thinking of your beauty, your goodness, your talent, or your spirituality in terms of pride, stop yourself! Then, because the words of our mouths are so powerful, just begin to confess that you are not anything without Jesus. Begin to say, "Without Jesus, I am nothing. Without You, Jesus, I'm nothing. I'm totally helpless. Whatever I am that is good, You are the cause of it, Jesus. Whatever I do that is truly good will be of Your doing."

Even those evangelists or preachers who operate under a heavy anointing from the Holy Spirit can be subtly brought to take the credit for their works. If they succumb to that kind of spiritual pride, to mixing flesh with the glory of God, their ministry will be destroyed. I could tell you of good men, evangelists, all over this country who used to operate in the power of God. They used to have a ministry or a mission, but you never hear of them anymore.

Perhaps they preach once in awhile, but their public ministry has essentially disappeared.

The reason this happened is because they allowed some demon to plant thoughts in them of their own abilities or their own goodness, and then pride rose up. Do not let yourself think that you are something in and of yourself, because if you do, you will fall. On the other hand, you are not an unworthy worm. You are a vessel which carries the greatest treasure in the world—Jesus Christ, and because of Him and His transforming power, you are valuable!

The Deceiver

Now let's look at Revelation, chapter 12:

And there was war in heaven: Michael and his angels fought against the dragon; and the dragon fought and his angels, And prevailed not; neither was their place found any more in heaven. And the great dragon was cast out, that old serpent, called the Devil, and Satan, which deceiveth the whole world: he was cast out into the earth, and his angels were cast out with him.

Revelation 12:7-9

Satan thought he was so big that he could take over heaven. He thought the angels would obey him, and some of them did. The other angels, the ones who remained faithful to God, fought the devil and his angels. And the devil and his angels were cast down into the earth. The earth where we live is full of demons taking orders from Satan to steal, kill, and destroy the human race, to deceive them in every way possible.

The devil has deceived nearly the entire Church world. That is the reason it scares other Christians if you say that demons are cast out of people in your church. That sounds like a foreign language to them. Yet it is supposed to be an everyday thing. Jesus did not put up with devils. He just cast them out and went on. If you do not believe that, read Matthew, Mark, Luke, and John—the four Gospels—and notice the number of different times Jesus cast demons out of people. Demons *had* to obey Him.

Some people have asked me, "Why don't demons obey me as quickly as they did Jesus?" They do not obey you, because you do not operate in as much power as He did. Yes, you have the Holy Spirit inside you, but you do not live your life the way Jesus did. Jesus lived His life so clean, so committed to the Father, so full of faith, that He left no room for doubt. He spent a lot of time in prayer, sometimes all night long. When is the last time most of us prayed all night? That is the reason demons moved when Jesus spoke. The power of the Holy Spirit had no obstacles in Jesus to flow around. There were no blockages of flesh and soul to hinder the Holy Spirit's power from coming forth.

Jesus told His disciples once that unbelief kept them from casting out a demon. (Matthew 17:20.) Also, He said that "this kind cometh out only by prayer and fasting" (v. 21). He knew they had not been praying very much. The more time you spend in prayer, the more power you have inside your life. Before you ever go to the street and witness for God, if you are on a witnessing team, pray, pray, and pray. Walk the floor, close your eyes, and pray in the Spirit, before you ever go out and face the devil on the street. If you would pray even thirty minutes pretty hard and strong, there is no devil in the street that can defeat you. You will be as if you have a one-track mind.

More than ninety percent of all Christians have never won a soul to God, and until they begin to pray, they will not be winning one.

The hunger God placed inside you was not placed there for your own benefit, but to win souls for the kingdom. No man or woman had better go out to build churches without spending time in prayer to fight the devil.

One of the easiest things for a human being to do is go to hell. Many, perhaps most, will go there because they will not listen to God. You have the right to go your own way, even if it leads to hell. It is not easy for God to get people to cast out demons, because most churches have not been teaching people how to do this, or even that it is possible in our day, until recent years. The denomination in which I grew up has thousands of churches with more than sixteen million members today. Those people know God and love God, but few of them cast out demons.

The Devil Must Obey You

If you stand on God's Word in the name of Jesus, the devil has to obey you. The only reason he does not is that you waver in your faith. The devil never has to obey someone who wavers. The Bible says that one who wavers will not receive from God (James 1:6-8). Of course, the devil does not want to obey, so he looks for every little excuse not to obey. However, Jesus gave us all power and authority over demons and diseases (Luke 9:1).

You have the power through the Holy Spirit inside you to take authority over any demonic influence on you. I am not talking about possession, but oppression. Many people stay oppressed all their lives and never get totally possessed. However, the way to become possessed is to enter into temptation and stay involved in some kind of sin. What does oppression mean? Oppression is demonic influence that takes the form of such things as fear, nervousness, depression, rejection, self-pity, and so forth. You can keep a relationship with God and still be oppressed by demons.

If you fall into some kind of temptation, repent immediately and ask for forgiveness. If you believe the Word and walk in faith without wavering, the Holy Spirit will empower you for victorious living. If you want the Lord to lead you, you must have the wisdom of God and the mind of Christ. Every case of demonic influence, oppression, or possession is different. Authority has to be exercised for different situations in different ways.

A thirteen year old boy was brought to me once. A friend of mine knew this boy's family and the trouble he was in, and thought I might be able to help. No school would allow the boy to attend, because he kept trying to burn down the school building. Demonic power drove him to set the schools on fire, and children could have been killed. You cannot begin to tell a thirteen year old, who does not know much about God, that demons are running his life.

When I met this boy, he seemed to be one of the nicest boys you would ever meet. He was well-mannered, and his parents were really nice people. I prayed for favor with him and for him to be able to trust me. I spent time with him trying to get acquainted, talking to him, off and on, about different subjects. I also talked to his parents casually, because I didn't want to put pressure on him, or the demon.

Then I said, "Let's go over, and I'll show you the church." After that, I took him back to my office to talk. The Holy Spirit gave me words to relate to him and I began to tell him of things I had done as a child, things that I could not tell my father. I told him of things that just happened, and how I could not seem to stop myself. Then a strange look came over his face, and he said, "I just had to set the schools on fire. I just had to do it. I just had to do it."

I just kept talking. I knew the power and authority was within me to cast out that demon that was trying to put this boy in prison for the rest of his life. I told him that I understood what he was going through. I told him when I was a boy, I knew it was wrong to get down in a ditch and smoke cigarettes, but I did it anyway. Then I said, "I'll bet you wish that power wouldn't come over you." He said, "Oh, yeah! I wish I didn't have to do it. I wish I didn't have to set schools on fire."

Then I asked him if he knew that Jesus loves us so much that He would do anything for us. I said, "Let's just pray in Jesus' name and bind up all the powers that try to destroy us." He agreed, so I laid hands on him and cast out that demon in Jesus' name. I told that demon that I would not let him drive this boy into anything again. I bound that demon up, and commanded him to go from the boy "right now, in Jesus' name." I said, "I have power over you, in Jesus' name." The demon left and the boy was set free from that pyromania compulsion.

You need to recognize that, as a child of God, you have power and authority over all the devils. You have to recognize that. You have to know that. In God, there is no wondering. You either know, or you do not know. God is saying, "I gave you My Son's name, the name of the Head of the Church, and the gates of hell cannot prevail against that name."

The truth is that every sick, oppressed, demon-possessed person who walks into a church building, ought to be set free. There is power available to do that, if you believe it and operate in it. You have the power and authority. The most important thing is to love the Lord, to worship and praise Him. But you also must know that you have power over devils in you. The Holy Spirit stays ready to move when you allow Him to. Take authority over devils. The name of Jesus is more powerful than all devils.

I was holding a meeting in Alabama one day, when a car pulled into the church parking lot. A man came running in looking for the pastor. There was a woman in town screaming in pain, so we went to her house. We walked into the bedroom where she was screaming in pain. I said, "In Jesus' name, I don't put up with pain." Then I began to walk through the house saying, "In Jesus' name, she is free." Then I jumped up on the bed with that woman and grabbed her and said five or six times, "Come out of her, pain, in Jesus' name."

The woman fell over as if she had died, and the glory of the Lord came into the room. I got off the bed and told her husband that she was healed, and that she was now free from pain. I told him she would be okay from now on. That night they were at the services. When people see the beauty and power of Jesus' name, they are hungry for it.

Curse Those Things

Brother Hagin was visiting me once, and we went to a neighbor's house, a denominational family, for dinner. My sixteen-year-old daughter, Zona, walked in. She was in high school and she had knots all over her. She had the worst looking hands I had ever seen on a girl. There were forty-two knots and warts on her. She had them for the past three years.

At that time, I had already studied the Bible on the subject of faith for years. I thought I knew what faith meant, until I ran into knots and warts on my daughter, then I found out that I didn't know as much as I thought I did. I knew the devil had put those things on my daughter's body, but I did not know what to do about them.

Brother Hagin said, "How are you doing, Zona?"

She said, "I'm fine, but it's my dad. You need to talk to him. I've been trying to get him to take me to the hospital to have these stupid warts taken off. Look at me! My hands look awful, but he won't take me. He just keeps telling me, 'We'll see, Honey.'"

Brother Hagin said, "I can curse those things and make them disappear."

I believed him, but I looked over at this woman in whose house we were, and I could see that his words did not go over big in a denominational home. I wanted to ask Brother Hagin how he would do that, but I didn't. Then for several days, I wondered why I didn't ask. Finally I realized that God wants us to be able to do that for ourselves.

The devil may go around your town messing up other people, but that is no sign he has to do it to you. If you, as parents, do not know any better, you will have to put up with the devil. He will come after your children. It was my own dumb fault that my daughter had those awful warts on her body for all those years. I got mad at myself and told God I wanted to know the truth. I found out something about God. When you get desperate to know the truth, the Lord will give it to you. He will teach you. The Holy Spirit inside of you is the teacher. If you listen, He will teach you all the truth.

I sought God for two weeks, and suddenly He began to talk to me. I could hear him talk to me in plain words. He said, "How long are you going to put up with those things on your daughter's body? Those are the works of the devil."

Let me show you something that I learned at that point. Jesus will put up with anything as long as you will. You must make an effort and take a step toward Him. Your faith must have some kind of action involved. You must press in on God.

I said, "I don't know how long." My ignorance made Him mad. Doubt makes God get stern with you, and He blasted me. He said, "You're the head of this house. You are the head of your house. If you go in there and curse those things in My name, they will die and disappear."

I was reminded of Brother Hagin's words. I had to do it myself. Brother Hagin does not have the time to go to everyone's house. We must learn to walk in the power and authority of Jesus' name ourselves. You have the right to use Jesus' name, just as I did. When the Lord told me that, I went right into my daughter's room and cursed those warts. I commanded them to disappear, and in thirty days, they were all gone.

One day, Zona was hanging up dresses, when all of a sudden she realized that she had brand new hands and legs. She had brand new shiny skin and it scared her. She came running in to me, and I saw brand new hands. She said, "I can understand God doing something for you, because you work for Him. But I don't work for Him, and He loves me enough to do this?"

Perhaps you have felt the same. *God will do things like that for Norvel Hayes, but not for me.* Perhaps you are saying that you are not a minister, a teacher, nor an evangelist. That does not matter. All believers were told by Jesus to cast out devils and lay hands on the sick, and He promised that if we did, the sick would recover and nothing would hurt us.

The Great Commission: Jesus' Greatest Words

Look at what we call "the Great Commission":

And he said unto them, Go ye into all the world, and preach the gospel to every creature. He that believeth and is baptized shall be saved; but he that believeth not shall be damned. And these signs shall follow them that believe; In my name shall they cast out devils; they shall speak with new tongues; They shall take up serpents; and if they drink any deadly thing, it shall not hurt them; they shall lay hands on the sick, and they shall recover.

Mark 16: 15-18

The first thing Jesus told believers to do was preach the Gospel to every creature, and right after that, His instruction was to cast out devils. That is how important dealing with the enemy is to the Lord. Even if you are not called to public ministry, you can cast out devils. Do it in your own home when the devil comes to steal, kill or destroy. You have to speak strongly and use the name of Jesus.

Dealing with Satan Through Faith

There is a lot more to casting out devils than just casting them out. Faith has a lot to do with dealing with the devil. In fact, faith is the number one thing. Your faith in God has a lot to do with how you take authority over devils. You have to learn that faith comes first. You must totally, completely walk in faith. You must stand up to the devil and refuse to waver. The longer you pray, the stronger you get. The devil never obeys weak people. *Never.* He only obeys authority, in the name of Jesus.

When an alcoholic demon has been in a person for years, he will not come out quickly. You must absolutely take authority over him. Speaking in Jesus' name, you can make that demon do anything. You cannot ask him to do anything, you must make him obey. So many people do not believe in the power of faith. If that person harboring an alcoholic demon wants to stay an alcoholic, there is nothing you can do. But if he wants to change, it can be done.

Homosexual demons are one of the hardest kinds to get rid of. Most of the ones I have dealt with have been in the men since they were little boys. So you parents of little boys, watch out who your children spend the night with. Someone might get hold of him, and in fifteen years, that will be the only thing they know.

Everything God has that is beautiful and sweet for you, the devil wants—he wants it warped or perverted in some way. The devil tells churches all over the world to read the Bible and make up their own doctrines. He has stolen God's Word away from so many churches. God told us in the Great Commission to do four things: *preach the Gospel, cast out devils, speak in new tongues, and lay hands on sick people who will recover* (Mark 16:15-18). Yet there are many, many churches that build great buildings, carry on a multitude of activities, hold revival services, and do not do any of these four things.

Even full-gospel people give up too quickly. Thirty minutes of praying, and they say, "Well, I guess God doesn't want him healed or delivered." ***Wrong!*** If that person wants to be free, and you do not get him free, it means your faith is not strong enough or your faith does not possess patience. The key to the whole thing is that faith must include patience. If you pray for someone and nothing happens, pray longer.

Deal with people in love first. Start out softly, but remember that some devils are very strong. You are still dealing with the demonic attitude that tried to take over heaven. Demons will try to take over the church service. I had a woman come into my service once who did that. Her daughters had brought her to the service, and about halfway through, she began calling me a profane name and walked around. I called to her to come down to the front and called the demon out of her. She kept calling me names, but we finally broke the devil's power over her.

Every time she spoke, I said, "Oh, shut up! You come out of her." I stood up there as if I had some sense. You are not supposed to get nervous about the devil. God does not answer prayers of nervous faith. If you want strong faith, you must obey Mark 11:23, "For verily I say unto you, That whosoever shall say unto this mountain, Be thou removed, and be thou cast into the sea; and shall not doubt in his heart, but shall believe that those things which he saith shall come to pass; he shall have whatsoever he saith."

Begin to say, "My spirit possesses patience. My mind, in Jesus' name, is quiet and settled on Jesus once and for all. I think the way the Lord thinks, I have the patience of Job and of God, and I have faith. Patience is mine, in Jesus' name." Repeat that, believing for four or five days, and patience will develop in you. From then on, spend time praying in tongues each day, and your nervous days will be over. I do not have any nervous, upset days anymore. I just rest in God and enjoy myself.

Resist Temptation

One year when I was at Brother Hagin's annual summer camp meeting, a man came from Nebraska to see me and get delivered. He said that he was demon possessed. He told me some of the bad things he wanted to do with women, and he wanted me to cast that thing out of him. I said, "Have you ever done any of those things?"

He said, "Oh, no. I've never done any of them."

I wanted to grab him and smack him, but I didn't because I'm a nice guy. I said, "You're not demon possessed. That is only temptation. But you have been listening to a dumb demon. Next time he approaches you, just say, 'In the name of Jesus, you stupid demon, go!'"

That young man had never obeyed the devil. But if he had kept listening to that demon for a year or two, he would have given in to what it said. Probably, he would have broken the law, hurt people, and ended up in prison. Resist the devil, and he will flee from you. First of all, submit yourself to God. Get on your knees and pray, worship the Lord, and tell Him you love Him. Then resist the devil, and he will flee from you.

There are certain things you must do to stay strong: raise your hands and praise the Lord, read the Bible, worship the Lord, and pray. If you are going to be a warrior and a servant of God, you cannot go around doing your own thing. "My brethren count it all joy when ye fall into divers temptations, Knowing this, that the trying of your faith worketh patience. But let patience have her perfect work, that ye may be perfect and entire, wanting nothing" (James 1:2-4).

The kind of faith that Abraham had can get you what you want from heaven. God can use you to minister to others, and you will be a blessing to many. He will give you orders of certain things to do. And, if you are obedient, you will be blessed. "By faith Abraham, when he was tried, offered up Isaac: and he that had received the promises offered up his only begotten son, Of whom it was said, That in Isaac shall thy seed be called: Accounting that God was able to raise him up, even from the dead; from whence also he received him in a figure" (Hebrews 11:17-19).

Years ago, a young man walked into one of Lester Sumrall's services in Chattanooga, Tennessee. He had tattoos all over his arms, a black bag tied to each arm, and a tooth hanging around his neck. He was wearing tight jeans and a sleeveless t-shirt. He was a hippie cult leader from Nashville. He walked right up to the altar and said "something" told him to come in. He said, "Something's been playing tricks on my mind. I was on my way to Florida to get acid, and my truck broke down up on the interstate. Something told me to come in here. Something spoke to my mind."

I said, "Yes, it was God. That's for sure."

Lester Sumrall and I began ministering to the young man, and when we said, "In Jesus' name, come out of him," that demon came out. He began to cry and said, "I didn't know God loved me." Thirty minutes later, he was still saying the same thing: "I didn't know God loved me."

He had been in prison twice, and had been going across the country making a living by robbing different places. No one had ever told him that God loved him. He wept and wept and became so bold for God. He even told the policeman by his broken down vehicle that God had got the demons out of him and that he had not known before that God loved him. Newspaper and television reporters found out about the incident, and he got a lot of coverage in the media.

During a television interview, he told exactly what had happened and how he had discovered that God loved him. I had never seen anything like this in my life and we decided not to close the meeting. Lester Sumrall went home to Indiana, but I continued for three more days. During one of those nights, television cameramen and local television stars showed up to see what was going on. By the end of the service, they were crying. God saved so many people that night, so we bought a house there where young people could come, and we left this young former hippie in charge of it.

The Body Affects the Mind

Later, when I was in my hometown of Cleveland, Tennessee, the Lord spoke to me and gave me orders to go to that house of young people in Chattanooga immediately. So I did, and when I got there, this young man ran out onto the driveway to meet my car. He had shaved, cut his hair, and was wearing long-sleeved shirts to cover up his tattoos. He said, "God sent you, didn't He? There is a crazy boy in the house."

We went inside, and there were two very distinguished looking men, one of them a doctor, the other, a college student. A few days before, this young man's mind had snapped. He was "streaking" (running around nude) across the campus, and he had been totally out of his mind ever since. He did not even know his own name. What you do with your body affects your mind. As long as you live, this will be true. All the demons or foul spirits cannot drive you crazy if you keep your body clean. Devils are such liars!

But when you have worked with as many oppressed people as I have, you know that the human mind cannot "go crazy" unless a person has been involved in an accident that has damaged the mind or brain, or has participated in abnormal sex acts or had addictions or compulsions—some misuse of the body. I have visited people in mental institutions many times, and every one of them had done something with their bodies that had resulted in addictions, perversions, or compulsions.

To keep your mind full of peace and joy, do not get involved in abnormal sex acts. Keep everything normal between a husband and wife, even. The cleaner you keep your sex life, the more peace of mind you will have. What you do with your body affects your mind. Many times, the things that happened with the bodies began at a very young age. Satan cannot drive you mentally insane if you do not give him the power. Do not ever say you are afraid of the devil. You will wind up oppressed if you do that. Satan will take advantage of your fear to come visit you. But when he comes to tempt you with anything—even fear—do not listen to him.

The doctor with this college student said, "A year ago I did not believe in demons or deliverance. But I saw this man on television, and he was so sincere and described demon possession so well that I have to agree that this student is demon possessed. Would you be willing to minister to him?"

I said, "I will, if you fellows will leave me alone. I cannot have you in the room, because you do not know enough about it. I cannot have unbelief in the room." So we walked into the room where the young man was, and the doctor introduced me and then left. The boy was looking strange, staring out into space. James 5:15 says that the prayer of faith will save the sick, and Mark 11:24 tells me to believe when I pray, that I will receive. The prayer of faith is important to you in dealing with demons. I walked up to the boy, just taking my time, and laid my hands on his head. I prayed, "Father, I claim in the name of the Lord Jesus Christ for this boy to be normal and for his mind to be restored to him." Then I said, "Satan, I break your power deep inside of him. Turn him loose. In Jesus' name, you cannot have this boy."

Then I thanked the Lord for the victory. Something that is important to remember is not to let the devil make you nervous. Exercise your faith in patience and believe deliverance already is available for the person with whom you are dealing. I just went over to a chair, sat down, and began to enjoy myself thanking the Lord for ten or fifteen minutes. Then I spoke to Satan again in Jesus' name, telling that demon he could not have the boy's mind. I thanked the Lord that he was free and his mind was restored. Then I rested for another fifteen minutes and started over.

How long did I sit there? Normally, I would not sit there that long, but this time I stayed all night. God had sent me, and I had no release to leave. I began to pray about 8 p.m. and I sat there until about 4 a.m. One time, the young man got up, went across the room, lay down in the corner like a dog, and began to bark and ask for water. The psychiatrist was in the room, and here he came with water, just like an English butler. I said, "What are you doing? I don't obey devils. I don't give devils a drink. Now, listen, sir, I love you, but leave me alone. Don't give demons anything they ask for."

The longer I stayed, the louder I got. About every fifteen or twenty minutes, I would tell the devil he could not have the boy's mind. About 4 a.m., he got up from the corner and walked across the room toward me. He stopped right in front of me and began to laugh without any sound, and he did this for about fifteen minutes. It may have looked as if nothing was happening, but I knew that when Jesus died on the cross and was raised from the dead, freedom was provided for this young man.

The young man began to stand on one leg and stayed that way for about forty-five minutes, then his tongue began to come out of his mouth — but it was the enemy's tongue. Then the young man's mouth came open and some white foam began to run down and puddle on the floor. During all of this, I just stayed steadfast and kept saying the same things I had been saying for the previous eight hours. After that, the demon loosed his mind, and he came to himself. Eight hours of praying in faith and claiming by faith, and this student got his mind back.

Refuse to Let Satan Push You Around

You can do this. Refuse to take anything from the devil. Be faithful and patient in the name of Jesus Christ. If you ever depart from having faith in doing the things that Jesus did or things He has taught you to do and begin to do things the way you want to do them, that is when you start getting into false doctrines. You would be surprised at how many churches are basically right in the things they do and believe, but the things Jesus did in the supernatural and told us to do, they leave out.

They tell the Gospel, but leave out casting out demons and laying hands on the sick. As long as a believer lives, it is his or her responsibility to lay hands on the sick and see them recover. God's power flows through people's hands. The "laying on of hands" is a doctrine of the New Covenant (Testament) Church. Faith in God is a doctrine of the Church. Without faith, it is impossible to please God (Hebrews 11:6). God honors determined faith. If you yield yourself to a certain type of demon, it will think you want it. If you obey it all of the time, it will not come out so easily.

Demons may growl at you, or you may not hear a thing. But make them mad, and make them get out. Sometimes it takes hours. I prayed for that one young man eight hours one night, all night long, because the Lord sent me. Do not get nervous. The Holy Spirit does not get nervous over devils. They are already defeated. Develop the patience of God if you are going to cast out devils. God does not know the meaning of defeat.

Nor does God know the meaning of poverty. When you are dealing with God, you are dealing with first-class things. There is total victory in Jesus' name. But you must have faith and learn to talk to the devil with authority. Be humble with God, compassionate with human beings, but be strong as an ox with the devil. You must have a one-track mind with the devil. You must have one goal, and that is to get that demon out of that person. Jesus came to set people *free*.

The Importance of the Word

I could teach a month on the importance of God's Word in dealing with the devil. There is no end to the goodness of God. So many people want to give their hearts to God, but not their lives. Years ago, when I first gave my heart to God, I could not believe He wanted me to teach the Bible in public. I told God I came from a religious background, and had no sense about the Holy Spirit's workings. He said, "I don't care. I'm calling you to cast out devils. I'm taking all of the shame of the Gospel out of you, and you'll be free to work for Me."

I promised Jesus that no matter where He took me, I would never stop casting out devils and praying for sick people. When I began to cast out devils, some people thought I had gone crazy. They just wanted to go to church on Sunday. They thought I was going too far. But I never did find out what life was really about, until I came into contact with Jesus. He will give you a precious life to share with Him all of the time. God's power follows the Word, and it makes the devil mad. Sometimes the devil will manifest himself through someone in the service, and if you are a speaker, that is where your authority and power comes in. Do not let the devil have any room to operate.

A few years ago, I was at a FGBMFI chapter meeting. The first woman at the altar held her head at an odd angle. As soon as I cast the devil out of her body, her head straightened right up and she began praising Jesus. But a demon in the woman next to her manifested and began to say, "I won't come out of her. You can't make me come out of her." After the devil says the same thing three or four times, it begins to "bug" you, so I excused myself from the congregation, gathered a few people around the woman who knew how to exercise faith, and began to command the demon to come out of her.

All of a sudden, she began to cry, and a denominational pastor who was there jumped up, took his wife by the hand, and said, "Let's get out of here." I did not stop him. I do not apologize for God, and I do not explain what He is doing — unless the Lord tells me to do so. Regardless of what we believe, God is still on the throne and the Bible is still true.

If we do not get anything out of the Word, it is because we did not approach it correctly. Do not apologize for doing what the

Word tells you to do. Get your teeth into Matthew, Mark, Luke, and John. Hang onto the Gospel, and tell Satan you've got it. I guarantee God will begin to teach you. But you have to watch your religious relatives, or they will talk you out of your healing or your deliverance. Of course, you do not want to offend them, but you are not obligated to answer their questions. Just think the way the Holy Spirit thinks.

That pastor and his wife just left. If he had simply gotten up and left because he had no understanding of what was going on, or out of fear because casting out demons was unfamiliar to him, then he probably would have been alright. But the next morning, he began to judge what went on and to make fun of it from his pulpit, in front of seven hundred people. He said, "I saw something last night that was insulting to my intelligence. I do not want any of you to ever go hear a man named Norvel Hayes. He thinks he can make the devil obey. Also, I do not want any of you to ever attend a FGBMFI meeting. I only went because I heard that Mr. Hayes was of our denomination, and the meeting was good until the end, until he acted like he could tell the devil what to do."

About a year later, there was a monthly meeting of the FGBMFI in that same place, and a man in dirty, ragged clothes came walking up to the front during the invitation. He said, "I was here a year ago, and you had a speaker named Norvel Hayes. He cast a devil out of a woman. I didn't understand what he was doing, and I made fun of him and warned my people not to go near him again. From that day on, my life began to go down. I began to lose everything. I lost my church, my wife, my child, and I started drinking. Here I am tonight, fallen from a salvation-preaching pastor to a wretched half-drunken guy who roams the streets alone. Please pray for me. I repent before God. I am dying. I need to be restored, and I know this is where my downfall started — by making fun of the Gospel." I am relating this story, because I would like all those who read this to remember that they are responsible to the Gospel and to the Lord, and not to men.

If you know that you have power and authority, you can make a demon leave, especially if the oppressed person has come to a gospel service and come to the altar. The person has to want to be free. Until the person gets sick and tired of that demon, there is no use for you to try to make the devil leave him. No doubt that preacher was a good man, but he saw something new, something no one had ever taught him before from the Word. But he should have been taught. It is in the Word. In Mark 1:23-25, you see it happening in Jesus' day. He was in "church" (synagogue), and a demon in someone began screaming out. It happened then, and it happens now.

Again, I want to say that no matter how long you have been involved in deliverance, sometimes you will run into things that you do not know how to handle. However, you can always begin to pray in the Spirit, and receive answers. If you want to stay built up in God, edify yourself by praying in tongues.

The Spirit Knows How to Get Victory

The devil cannot stand against God's power. Remember: Where the devil has been before and done damage, he will try to come back. If you are cured of alcoholism, but you used to love whiskey, the same demon will return again and try to tempt you to just take one drink. He will tempt you with the sin that he knows is your weakness.

I admire anyone delivered from the world of society. I know what social drinking is like. It is not easy to get delivered from all that. I made up my mind I would not go back into that kind of life after

I got saved, and it cost me my family. Some people will not give up the world of cocktails and social life, because they want to be with the "big shots." Porterhouse steaks, cocktails, and dirty jokes—that's what I was delivered from (not the steaks, but the rest of it). Praying in tongues will keep you strong enough in God that the devil cannot drag you back.

I was in the ministry of helps for many years before God called me to public speaking. He sent me down to the town dump to pass out tracts. When He called me to public speaking, He told me He would be with me day and night, and He has been. The things you cannot figure out, call out to God and pray in tongues. The Spirit of God knows how to get victory in every instance. If you will let Him come through you and pray in tongues, He knows how to get the will of God in every situation. You can be sick in any form or fashion, and the power of faith in Jesus' name will get you your healing.

A sixteen-year-old girl called a prayer counseling line once and asked for help. She said something was making her try to kill her relatives. Her father belonged to a motorcycle gang, and her mother was a prostitute. So the prayer-line leaders called the girl's home and found that, yes, she had tried to kill her aunt with a knife. Apparently, she was totally demon possessed.

The people running the prayer-line did not know how to handle this, so they called me. I went to see this girl and got her to come to church. She looked like a "Miss Teenage America." The girl was beautiful just like her mother, who looked like a movie star. When the girl and I were introduced before church, I said, "Nice to know you," to which she replied, "I'll kill you."

I said, "No, you won't. I don't die easy." Then I asked her, "Do you want me to pray for you?" She said there was nothing wrong with her and that she did not want me to pray for her. Many people would have left when she said that she did not want prayer. But I learned a long time ago, that you have to trick the devil sometimes. So I acted as if I were not going to pray for her. We took her into a Sunday school room where we sat around and talked. Then all of a sudden, I grabbed her head and said, "Satan, in Jesus' name, you let her loose."

When I did this, she jumped into the air and said, "Ouch! Don't do that!" At that time, I went into the hall and told the people who had brought her that it was going to take some time to get that thing out of her. "Are you willing to stay until I get her free?" I asked, and they said they would stay as long as it took. About that time, the girl came out where we were and said that when I prayed for her, a big black thing jumped out of her and stood in front of her. She said, "I went weak, but when Norvel let me go, it jumped back on me again. What is that thing?"

I heard the music begin for the church service, so I suggested we go on up for the service. This was a good church, but they did not cast out demons. The pastor began to read the Bible, and the girl said to me, "Tell him I said to be quiet."

That shocked me, and I said, "Who?"

She said, "Him, the pastor, I don't want to hear him."

I told her, "You be quiet yourself."

But a few seconds later, she said it again, "Please make him stop. It's not true. It's not true. Please tell him to stop. I don't want to hear it. I want to scream." Finally the pastor finished his Bible reading, and she said, "Oh, good!"

A young evangelist from Florida was the revival speaker. He was bold, and when he began to read the Bible, the girl got upset again. She wanted me to tell him to be quiet, but I kept telling her to shut up and sit still. Then she decided she wanted a drink of water. Devils always want water. So we went for a drink of water. She tried to get away, but I dragged her back to the Sunday school room.

Her relatives had said that if she got away, she would run up on the mountain in the woods and dance all night long. They said demons would come get her every night at midnight and make her dance. At sun-up, she would lose her strength and the demonic energy would lift. Then she would walk back home and sleep all day long. She had not slept in her own bed one night in three months.

When I closed the door, she looked at a picture on the wall and said, "I bet you think the devil's in me, don't you?"

I said, "What do you think?" Then her voice broke. You can be possessed, but there is a part of you — the spirit man, the real you — that the devil can never take over. That part of you always yearns to be free. But when a demon is allowed into your body, it will run you.

She said, "I know it's the devil that's in me. I wish he would leave me alone. I'm just a slave!"

Then I knew that she really wanted to be free, but she did not know how. I knew I could get the demon out of her, and the Lord taught me something new that night. The demon in that girl could not stand the Bible. I had never had any experience before that would have shown me that. I asked her again if she wanted me to pray, and the demon took over again and said, "No, I keep telling you I don't want you to pray." Again, I tricked that demon. I casually walked over close to the girl and then grabbed her by the head. I pulled her face up to me and said, "In Jesus' name, you get out of her, you demon."

When I turned her loose, the girl screamed and ran into a corner of the room. About that time, the young evangelist walked in with his Bible in his hand. I realized the Holy Spirit had sent him in there, so I told him to read the Bible out loud. It did not matter what he read, all of the Word is full of power. So, he began to read hard and strong for about ten minutes, and the girl was in the corner all that time.

She experienced one of the most beautiful conversions I have ever seen. After a few minutes of hearing the Word, I saw a tear come out of her eyes. Then her whole body began to slide down the wall very slowly, inch by inch. The boy was still reading the Bible. Then she began to cry real hard for about fifteen minutes. Suddenly she stopped crying, picked herself up slowly, and we saw her face for the first time. Sitting in the corner, all of her long hair had hidden her face. Now she looked like a different person — she looked like an angel. She said, "I'm free! They're all gone. I'm not a slave anymore. I'm free."

She reached up, hugged my neck, and laid her head on my shoulder, and right there, the Lord filled her with the Holy Spirit. That night I learned that the Bible is more powerful than Satan and all his demons. The devil cannot stand against the Word of God. The Word will put the devil on the run. The Word will bring the presence of the Holy Spirit onto a person, and when His presence goes on a person, the devil has to leave. The Word of God is powerful enough to set free the demon possessed. The Word of God is powerful enough to heal the sick. His Word will never fail. His Word is not weak; it is strong and powerful. *The Word of God will set people free.*

Devils do not listen to weak Christians. He beats them to the ground in spite of the authority Jesus has given them. Having authority and exercising it are two different things. Casting out demons and laying hands on the sick is supposed to be the normal Christian life. Learn about the power that is in you.

The Holy Spirit does not think as we think. He thinks according to the reality of heaven: no sickness, no confusion, no nervousness, no cripples, and no blindness. Until you get your mind renewed with the Word of God and stop thinking about yourself, you cannot even get healed. Remember, the Holy Spirit is not ignorant. If you are not receiving the blessings of God, it should be evident to you that you are ignorant. The Kingdom of God is total victory, and if you are born again, you have inherited heaven. The entire Kingdom of Heaven lives in you.

God only blesses people mightily who want to learn and who will yield themselves to Him. It is hard to get free from the devil if you go to church where they refuse to cast out demons. Luke 9:1 says that Jesus has given His disciples all power and authority over all devils and over all sicknesses and diseases. All devils include the ones that have been robbing you of heaven's blessings. You have a right to be free.

Do I think the Lord will heal you? Yes, I know that He has already healed you. Healing, as well as salvation and freedom from demonic influences, was provided on the cross. However, just as you have to choose salvation and believe on Jesus to receive, you must receive healing. If you will not believe the Scriptures, you will not be able to receive healing. Faith is not believing what can be seen, but believing what is not seen because the word says it.

If you want to be free from demonic oppression, act and talk like you are free. God will honor what you do in His Son's name, but He will not honor a false doctrine. Wondering in your mind and wavering to and fro between opinions will put you in an early grave. If you are a pastor who's afraid to cast out demons because you might lose some members, just obey the Word of God and let those go who want to go. The Lord will bless your obedience.

The Lord told me one day, "Son, do you want to know what real faith is? You have been teaching it, you ought to learn what it is. Anything you will give Me thanks for with joy and not let your mind wonder, I will see to it that you get it." Always remember, God loves you as much as He loves me. If you need something, start thanking Him for it right now and every day. One day, all of a sudden, you will have it. Let Jesus hear you thanking Him.

I bought a block of property in Cleveland, Tennessee, for the Bible school. I paid $10,000 down on it, and for a year and a half, money came floating in from everywhere. I never took up an offering. I have bought property that the Lord told me to, and built buildings the Lord told me to build, and never took up an offering. Money to pay for those things just came in. People would call me and say that the Lord had told them to give me certain amounts of money.

For God to perform financial miracles, He has to have time. He does not mint money in heaven and drop it down to you. He has to work through the world's system, so it takes time to work out circumstances. However, if you keep giving Him thanks for anything He promised you in the New Testament, continually every day, and do it joyfully and reverently in Jesus' name, He will get that thing for you. When I have a need in my life and go to God in Jesus' name, thanking Him, He gives it to me. He hears me, the devil hears me, and the neighbors hear me! I am telling you, *this works.*

Jesus said to me once, "Son, if you will get people who are devil possessed to confess their freedom, they will get free quicker. If you say, 'In Jesus' name come out of him,' and nothing happens, get them to thank Me for their freedom." If you believe Jesus and thank Him for what He has promised, He will do anything for you. But do not forget to thank Him for everything He has promised — that means, in advance. Faith means that you believe you have something in advance. Begin to thank God for it before you ever see it.

Do not ask God how He is going to do something. That is departing from faith. When you try to figure God out, you are departing from faith. Boldly and totally throw yourself over on Jesus, claim what you need or want and God's power will come on you and give you what you want. But you must do it every day. Faith in God's desire to bless you and His ability and willingness to do so is a way of life, not a one-time occurrence.

Unless you resist and rebuke the devil, demons are not going to go anywhere, *ever.* Do not be ashamed of the Gospel or the power of Jesus' name. It does not matter how you feel or do not feel. Every day, resist the devil in Jesus' name. You cannot cast out demons without faith. You cannot cast out demons without the Word. You cannot cast out demons without boldness.

The Holy Spirit inside you knows all truth, has all knowledge of heaven, and has all the power you need to operate in the authority you have been given. Those who seek Him will find Him. It is an awful thing for a ten year old to have his mother die, then stand by the coffin and try not to cry. I loved her so much and did not want to say goodbye. My mother died of cancer at the age of thirty-seven. That is why I am so bold and ruthless against the devil, and particularly against cancer.

You have to make cancer get out of you. Cancer is a work of hell. All diseases come from the devil. All heartaches come from the devil. All spirits that entice your children into taking drugs or becoming alcoholics come from the devil. But Jesus came down from heaven to bring us eternal life and life more abundantly here on earth. Stick with Jesus, and you will have a life full of peace, joy, and power over the enemy. "Whom the Son sets free is free indeed" (John 8:36).

God wants you free to believe the whole Bible, not just the parts that fit the doctrines of men. Some denominations have not departed from the doctrine of salvation, yet they don't believe the whole Bible, because they have departed from the doctrine of healing and the doctrine of deliverance. Whatever Jesus did is what I want to do. Jesus is the Head of the Church. All pastors are "under-shepherds" of the Lord Jesus Christ. All pastors are supposed to obey Jesus and do what He did. As a member of a local church, you are to obey your pastor in Christ. However, you do have a right to check on what your pastor is preaching to see if he is obeying Jesus or not. A good pastor will want you to bring your Bible to church and check up on him.

Once I went to a minister's conference where I was a speaker. I wanted to have a healing service, but the Lord said He wanted me to have a deliverance service. So I had to go in there in front of full-gospel ministers and speak on deliverance and then minister deliverance. I spoke and gave the invitation. About one hundred and fifty people jumped out of their seats and came down front.

I taught the pastor and the evangelist holding this conference, saying, "See all these people? Outwardly, they look as if they are in pretty good shape. But I have not prayed yet. It is amazing how good a church looks until you have a deliverance service."

I began to pray and bind the devil in Jesus' name, and demons began to scream out in those people. They began to fight and to fall on the floor. A demon can be in you for twenty years and never scream and fight as long as you do what he wants. He will not manifest twenty-four hours a day—only whenever he needs to in order to keep you in line.

The Sign of Holiness

The sign of holiness is not any outward appearance, but is keeping your mouth shut and obeying Matthew, Mark, Luke, and John; loving everybody, praying, and reading your Bible. The sign of holiness is walking in faith in everything you do. Faith means obedience. When you obey God, you have faith. When Jesus tells you to do something and you do it, you show God you have faith in his Son. If you do not show Him by your works that you have faith, you are going to have nothing but trouble. Then you will be wondering why good things do not come your way.

Show God that you can be patient and content where you are. If you are patient and content, this is a sign that you know God. I am never sure that nervous people know God. God is not nervous. Obedience means faithfulness in doing what the Word says, answering whatever call is on your life, and being a good steward of your time, as well as your money. If you are not a good steward of God's money, your bills will never be paid. Do not spend your life wondering what God is going to do. If you can read, then you should know what He is going to do. *He is going to confirm Matthew, Mark, Luke, and John.*

God is not going to write any new books to the Bible for you. For two thousand years, He has been confirming Matthew, Mark, Luke, and John for those who believe it. You can have your own doctrine if you want to, but nothing but God's is successful. If you are not successful, do not check up on God. There is nothing wrong with Him. Check up on yourself. The Bible is never wrong.

You want to cast out devils? Build yourself up and use your heavenly language. God gives it to you for you to talk to Him and for you to edify yourself, or build up yourself. If you do that, you will be doing what God says to do. If you are sick, Jesus will heal you-every time for everybody who will receive it. But you have no right to judge God by how He deals with your friends. Once you refuse to do what Jesus tells you and refuse to trust Him, and do your own thing, you allow seducing devils and doctrines of devils to come in and cause you to believe all sorts of things.

Faith is not seen. I do not cast out demons because I see or smell or feel something. I cast them out because the Word of God tells me to cast them out. It is by faith that you do things for God. When you depart from faith, you open the door for seducing spirits. Your mind is in danger of being sucked up by the devil. If you don't believe the right thing, you will accept the wrong thing. God does not honor wondering. He honors faith. If Jesus tells you to do something, you had better do it. Right before Jesus went to heaven, He said, "they shall lay hands on the sick, and they shall recover . . ." (Mark 16:18). Then He went right on to heaven.

Yet there are ministers who will tell their congregations, *"That's not the way we do things around here."* I know God does not think too highly of that attitude. If you refuse to obey Jesus, you are in trouble with God already. It does not matter what is involved. Get started in obedience. Nothing is too difficult or too hard for the Lord.

No Cases Are Too Hard for God

In the late seventies, I was preaching at a big church in Dallas, Texas, when this girl came running down the aisle, screaming. After we got her delivered, she told us that she had hitchhiked there, because she had heard that I was going to speak. She heard that I made devils leave people, and she was a lesbian. Demons that infest lesbians and homosexuals or addicts do not always give up easily. To stay clean, a person must receive the right kind of teaching.

The love of God saturated that girl, and the demons left. But they kept trying to come back for a long time. She showed up in Cleveland, Tennessee, at the Bible school I started. For a while, she would be okay, but then she would go back into that oppression. She went back and forth for months. We kept loving her and talking to her. We would lay hands on her and pray. Then those spirits would try to get her again.

Once, she stood in the parking lot during the services for days. She would not come inside. This went on for more than a year. We could not keep her still long enough to get the teaching in her, but we kept on and on patiently, and today she is full of the love of the Lord. No matter what the devil tries, if there is someone who loves you and keeps persisting, the devil will lose. Sometimes the flesh gets tired, but the Holy Spirit never gets tired of loving. It is wonderful to see what God does.

The greatest thrill of my life was seeing my daughter sitting on the front row at church and Christian meetings, and later, seeing her get up and speak at meetings. For three years, I went through hell with her. She did not darken the door of the church during that time. She would not even go to one service. Sometimes a case may seem hopeless, but the love of Jesus works for everybody. Just keep on loving them, but do not allow them to cause confusion for others.

If you are asked to participate in church, you should be thrilled. It is an honor for you and me to have the privilege of doing something for God. If you want to sing, you had better be just as satisfied singing in the nursing home as on Sunday morning in front of the church. Many times, old people in those homes are oppressed by demons. One song or one prayer can set them free. Do not think that you're too good to visit nursing homes and jails. If you cannot preach, you can at least give your own testimony in detail.

Two Ways to Cast Out Devils

There are two ways to cast out devils: One is to say "Come out of him," and the other is to say, "Go!" Both ways require faith and obedience, the signs of holiness. You cannot do anything without faith. You must have faith in the name of Jesus, that name is more powerful than all devils. Your faith in Jesus' name can get victory for the person you are praying for. Every bad thing that happens is the work of hell, but the work of hell has to bow to the authority of the name of Jesus.

On earth, the closest thing to hell you will ever see is your state mental institution. Take a stroll through one sometime. See the shape the patients are in. Some will laugh, some will hide, and some will be bold. All are full of devils, making fun of God. Many of these people do not know where they are, because so much of them, has been taken over by the devil.

As I said earlier, however, their demonic oppression usually began with some misuse of the body. What you do with your body affects your mind. For years and years, all of the mental patients, with whom I've worked with have done strange things with, or to their bodies. A person involved in addictions, perversions, or compulsions will eventually lose his mind. He will lose all self-respect. His thoughts will get fuzzy. One of these days, his mind will snap.

Regular hospitals may have empty beds, but most mental institutions in America have long waiting lists. If you will give your life over to the Lord Jesus Christ, keep your body full of the Holy Spirit, and praise the name of Jesus, then your mind will never snap. But even lying, cheating, and gossiping will affect your mind eventually. You will not be able to know the truth when you hear it because you have given place to a lying, deceiving spirit. Your body is the temple of the Holy Spirit. God wants you to have a sound mind — a mind full of peace, power, love, and joy. Begin doing strange things with your body, and you will totally lose the precious life of the Spirit. Teach your children how important it is to have friends who are godly. Turn your children away from the wrong crowd.

We were passing out tracts once, and a girl said, "Stay away from me!"

We said, "We just want to give you a tract and tell you that Jesus loves you."

She said, "I know all about God. I used to sing in the choir and attend church. Every Sunday, when the doors opened, I was there. I was a 'goody, goody' all my life. I got tired of it and wanted to see what the rest of the world offered. But I didn't want to become like this."

We said, "Jesus loves you. You can repent."

She replied, "No, He doesn't love me! Jesus doesn't love me. I've gone too far. I've committed the unpardonable sin. I live in the valley of the damned forever."

"In Jesus' name," we said, "you can be free."

She said, "No, I can't be free. But, mister, please tell all the young people you see everywhere, not to get tired of going to church and singing in the choir. Don't get tired of going to church and being good. You see that girl on the corner over there walking back and forth like a mad dog? I'm 'married' to that girl, and she's mad because I'm talking to you. So you see, I'm damned," she said, and whirled around, disappearing into the dark.

She was doomed, but all she would have had to do was fall on her knees and ask Jesus to forgive her and make her clean. So many people believe what the devil says and think they are too bad to come back. But I'm telling you the Spirit of God can break the shackles of sin. You can be a totally free human being who can praise Jesus from your innermost being. Do not ever leave the doctrine of faith, because if you do, then you will get messed up for sure. Showing your faith in Jesus is what brings you victory every time.

Keep yourself filled with the Holy Spirit, so that you have the power to cast out devils. "But he that speaketh in an unknown tongue speaketh not unto men, but unto God; for no man understandeth him; howbeit in the spirit he speaketh mysteries" (1 Corinthians 14:2). First of all, God gave you your heavenly language to talk to Him with. If you speak in an unknown tongue, you edify yourself. You build yourself up in God. You become strong. The devils are weak. If you build yourself up, you will be able to exercise in power, the authority Jesus left us. Do not attend a church that makes fun of tongues and of casting out devils. That church is making fun of the Gospel. Go where the Lord has freedom.

Chapter 9

The Number One Way to Fight the Devil

The following teaching was taken from one of Norvel's books entitled, *The Number One Way to Fight the Devil*. This message is one that God unfolded to Norvel supernaturally, and told him to teach to the Church.

The Number One Way to Fight the Devil

You know by this time that Jesus loves you and He causes you no harm. He comes to bless you. He comes to give you life and give it to you more abundantly. All the bad things: the harm, heartaches, and other things of this nature that have happened to you—did not come from God. They came from the devil.

Now it is one thing to learn who Jesus is, and it's another thing to learn who the devil is.It's like this one family that said they had trained their children to know the Lord Jesus Christ all of their life. They were a good, sweet, precious Christian family. They received a phone call one night from the police station. The policeman said, "Is your name So-and-So?"

"Yes, it is," the mother said.

"Well, this is the local police station and you better come down here. We're fixing to lock up your son (he was seventeen years old) and he's going to be here a long, long time."

"Oh, no, not our son! It couldn't be our son. Our son is a Christian. We've taught our son all about Jesus all his life. He's never caused us one minute's trouble. He knows the Lord Jesus Christ personally."

The policeman said, "I don't know about that, ma'am. I'm just telling you that your son's down here, and he told us to call you. He just shot somebody, tried to rape a girl, and robbed a place—practically all at one time. We've got about three big charges against him. He's going to be here a long, long time. You better come down here if you want to see him."

So the woman got all shook up, and started wringing her hands asking, "Why, God? Oh, why, God? Why did this happen to us?" That's what Christians usually always say, "Oh, God, why did this happen to us?" when God doesn't even have anything to do with it.

They went to the police station to talk to their son. The mother was so shook up, that she decided to call a Bible teacher for some words of comfort. When I got there, the mother began, "I don't know why this happened to us. We've taught our family all about Jesus. Oh, God, why did this happen to us? Jesus, why did this happen to us?"

I said, "Wait a minute, lady! Wait a minute! What do you mean talking this over with Jesus? You picked the wrong one."

"Ah, I have?"

"Yeah, that's right; you have. Why are you blaming God for this? God didn't have anything to do with this."

"Oh, but I've taught my son all about Jesus all of his life."

"But Jesus doesn't make people rob places, rape girls, and shoot people. Jesus is not guilty of that kind of junk. Let me ask you a question, ma'am: 'Did you ever teach your son about the devil?'"

She answered, "No, I never did teach my son about the devil."

"Well this is a result of your teaching. Jesus is not guilty of making people do those things, the devil is. How would you like for the United States Army to draft your son at eighteen years old and send him overseas in the battlefield with no basic training at all? He doesn't know how to dig a fox hole or even know to wear a helmet. How long do you think he'd last? Why, he'd get killed in thirty minutes. He wouldn't even know what to do."

The Devil Is Crazy

I want you to know that the Bible says you're in a battle. Now Jesus himself, the Head of the Church, teaches you how to fight the devil. God says in the Bible also, through Paul, that you better know who your enemy is, and you better put on the whole armor of God so that you might be able to stand against the wiles of the devil. (See Ephesians 6:11-18.) You have to stand against the wiles of the devil. *The devil's wild, crazy as a bat! He's wild.*

I've worked in penitentiaries and mental institutions for years. You talk about crazy, I mean, the devil is goofy. I've worked in penitentiaries where they gave me a room, and the prisoners would just sit around. I'd have a question and answer session for an hour. Most of them don't know why they're in there.

I asked a young man, "How long are you in here for?"

"Twenty-five years."

"What did you do?"

"Well, I'm in here for rape."

"Who did you rape?"

"A 70-year-old woman."

"How old are you?"

"Twenty-four."

I said, "Now, you're a sharp-looking young man. You could get most any girl. Why would you rape a seventy-year-old woman? Why would you do that?"

"I don't know; something made me do it."

I'd ask another inmate, "How many years do you have?"

"Fifteen."

"What are you in here for?"

"I'm a bank robber."

"What made you rob the bank? Are you lazy? Don't you want to work?"

"I just got hung up with the wrong crowd, I guess, and started drinking; and something got in me."

It's the same way with all of the inmates; they don't even know why they're in prison. They know something did it. But every time the guard walks them down those long corridors and opens the steel door and pushes them in their cell, locking it and walking off—some of them in for ten years, twenty years, thirty-five years, fifty years— they stand there and think, *Well, this is stupid. Why am I in here? What made me do that? How dumb can you get?*

The inmates don't even know why they're in there. I start telling them that the devil did it; and unless I can get that devil out of them and get them filled up with God, they'll do the same thing when they get out of there. But eighty to eighty-five percent of them go back to prison again.

It's good to minister in penitentiaries. Most of the prisoners are pretty nice fellows; they really are. They just listened to the devil. Those inmates, for the most part, had nobody to help them, nobody to warn them about the devil. They don't even know who the devil is. When you start pointing out to them how the devil operates, they say, "Yeah, that had to be the devil." It's good to teach people about Jesus, but you better also teach them about the devil and how to combat him.

The Easy Way to Fight the Devil

I tell you, Jesus has the perfect solution and the perfect way to fight the devil, and He wants to teach you how to do it. It's very simple, but you have to do what God says. Looking at Matthew, Chapter 4, you will see from the Bible how Jesus fought the devil. *Jesus told me to teach you how He fought the devil, and to tell you that you better learn and learn quickly to fight the devil the same way He did.* Do you understand what I'm telling you?

Let me say that again so you won't forget it. Jesus told me to tell you plainly, that He wanted me to teach you how He fought the devil. And He told me to tell you to learn quickly how to fight the devil the same way He did. The Lord Jesus Christ is an example for us. We're supposed to fight the devil the same way that Jesus fought the devil. Now this is the easy way to fight the devil. There's nothing that the devil can do with the Word of God—*nothing!*

All through the New Testament, Jesus offers you things and tells you about all the benefits you can have, but you can't have them unless you believe the Word and claim the benefits, chapter and verse. When you claim something, remind God of the chapter and verse that you're standing on and claiming in Jesus' name. Remind God. Quote the Bible to God. God likes for you to quote the Bible to Him. God likes for you to go to Him and say, "God, I come in Jesus' name. The Bible says in chapter so-and-so, verse so-and-so that this is mine."

Start quoting what the Bible says, claim it in Jesus' name, thank God for it, and walk off like you got it. Boy, I tell you, God loves that kind of praying. Why? Because He knows you've been reading the Bible, and you haven't just dreamed up a bunch of things in your mind. God left the Bible on the earth to get your thinking straightened out. I'm going to teach you the fourth chapter of the book of Matthew to get your thinking straightened out on how to fight the devil. If you can't follow the example of the Lord Jesus Christ, you might as well hang it up, go home and get under the house. You'll never be in victory anyway.

Now the battle always starts *after* the Spirit of the Lord comes upon you. That's when the battle starts. That's the way the devil operates. A lot of times, a young man who doesn't know anything about God, will go out with three or four young boys on a Saturday night and try to pick up girls if they don't have a date. They'll try to pick up girls. That's just the way young men are. And a lot of times it's hard to pick up girls. When they get saved and baptized in the Holy Ghost and start working for God, then girls try to pick them up all the time. Isn't that wild? A young man who doesn't know God can go out on a Saturday night and try to pick up a girl, and some Saturday nights he can't even pick one up. He gets saved and baptized with the Holy Ghost, and there will be six girls trying to pick him up. *The devil's nuts, man—I'm telling you.*

After the Spirit of the Lord comes into you, then the battle begins. That's the reason it's very important for you to know the Word of God. Learn to do things like Jesus did them. Matthew 4:1-3 says: "Then was Jesus led up of the Spirit [this was after John baptized Him] into the wilderness to be tempted of the devil. And when he had fasted forty days and forty nights, he was afterward an hungred. And when the tempter [that means the devil] came to him, he [the devil] said, If…" (explanations mine).

About two thirds of the devil's conversation with you will be "IF So-and-So," or, "IF such-and such." Now notice what the jerk says right here, "If thou be the Son of God [If thou be the Son of God— he knew that Jesus was the Son of God; he was in heaven with Him], command that these stones be made bread" (v. 3, explanations mine).

Why would the devil say that?

Well Jesus had been fasting forty days and forty nights.

"But he [Jesus] answered and said, IT IS WRITTEN…" (v. 4, emphasis added).

Say that out loud, "IT IS WRITTEN." Say it again: "IT IS WRITTEN."

Now that's your answer for the rest of your life. Do you understand that? That's your answer for the rest of your life. In the Bible is where all of your answers are. Whatever is written in there, that's what you've got.

Now you might say, "Well, it's in the Bible, but I don't have it." You haven't claimed it then. You have to learn how to apply the Word of God. The Word of God doesn't work for you *unless you apply it*. Let me break this down for you so I can teach it to you. When is the last time you read the Bible to the devil? Every Christian should read the Bible to the devil. If you'll read the Bible to the devil, he will never be able to steal the patience of God away from you. And for you to possess patience is so important in your life. I don't mean have it every once in awhile, I mean to "*possess*" patience.

The devil will bombard your mind and give you all kinds of excuses why you're not going to receive something from God. But if you'll just stand steadfast with patience and say, "Well, it is written devil, that it's mine. The Bible says I have it!" that will get rid of temptations in your mind quicker than anything else. Just say it boldly: "The Bible says I have it!"

He Won't Quit the First Time

Now, the devil won't quit the first time. The Lord told me to tell you and to show you in the Bible that he won't quit the first time. Suppose you go to a service and walk up to the front and say, "Lay your hands on me Brother, I want to be healed." Someone lays his hands on you and maybe the power of God comes on you so strong that you fall flat on the floor, and the healing power of God just surges through you. If you think you're going to get away with that with the devil, I've got news for you.

I guarantee you that the next day, or in just two or three days, the devil will come to you and tell you that you didn't get healed. He'll try to make symptoms show up again. When the symptoms come on you again, that's when he tells you, "You didn't get it. You are not healed. You did not get it. You did not get it." Now that's when you need to rise up, right then, and say, "The Bible says I did! It is written in the Bible that I did!"

If the devil keeps on bugging you, just turn in the Bible to Mark 16 and read it to him. Say, "Devil, Jesus said right here to lay hands on the sick and they shall recover. I walked up there by faith, and I got that Brother to lay his hands on me. He laid his hands on me so therefore, I got it. It's mine. It is written in the Bible that it's mine. I've already got it."

You are healed *because that Scripture was fulfilled*. It is written that you have it. It is written. It says to lay hands on the sick and they shall recover. The moment that he laid his hands on you, I don't care how you felt, you were healed. That split second when he laid his hands on you, you were healed.

Why? Because it is written; that's the way it is.

Lets read on in verse 4: "But he [Jesus] answered and said, It is written, Man shall not live by bread alone, but by every word that proceedeth out of the mouth of God." See, He said "by every word"—*every* word, *EVERY* word—"that proceedeth out of the mouth of God." That's the reason you need the *whole* Bible. You need to study the Bible and find out what it says.

Don't think the devil is just going to walk off and leave you alone and never come back and tempt you again, because I've got news for you: He'll be back! Now the fifth and sixth verses say: "Then the devil taketh him up into the holy city, and setteth him [Jesus] on a pinnacle of the temple, And saith unto him. . . ." This is what the Lord told me to point out to you, look what the devil says—"IF

THOU BE THE SON OF GOD" (emphasis added). See, he said the same dumb thing again—*IF*. Now notice the devil mocking Jesus here: "If thou be the Son of God, cast thyself down: for it is written, He shall give his angels charge concerning thee: and in their hands they shall bear thee up, lest at any time thou dash thy foot against a stone" (v. 6).

This is the second time the Lord told me to tell you that *you must obey the Bible and do what He did*. Don't let your mind wander away from God's Word and come at it a different way. Jesus told me to point out to you what He did and teach you to do what He did. In the seventh verse it says, "Jesus said unto him [the devil], IT IS WRITTEN…" (emphasis added).

Say that out loud—"IT IS WRITTEN." Say it again—"IT IS WRITTEN." Now, remember as long as you live, that this is what you always say to the devil, "It is written, devil. It is written, devil." Get your Bible and read the Bible to the devil. When you open up your Bible say, "Devil, I do have it, because it is written, and I'm going to read it to you right now." And then read it to him.

The Word Works

I ministered to a lady in San Antonio, Texas, several years ago. She came forward one morning in a service. She had a great responsibility in a big corporation. She had a lot of people working for her. She said the pressure on her was so great that she could hardly stand it. I ministered to her, and God really moved on her and set her mind free. Her mind became so clear, she was weeping, crying, and rejoicing in the Lord.

She came up later and said, "Brother Norvel, I've been a Christian for years, but the pressure on me, as far as my job is concerned, is so heavy that I can't hold onto this feeling. If I could just stay like I am right now! But when I go back into my office and that pressure comes back on me, my mind gets so messed up and confused."

I said, "Do you know what that is?"

She said, "What?"

"It's the devil," I said. "The devil comes to confuse your mind. Now I'm going to tell you what to do. I want you to read the Bible to the devil. You have received the joy of the Lord according to Mark 11:24. We have prayed and you have received. Jesus said whatever you believed for when you prayed, believe that you received it and you shall get it. You will get it. All right, you believed and now you've got it, and you know you've got it. Don't let the devil rob you of your joy. Now I want you to take your Bible to work with you tomorrow and lay it on your desk. When the devil comes to you, tomorrow or the next day or whenever he shows up, take your Bible and open it up, and read it to the devil. Tell him that you HAVE RECEIVED, not GOING TO. YOU HAVE RECEIVED! Just sit there at your desk and say, 'I've got the joy of the Lord. I have received the joy of the Lord in my mind and in my spirit. I possess joy. I won't accept confusion. No pressure can put confusion on me. My mind belongs to God in Jesus' name. Devil, you won't rob me of this joy.' And start reading the Bible to him."

The lady came back to church a day or two later and jumped up one night and started testifying, rejoicing, and shouting. She said, "I have never seen anything like that in my life. You never could have made me believe that something that simple could have worked like that. The devil tried to come back and confuse me and mess me up, just a few hours after I got to work. I did exactly what Brother Norvel told me to do. I took my Bible and laid it on my desk, open. I said, 'No, devil, you're not going to rob me of the joy. The pressure is not going to have any effect on me. I've got the joy of the Lord, and you're not going to rob me. It is written in the Bible, I have the joy of the Lord.' I read the Bible to him. I said, 'Listen, devil, to what the Bible says.' Then I began to read it to him.

"I'm telling you, people, it works. The devil left. I sat there all day with the joy of the Lord in my mind, and my mind was clear. All the problems came in on me, all the secretaries, all the work like it always did, at one time, just continually, but I just waded right through it calmly. Glory to God! It works! It really works!"

You're not supposed to let the pressures of the world rob you of the joy of the Lord. Listen, the devil wants to do it. He wants to rob you. But you don't have to let him. Tell him like Jesus did the second time, "It is written." Jesus said, "It is written *again, thou shalt not tempt the Lord thy God*" (v. 7, emphasis added).

You Need the Word

Remember, the devil always comes back; he's not dead. So you need the Word of God and the name of Jesus as long as you live on this earth. Don't think you'll get to be a strong Christian sometime, and the devil won't ever tempt you again. Sometimes he will leave you for several weeks, or even for several months. But don't you ever forget, he's going to come again one of these times—maybe through your child, or your business, or something else—and try to mess you up.

"Again, the devil taketh him up into an exceeding high mountain, and sheweth him all the kingdoms of the world, and the glory of them; And saith unto him, All these things will I give thee, if thou wilt fall down and worship me" (vv. 8-9).

The devil offered Jesus the whole world, but he offers you and me a whiskey bottle and an X-rated movie—big deal. The devil offered Jesus the whole world. He doesn't offer you and me anything but a bunch of junk. Jesus told me to show you and teach you that *you've got to get mad at the devil.* You've got to get tired and fed up with his temptations, and then tell him what to do. "Then saith Jesus unto him, Get thee hence, Satan: for it is written, Thou shalt worship the Lord thy God, and him only shalt thou serve."

What did He say? Jesus said to the devil, "Get thee hence Satan, for it is written…" Now remember, every time you must say, "IT IS WRITTEN; IT IS WRITTEN; IT IS WRITTEN. It is written in the Bible that I've got it. It's rightfully mine. It's mine. It is written."

What does that mean? That means that *you fight the devil with the Bible.* You use Jesus' name and come against him and use the Bible. Quote the Bible to the devil. Make up your mind. Be determined. What happens when you just keep telling the devil in his face, over and over and over and over again, "It is written, devil. It is written"? I'm glad you asked, because the eleventh verse shows you exactly what happens to you, and the Lord told me to tell you it will happen to you exactly the same way it happened to Him—*IF* you'll do the same thing He did.

"Then the devil leaveth him." That moment when the devil left him, glory to God, "behold, angels came and ministered unto him." Angels came and got around Jesus and began to minister unto Him—

angels did! If you'll stand and resist the devil in Jesus' name and tell him what the Bible says, he'll leave you. If you keep on quoting the Bible to him and telling him, "It is written," he'll leave. Then the angels will come and begin to minister to you. I guarantee you the angels will come and begin to minister to you. Praise God forever!

But you have to stand in the devil's face and learn how to fight him. You have to stand in the devil's face and quote the Bible to him. He'll bombard your mind and dog your tracks as long as you live, if you allow him to do it. You have to stand up steadfastly and say, "It is written. The Bible says I have it. The Bible says I have it. The Bible says I have it." If you can get a deaf man to do that, his ears will pop open.

Of course, I understand the problem is getting people to do it. *It only works for people that do it.* The fourth chapter in the Book of Matthew doesn't work for people just because they read it. It works for those, and only those, that do it. The devil only leaves people that stand like Jesus did, in the face of the devil, and say, "It is written Satan." But you have to SAY that. Don't just THINK it.

You may think, *Well, I'm going to hunt a good spiritual service to go to.* Well, that's good, I'm not knocking that. You need to go to good spiritual services. But see, you're only in services a little while on Sunday and Wednesday. What are you going to do on Tuesday afternoon at two o'clock? What are you going to do on Friday at 11:30 at night? The devil's not dead on Thursday morning, you know. You have to understand that the Word of God works for you all the time, not just part of the time—*all* the time. The Bible will stick closer to you than a brother. The Bible works for you all the time—twenty-four hours a day, every day—*but only for those who obey it.*

I tell you, God gives you life, but you've got to find it. And you can't find it by just watching some popular program on TV. You find it by opening up the Bible and studying it. Ask the Holy Ghost to unfold it to you and show you what you need. He will, because He is the great Teacher. Praise God forever! *You can have what you believe the Bible for.*

Don't Doubt

I was in a fellow's church some time ago teaching the Bible. I had been there for about three days, when all of a sudden one night, a woman in the back of the congregation just stood up and challenged me. She just stood up boldly and said, "Brother Hayes, you talk like God would do anything for you. I've been listening to you for three days, and you talk like God would do anything for you."

I said, "Well, I believe that for anybody who will trust and believe Him."

She said, "Well, my husband and I are parents of a seventeen-year-old girl who went to the drug store six months ago and never came back. Doesn't God know where she is?"

"Sure God knows where she is," I said.

She continued, "We're Christians, Spirit-filled, and we love God. I've been praying and wringing my hands, about to go crazy, for six months."

"Yeah," I said, "but you've lost the peace of the Lord and the patience. God will show you where your daughter is at, if you'll do what I tell you to do. I imagine the devil's already told you at least five thousand times that she's dead."

"That's right! He's told me thousands of times that she's dead."

I said, "Alright, let's pray. Jesus said believe that ye receive when you pray. (Mark 11:24.) Now stretch your hand out here to me." So we prayed and agreed in Jesus' name.

I said, "God, I ask you in Jesus' name to move upon this girl wherever she is and have her call her parents. And thank You, Lord, for doing it for her."

When the lady started to sit down, the Holy Ghost moved on me and let me know, "she doubts." So I said, "Don't sit down lady; stand up." She stood back up. "I'm warning you lady, you better not doubt. You better not doubt."

She said, "Oh, okay, alright, I won't doubt."

I went back to that church six months later to hold another meeting. Right before I spoke, a man stood up and said, "We've got a testimony for Brother Norvel. Can we give it to him? Honey, you give it, because he's the one who taught you what to do."

So this lady said, "After you left here the last time, Brother Norvel, I did what you told me to do. I walked around the house for about two weeks saying 'Thank You, Jesus, for showing us where our daughter is at.' But nothing happened. The devil told me that you were crazy and not to believe anything that you said. He reasoned it out to me that my daughter must be dead. She never did cause us any trouble at all. She's such a sweet girl, and you know that she wouldn't have just run off like that and still be in good shape. The devil said my daughter must be dead, because she wouldn't have done that. (The devil always does that.)

"I started to fold up, just like I had done before you came to our church and taught the Bible. I started to fall on the floor, like I had done several times before, and say, 'Oh, God, why us? Lord, why us?'

I just couldn't stand it any longer. I started to fold up, when all of a sudden (Boy, I tell you the Holy Ghost is inside of you to help you) I saw you inside of me. You were standing behind that pulpit in the church and you were saying, 'I'm warning you, lady, you better not doubt. You better not doubt. You better not doubt.'

"When I saw you doing that, I jumped and said, 'OOOOOOHHH! I'm not going to doubt. I'm not going to doubt. Thank You, Jesus, for showing me where my daughter is at. You said I could have whatever I desire, and God I desire so much to see my little girl. I believe Jesus, I believe. It is written in the Bible that I can have my desires. Thank You, Jesus, for showing me where my daughter is at.'

"I kept on doing that for about another week, and one day the telephone rang. I picked it up and the little voice on the other end of the phone said, 'Mama, do you know who this is? Mama, something has happened to me. I feel so bad the way I've treated you and Daddy. Mama, I want you and Daddy to come to such-and-such city and pick me up and bring me home. I want to sleep in my room. I want to come back home, Mama. And, Mama, something else has happened to me, too. I want to get saved and give my life to Jesus.'

"Needless to say, we jumped in the car and drove to the city where she was. Jesus not only showed us where our daughter was, but He already had her under conviction.

"And do you know where she is tonight?"

"Where?" I asked.

"She's sitting right over there, saved, and filled with the Holy Ghost."

I looked over across the aisle from there, to where she was sitting and she looked like "Miss Teenage America". She had long, straight hair—just as cute as she could be. As I looked over there to her, the Spirit of God fell upon her supernaturally and she broke and began to cry and weep. Her hands went up in the air. She was the only one in that audience of several hundred people, doing this.

I saw that it was a holy thing, and I backed away from the pulpit. And when I did, God raised her up out of the seat, and she walked slowly up the aisle and behind the pulpit, under the supernatural power of God. She walked up to me, put her arms around my neck, and put her little head on my shoulder. The glory of God was on her so strong and she was just rejoicing, and rejoicing, and rejoicing in the Lord, crying with tears of joy. And when she put her head on my shoulder, it got on me. Glory be to God! I tell you, the glory of God dropped on both of us and we stood there for about ten or fifteen minutes, rejoicing in the Lord. The congregation just had to sit there and eat their hearts out.

I'm telling you, when you look the devil in the face and hold the Bible up to him and say, "It is written, devil. Devil, it is written. Jesus said I could have the desires of my heart. I am a believer; I'm not a doubter," then the angels of the Lord will come and minister to you. Glory be to God!

Now, Do the Word

If you'll just be honest now, you might say, "Yes, the devil has been trying to mess me up. And I see it; I see it. It is written in the Bible that there is victory for me. It is written in the Bible that I don't have to put up with this mountain."

Do you want to get rid of that dumb mountain?

Begin to confess with your mouth: "It is written in the Bible, I have victory. I've got the victory. It is written, I've got the victory. It is written, the victory is mine. The victory is mine."

The victory is yours because you said this in Jesus' name. The Lord Jesus Christ has bought for you and me abundant life, not a bunch of junk. Jesus didn't pay the price for you and me to live a junky life and to put up with a bunch of junky stuff. That's not the price that Jesus paid. Jesus paid the price so you could have patience, contentment, peace, and joy and so that you can stand steadfast and not waver.

You have the nature of God in you, and it is not His nature to be climbing over mountains all the time and falling into gullies. You have a right to live in peace. You have a right to have the kind of life that Jesus has offered you. You have that right. You inherited it. You are an heir of God, a joint heir with Jesus Christ. Jesus is complete victory. Receive that peace.

Say it gently to the Lord, "It is written, I do have what I desire in Jesus' name. It is written. Thank You for the Bible because the Word is truth. And only the truth will set me free and keep me free in Jesus' name." Say, "The words from my lips will be from this day forward, 'Satan, you thief, IT IS WRITTEN, I am victorious in Jesus' name!'"

Chapter 10

Stand in the Gap for Your Children

"I sought for a man among them that should make up the hedge, and stand in the gap before me…"

Ezekiel 22:30

Sometimes Zona sits down beside me, lays her head on my shoulder, and starts to cry, saying, "I thank the Lord all the time for giving me a daddy like you. Sometimes I pinch myself to make sure I'm your daughter. If it hadn't been for your faith, I'd be dead now."

She is referring to the time I used my faith as head of the house to bring her back to God after she had backslidden. She had gone so far away from God that she had joined a gang. Five members of her gang—young people—had died. I got half-beaten down trying to stand in faith to bring her back to God.

When I was holding a meeting in Texas, the Lord manifested Himself to me. He said,

"Your faith is strong for healing and in other areas, but it isn't strong enough to get your daughter back. She'd like to come back to

Me, but she can't. The little bit of faith she has left in Me isn't strong enough for Me to be able to manifest Myself and come to her. It's not strong enough for her to give up the nightclubs, the new set of friends, and the worldly desires she's been involved in for three years. Those spirits of darkness have grabbed her."

As head of my house, I was willing to obey God when He told me to confess for Zona's healing and later for her deliverance. The Lord told me that even though my faith wasn't strong enough to get Zona to come back to Him, it was strong enough to enable Him to manifest Himself to her. As a result, He brought her back and she was healed and delivered through my faith as the head of my house. The following was taken from the book entitled, *Stand in the Gap for Your Children.*

Standing in the Gap

Standing in the gap is serious business. The eyes of the Lord go back and forth, looking for someone who will stand in the gap for someone else. When someone is away from God, there is a gap between that person and God. He is not able to close that gap and come to God because his faith is too weak. Someone else is needed who is willing to pray and stand in faith in the gap between that person and God. By praying and standing in faith, that Christian builds a bridge for the weak person to come to God. This can be done for groups of people or even for entire cities; but, in this particular teaching, I want to instruct you in how to stand in the gap for your children.

I learned how to stand in the gap by praying for my daughter. When Zona was sixteen, she started dating a boy in our church. His name was Bobby. Both of them had already received the baptism of the Holy Spirit. I never had any problems with this young man. When Zona was seventeen, I allowed her to stay out until 11:30 p.m., if she and Bobby went to get something to eat after church. Bobby took her to church regularly and always brought her home on time, never questioning me about my guidelines for Zona. He was just as nice and kind as he could be.

One day I was told that Bobby was going into the service. He had already graduated from high school and gone to college. Bobby and Zona had decided that after Zona went to college for two years and Bobby got out of the service, they would get married. So I said, "Fine." When Zona graduated from high school, she enrolled in a Full Gospel college in town. One morning as I was getting ready to leave town, the Spirit of the Lord spoke to me and said, "I don't want them to get married. Beware! Watch that boy."

The Holy Spirit Knows Everything

You could have knocked me over with a feather, but I knew it was the Spirit of God. The Holy Spirit knows everything and can reveal the truth to us. To be successful, all we have to do is get the mind of the Lord. I kept what the Holy Spirit had told me secret for awhile, until I heard that Zona and Bobby were thinking about getting married earlier than they had planned.

One night I went over to the college and called Zona down to the lobby. I told her how the Lord had spoken to me. I said, "It's not God's will for you to marry Bobby, at least not now. Don't ask me to explain anything, but I'm just telling you what the Lord told me."

Zona said, "It may not be God's perfect will for me to marry Bobby, but I think I'm going to anyway."

"Get your fighting clothes on then, because you're going to need them," I told her. When the Spirit of God tells you not to do something, you had better not do it! I don't care who you are or where you come from, *if God says, "**No!**" then He means, "**No!**"* You may never know why He says it; He doesn't have to tell you why. Sometimes He may show you; sometimes He may not. But if God says, "No," then don't do it!"

In spite of what I told Zona, she and Bobby started planning the wedding. Bobby's mother wanted them to get married. She liked Zona and thought she was a sweet girl, so she promoted the marriage. Bobby was coming home every two or three weeks, and Zona was living in the college dormitory. She wasn't supposed to leave without me signing out for her, but one Saturday night, Bobby's mother signed Zona out and took her home. They found two preachers who would marry them. I went to both pastors' homes and talked to them. I said, "It's not God's will for you to marry my daughter to this boy. I just thought I would come and tell you so that when they get a divorce, you can say I had told you so. God said, No!"

Then I said, "I'm not going to cooperate with the wedding. I'm not going to give Zona away. Jesus said, No! So I just can't do it. I like the boy myself, but God said that Zona shouldn't marry him."

I told both pastors that the decision to perform the ceremony was between them and God. The plans continued, and when Zona asked if I would give her away, I said, "No. God told me He doesn't have anything to do with it, so I won't have anything to do with it. I love you, honey. Because I love you so much, I'll walk you down the aisle, but that's as far as I'll go."

On the day of the wedding, I stood out in front of the church as "Here Comes the Bride" started playing. Zona was standing there in her wedding gown. I said, "Zona, Honey, this is your last chance. Jesus said not to do it! My car is full of gas. If you'll get in the car, I'll go up in front of that full auditorium and say, 'There isn't going to be a wedding tonight!'"

Zona started laughing and said, "Daddy, you just love me so much, you don't want to give me away."

"No, that's not it. Jesus said, 'Don't do it! '"

"Daddy, everything is going to be alright."

"No, it won't, Zona. God said it wouldn't; and if God says something, that's the way it is. I don't know what the future holds, but He does."

Our walk down the aisle was a long one for me. When I got down front, I just turned around and sat down. I went to the reception and acted like I was enjoying it, but I wasn't. I was just putting up a front. Why? Because the Spirit of God in me had said, *No!*

One Sunday morning about three or four weeks later, Zona came to church alone. Bobby had never missed church in the two years before that. After that, he missed some night services—then another Sunday morning service, then another. By that time, Zona had begun to see the light, and see what was happening to her. When she got home from church, she would find Bobby dressed up. He would say, "Come on. I'm going to take you out to dinner."

But Zona would say, "No, you're not. If you can't go to church with me on Sunday morning, then I won't go with you to the restaurant after church."

She Just Did What She Wanted To

A year later, Bobby and Zona were divorced. At age nine, Zona was surprised at her mother. As an adult, she was surprised at her husband. Finally, she decided to quit going to church and start going her own way. She got her own apartment and got involved in drugs. She started taking speed. For two years, she dropped pills and didn't darken the door of a church. I had been praying for her, so I just kept on praying!

When she came to the house, she barely spoke to me. Sometimes I wouldn't see her for a month or two, even though we were living in the same city. I had to stop her credit cards because she kept running up charge accounts. She just did what she wanted to. I began to pray even more. Sometimes the devil would make me feel like a failure and a phony. He would say, "You're a good one! You've lost everything. You don't have a home anymore. Here you are sitting alone, with your daughter living in the same city."

For nearly two months, I felt like all the blood had been drained from my body. Though I felt like a failure, I kept going on. "Oh, no, Satan," I said. "I remember how Jesus visited me in His mighty power." Saying this began to melt and burn the junk out of me. I said, "No, you don't, Satan. Jesus has never let me down, and I'm not going to let Him down! I can't help it if all my relatives go to hell—I'm not going to hell!"

I just kept on going. I went to the Florida beaches to pass out tracts. I gave my testimony across the country. I went everywhere I could to work with young people. One day as Zona strolled through the house, she said, "Where are you going next weekend?"

"I don't know," I said. "Maybe New York or maybe California."

"I bet it makes you feel funny, Daddy, going around the country trying to win other kids when you can't win your own."

The Lord told me to tell Zona like it is, so one day I sat her down and said, "Zona, Honey, listen real close and believe me. I'm not going to hell. If I did what you wanted me to do, I would go to hell. But I'm not on the same path you are and I won't be on it, either! And you aren't going to stay on it, Zona, because I'm going to pray you out of it!"

So I just kept praying and praying and praying. I kept crying out to God. I wondered, *When will my daughter get out of darkness? How long is it going to be?* I prayed so long and so hard that I didn't even know how anymore. After you pray for something for six months, you begin to wonder if God even hears you. After a year, you begin to believe He doesn't hear you. After two years, when things get even worse, you *know* He doesn't hear you!

You Haven't Been Loving Her Right

After holding a meeting in San Antonio, Texas, for ten days, I went to Houston to catch a plane to Chattanooga. Fifteen minutes before I had to leave, the Spirit of God came on me suddenly *(that's what makes the difference—the Spirit of God!)*. He told me to call Rev. J. R. Goodwin. Rev. and Mrs. Goodwin were pastors of the First Assembly of God Church in Pasadena, Texas, just outside of Houston. I hadn't seen the Goodwins in five years.

When I called, Rev. Goodwin asked me to come see him, so I went. The missionary who had taken me from San Antonio to Houston was there. We hadn't been in the Goodwins' living room more than five minutes when the Spirit of God came on me. The missionary began to speak in tongues and interpret. After the second message, I began to weep. The Lord began to speak to me. He told me to go to Tulsa, Oklahoma. He said, "I will show you two things after you get there."

As I was on my way to Tulsa, He said, "The things you love the most on Earth will not come to pass as long as you continue living and praying under your present conditions. There is something more you need to know."

"What is it, Jesus?" I asked.

He answered, "Your daughter is in so much darkness and her faith is so weak that she will never be able to get out of that darkness. Her faith is too weak for me to bring My power to her to break that darkness, but your faith has been wavering and it won't work."

"Where has my faith been wavering, Jesus?"

"You have been wondering why I don't hurry up and do it," He said. "I have to be pleased with your faith before I can do what you are asking. Stand in the gap for your daughter with an unwavering faith, and I will come to her. I will manifest Myself to her."

When you pray for something for two years without getting it, you will become nervous if you aren't grounded in God's Word. God wants you to trust Him with patience. Anything outside of patience is doubt. If you don't have the peace of God about what you are asking God for, you are in doubt and it won't work.

"Besides that," the Lord said, "you haven't been loving her right. When Zona comes in at one or two o'clock in the morning, you haven't been reaching out to her like I reached out to you when you were in sin. I didn't come against you when you were in sin. I want you to reach out to her when she comes in. I want you to tell her how much you love her." I found out that I was the one who had to change. I began to watch my mouth and stand with an unwavering faith. When Zona would come in at one o'clock, I would say, *"Come here, honey."* I would have her sit beside me and then I would tell her how much I loved her.

As I watched her back out of the driveway at night, I knew she was going to the dance hall. Her girlfriends told me that she would completely take over the dance floor and do the "Funky Chicken." *(That's a screwy name for a teenage dance.)* No matter what her friends told me, I refused to let my faith waver. Every time Zona would put on her mini skirt and walk out the door, I would go to the window. As I looked out, I would stand on God's Word, quoting His promises. I got my spirit grounded in God's Word. As I watched her drive off, I would tell the devil, "I won't let you have her. You can't have her. You're not going to kill her." I would say, "Thank You, Jesus, for bringing Zona back into the kingdom of God." I just kept on thanking and praising God that Zona was coming back into the family of God. After several months of that, Zona began to date Bobby again. I thought, *Oh, no! This can't be real!*

I Had to See It and Confess It

When God had told me that Bobby and Zona shouldn't get married, I didn't know why. But even though they loved the Lord, He knew what was going to happen. When Bobby started dropping out of church, Zona backslid, too, because she loved him so much. Now here I was, facing the same crazy mountain again—*that goofed-up boy!*

I told Zona, "God told me that you shouldn't marry Bobby, but you did it anyway. I know how old you are, but I'm not going to put up with it again." She kept seeing Bobby, so I told her he couldn't come into my house. I said, "I'm not going to let the devil just walk in and take you off!"

I stood my ground! My relatives told me I was making a mistake. "I don't care!" I said. "I'm not making a mistake. When God tells me differently, I'll let Bobby come in."

For months, when Bobby came to get Zona, he would stop in the driveway and she would meet him there. I refused to give in! Before long, Zona began to talk about marrying Bobby again. I couldn't believe it! "You don't really mean that, Zona. You aren't that dumb!"

"My girlfriends told me I couldn't get him back, but he wants to get married," she said.

In spite of all this, I just kept standing steadfast in faith and claiming her complete deliverance. I praised God that Zona was back in church and completely delivered. I had to see her deliverance and restoration in my spirit and confess it with my mouth. I just kept on praying and praying and praying!

One day as I was walking back and forth across my living room praying, I felt like laying my hands on Zona's bed. As I did, I said, "God, this house belongs to You. Everything I have belongs to You. I'm not trying to tell You how to do anything. Just do what You want to do. As she lays in this bed tonight, Jesus, work her over. Shake her up."

About four o'clock the following morning, Zona woke up screaming. When I went to her room, I found her standing by the door, trembling. She had opened her eyes to see an angel sitting on the floor, looking at her. He was sitting there with his legs crossed, staring straight at her. "Daddy," she said, "I got so afraid that I couldn't scream. When he saw that I was afraid, he got up and walked out of my room. I know I wasn't dreaming. It was real! I jumped out of my bed and watched him walk down the hall. Then he turned and walked right through the wall! He was wearing clothes, but he just walked through the wall!" She was scared half to death. I told her what had happened to me—how the Lord dealt with me and how I had prayed for her—and that it was her angel that had been in her room. She started screaming and crying out to God.

Despite everything, Zona and Bobby got married again. They moved to Alabama, but God wouldn't let her get away from that angel. When she slept, her angel stared at her. She got so frightened that she wrote me a letter, begging me to pray. She said she couldn't get away from that angel, and that he was about to scare her to death.

About that time, Kenneth Hagin came to town for a seminar. He came a few days early to stay at my house and pray. One night around midnight, he and I were sitting in my den. We began to pray together. We had prayed in tongues for almost an hour, when Brother Hagin received the interpretation. I began to shake.

The Lord told me through this interpretation that He had dealt with Bobby, but that Bobby had not listened to the wooing of His Spirit. He said He was fed up with Bobby's rebellion.

God gets tired of continuous rebellion. You can only push God so far in anything. When you step over that last step, you had better watch out, because destruction will be there waiting for you. Bobby was a stubborn boy, and God was getting tired of his three years of rebellion. Through Brother Hagin's interpretation, the Lord said that Bobby was about to step into a deep, dark valley.

Then Brother Hagin began to weep and say, "Oh, it will be so dark, so dark."

Then God said He wanted to use me to rescue Bobby, to warn him, before he went into that dark valley. I wondered how in the world God was going to use me. God's power was so strong that night. The Lord told us that the best way for a child of God to get an answer to prayer was for him to simply ask for what he needed. As James 4:2 says, "Ye have not, because ye ask not." Just ask in English then pray in the Spirit. Brother Hagin said he had never understood the simplicity of this before. "You know," he said, "we've got hold of something I've never had before in my life."

I had been praying about this situation with Bobby for over a year with an unwavering faith. I thought I had been praying for it for three years, but the first two didn't count. God told me my faith wouldn't work because it was wavering. When God says it won't work, it won't work!

Saturday night was Kenneth Hagin's last service. As Brother Hagin's son, Ken, was leading the singing, Bobby and Zona walked in. Ken saw a dark cloud over Bobby, which he had never seen before. Brother Hagin spoke and then gave the invitation. He tried to close two or three times, but God wouldn't let him. He just kept on giving the invitation. About that time Zona, weeping, stepped out alone and started walking toward the front. The power of God was all over her.

As I was standing at the side of the church, I found out how the Lord was going to use me to rescue Bobby from that dark valley. The word of the Lord came to me saying, "Get on your face." Then He told me to have the pastor of that church agree with me for Bobby's soul. The Lord said, "He's on My territory tonight." So the pastor and I prayed together.

When we finished praying, the Lord told me to go to Bobby, put my arms around him, and tell him, "Bobby, the past is in the past; and the future is in the future." The Lord told me to tell Bobby that if he didn't heed that night, a valley of darkness was going to come on him. I also told him the only thing that Zona had ever wanted was a Christian home. "Won't you give in, Bobby? Won't you give your life back to Jesus tonight?"

Bobby agreed and started walking to the front. When he got there, the Spirit of God came upon him. Brother Hagin put his arms around Bobby and Mrs. Hagin put her arms around Zona, who was standing there weeping before God. Mrs. Hagin gave a message in tongues, and Brother Hagin gave the interpretation. I had my hands on Bobby's back.

The Spirit of God was in that place so strong! I almost had a fit! God began to melt Bobby and Zona. When Brother Hagin put his hands on Zona, she just melted onto the floor. Bobby just kept speaking in tongues. He must have spoken in tongues for forty-five minutes under the supernatural power of God. Brother Hagin said Bobby was preaching a sermon in tongues. *That was a beautiful service!* Afterwards, we went to my home for fellowship. Bobby couldn't even eat because the power of God was still on him so strong.

Sometime later, Bobby and Zona came to a Memphis convention where I was in charge of the youth. As we were beginning, Bobby came up and asked for prayer. Richard Shakarian, Hoyt Elliot and I took him aside. When we laid our hands on him, God knocked that two hundred-pound young man onto his belly. He just fell across a table. He laid there for over three hours, unable to move. For three hours he saw little children who were naked and crying out for help.

God showed him that, because Zona had a call on her life to work with children. She had a missionary call on her life, and she knew it.

Some missionaries who came by said that Bobby was speaking in five languages. They gave a couple of interpretations, then left. When Bobby was finally able to get off the table, someone had to help him to his room. From that day forward, Bobby was a changed person. You could never meet a sweeter boy! The Spirit of God came on him and cleansed him of all past sin. *Let the past be the past and the future be the future.*

Chapter 11

A Daughter Is Rescued

The following is taken from, *Standing in the Gap for Your Children*. However, this part is from Zona's perspective of the previous chapter.

My Story

I really don't like to talk about the things I'm about to reveal. However, I, too, feel the time has come to expose the devil and his works. First of all, I want to thank my father, Norvel Hayes, for praying for me without ever giving up and for never leaving me. I love him greatly.

My home was split apart when I was nine. At the time, I didn't understand what was happening. I only knew that my father looked different, and that my mother was not around anymore. Dad explained the situation to me the best he could for my age, and he did a really good job. He never said anything bad about my mother. So my later rebellion was not against my parents.

The only reason I went through hard times in my teenage years is that I would not listen to anyone, except my dad, and sometimes not even to him. When someone told me to do something, I rebelled.

Even Dad had to use a certain tone and a particular look before I would give in to his requests. Many nights I left home with my white, bleached hair, wearing heavy eye make-up and a mini skirt, leaving my dad kneeling in prayer on the living room floor. I thought that because he was a "real religious man," I would go to heaven, too.

I had once been Spirit-filled, though now I knew I was in a backslidden state. I thought, *God would not let Norvel Hayes' daughter go to hell. Look at the people he has gotten saved for the Lord. That would be a disgrace!* I thought I could get by on my dad's relationship with the Lord. But I couldn't. If you believe you will get to heaven because of your mother, father, brother, sister, or grandparents, then you are mistaken; you will end up spending eternity away from God.

If you are a young person, I hope you will learn something about the devil's traps as you read my story. Or if you are a parent, I pray that you will learn something about the importance of interceding—*standing in the gap*—for your children.

I Knew the Holy Ghost Was Real

I received the Holy Ghost when I was fourteen, even before my father received Him. We had started going to different churches—that's what my relatives called them, "different churches." As I was praying for a lady who had asked to receive the Holy Ghost, I received Him also. Dad saw me down in front of the church, praying in tongues, and said, "Oh, no! That's my daughter down there!" At that time the baptism in the Holy Spirit was new to him, too.

Some people don't feel anything when they receive the Holy Spirit, and some people do. I did, and I loved the feeling. From that experience I learned that if you pray for somebody to receive the

Holy Ghost without having Him yourself, God may give Him to you also. When I received the Holy Spirit, I didn't even know what had happened. I just knew that I liked the feeling I experienced. It was so warm in my stomach, in my spirit. But at the age of fourteen, I didn't know what the Spirit was. I just knew that the baptism in the Holy Spirit was real. It meant a lot to me. And all those days later on, when I was in sin, I remembered that experience and thought about it often.

As a teenager, I didn't like people—I only acted like I did. However, I wanted to be accepted so I became part of a group. It wasn't a gang in the sense of "Hell's Angels", but it was made up of young people who didn't care about anyone but themselves. All they were interested in was "having a good time." I had never been part of what might be called the "in crowd"—which is what these young people were to me. Because they were paying attention to me, I was pleased and thought it was a really big deal. I thought they were my friends and that they really liked me for myself. But later, I realized they didn't care about me the way I wanted people to care. Otherwise, they wouldn't have given me drugs.

In Search of a Mother's Love

I guess I always wanted a lot of attention because I was from a broken home. My dad gave me as much attention as he could, but still I longed for a mother's love. All of my life I had wanted to be the center of attention, to be in the middle of everything. I was happy-go-lucky.

I got married at an early age, even though my dad told me that the Lord had warned him that I was making a mistake. I didn't listen.

Bobby and I got married anyway. When he was sent to Vietnam, people started telling me that he was probably being unfaithful to me. That is when the trouble started.

Bobby never explained to me where he was and what he was doing. People said that he would probably find a Vietnamese girl and be with her. I believed that nobody was ever faithful to anybody. Everyone I knew had been untrue to me, except for my father and a few close relatives. I felt that Bobby had slipped away from me, because I hadn't heard from him in months. I didn't understand what it meant to be on the front lines in Vietnam.

Both Christians and non-Christians told me that Bobby probably wasn't being faithful. I was barely eighteen and wasn't confident enough in myself to believe that my husband (or anyone else) would ever stay true to me. Deep within my heart, I knew Bobby loved me. I also knew he would never do me wrong, but I listened to my "new friends." This is an example of why it is so important for parents to watch the company their children keep.

I went to work in a restaurant where I met people who later influenced me to start taking drugs. They really seemed to like me. I wanted their attention so badly. Their acceptance of me drew me to them and consequently pulled me away from church. They were doing all the "fun things," like skiing at the lake on Saturday and Sunday. I couldn't go with them on Saturday because I had to work, so I went after work on Sunday. Gradually, I started doing more and more things with them. Then we started going to night clubs together.

I remember the first night I took drugs. It was the most awful feeling I had ever experienced. I felt as though I had killed somebody, because I had not been raised to do things like that. The first time I went with the group to a club, I thought we were just going to ride around. I was nervous. I had not been brought up in that kind of lifestyle. I was also nervous because I wasn't old enough to drink. But my friends arranged for me to get into a club anyway.

They said, "Oh, come with us, Zona. You'll have a blast! The things we do aren't really bad!"

But they were bad, and at first I was miserable. By the time I got home that first night, I thought I was going to have a heart attack. I begged God not to let my father find out what I was doing, "because if he does, he will kill me!"

I was busy with my job all week, and my "friends" didn't bother me again until Friday. Then they came to the restaurant where I worked and hounded me to go out with them again. "I can't go! I can't go!" I insisted; but they kept saying, "Yes, you can! Come on!"

I tried to find an excuse not to go. I persuaded the people I worked for to assign me to clean-up duties. It was a big job, because I worked at a restaurant where there were ice cream machines, grills, and other equipment that had to be cleaned after hours. I wanted that cleaning job to take all night. But when I finished, the group was waiting for me, so I wound up going out with them again. That's how I started living a wild life in my teens. After that night, the group even helped me clean up so I could go out with them.

In the beginning, I was miserable the entire time I was with the group, because I was afraid someone would see me and tell my dad. The third time I went with the group, one of the girls brought me home afterwards. I went in and lay on the floor and cried. The next morning, I didn't want to see anyone. I was so ashamed! I was from a nice family. My dad always liked people and was friendly to everyone, and I had not been brought up to party all night.

However, it became easier and easier to go out with my new friends. I liked them because they were giving me the attention I craved, and they were paying my way. I loved the attention I was receiving. *My mother and Bobby rejected me*, I thought, *but these people accept me.* I believed they really cared about me. Going out with them started to be fun, and I loved it.

After I became comfortable with this crowd, I would head straight for the dance floor as soon as we got to a club. When I was on the dance floor, I would "get into" the music, and all of the hurt from my mother's rejection would be blotted out. I told myself that I was having a great time. Sin is fun for a season. That's how people get hooked on it, but Romans 6:23 says, "the wages of sin is death." I know this is true, because of what I saw sin do to me and my friends.

I really liked the people I was involved with. Still, what I was doing bothered me because of my upbringing at home. It disturbed me when I began to backslide. Even when I was on drugs, I drew the line at some things. For example, I would never go to clubs on Sunday.

Descent into Drugs

The first time my friends gave me speed, it was one of the strongest types, called "the black widow"—the kind truck drivers take to stay awake on long hauls. I thought it had worn off, so after three hours, I took another one. I was up all night! The next day, I went Christmas shopping and was "wired" to the sky. I loved the feeling and soon became a "speed freak." I did speed every day for almost three years, and worked my way up to twelve pills a day. I worked sixteen to eighteen hours daily managing a restaurant in town, and could not be without my constant dosages of speed.

By then, I had become thoroughly convinced that Bobby had been untrue to me in Vietnam. Someone who knew me wrote him about the kind of wild lifestyle I was leading. He got an emergency leave to come home and see for himself. Our marriage disintegrated. Although Bobby assured me that he loved me and that he had been faithful to me, I couldn't believe that he wasn't untrue. Finally, he filed for divorce and I kept on partying.

I was a partier all right, but I convinced myself that I wasn't doing anything immoral—after all, I wasn't even drinking, although my friends thought I was. I just loved all the attention I was finally getting. The truth is, alcohol made me sick. One night, not long after I started going to night clubs, my friends gave me wine instead of Kool-Aid. After I had drunk several glasses of it, the room began to spin around. My friends stood around me and laughed. Their faces looked distorted to me—all large noses and big mouths. They carried me outside to a van, and one of the girls sat with me all night while I threw up.

The gang thought the trick they had played on me was hilarious. So I started playing a trick of my own. When we were in a club, everybody would be "half lit"—like the club itself (it was always so dark in there that it was hard to see what was going on). The group would order me screwdrivers—a mixed drink made with vodka and orange juice—and in the darkness I would pour them down onto the floor beside me. They would order me twelve to fifteen drinks in one night. After awhile, they started calling me "little alchy," because they thought I held my liquor so well. Actually, I never drank even one of them. There were lots of "friends" who gave me speed. Nearly all of them are dead now and I'm only alive because my dad prayed and stood in the gap for me. I believe many of my friends are dead, *because no one prayed and interceded for them.*

Parents, Stand in the Gap!

If you do not stand in the gap for your children, they may die and go to hell. You must give your children positive words and the Word of God to hear in order to build faith in them. The disgrace being brought on the family is not the most important thing you should be concerned about. What about your children dying and going to hell? If you do not want their blood on your hands, pray for them and confess the Word of God over them.

Over the next three years, my life became progressively worse and my drug habit became progressively stronger. Yet there was always a line that I wouldn't go past. The Holy Spirit was always tugging at my heart. There were many times when bad things could have happened to me. I might have even died, but I believe my dad's prayers prevented those terrible things from taking place.

One time I went to a house where two or three of the girls I ran around with used to hang out. There was plenty of food, so we got something to eat. Then we just sat around outside with the rest of the gang. I noticed there were several horses on the premises. When I went back inside, I saw home entertainment centers, a bedroom suite which had been taken apart, and all sorts of appliances including kitchen stoves. I knew the house had a range because I had seen it, so I thought that was strange. Out back, I noticed there were pigs, chickens, a car, and a motorcycle.

"What's going on?" I asked. "Are we going to have an auction or something?"

My friends rushed me back outside saying, "Don't let anyone know you saw any of that stuff!"

After I got home, I realized that all of those things had probably been stolen. The next day, we went back to the same house. We were just sitting around talking. The guy who had been stealing most of the articles found out that I knew about what he was doing. I'll never forget how scared I was. I was shaking from the inside out. My knees were knocking together; and I thought to myself, *Where's my daddy? Where's my upbringing? What am I doing here?* But outwardly, I was trying to act "cool."

All of a sudden, the guy came over and spoke to the people with me. "If anyone knows anything that is going on around here…," he started to say. Then he slapped me across the face, knocking me right out of the chair. He looked right at me and said, "If you say anything, I'll kill you. No matter where you go, I'll find you. I'll track you until the day I die."

The Fun Didn't Last

There were ten friends in my group. Seven of them are dead today. It is their stories that I want to share. Three others had bad things happen to them, but they aren't dead. One girl has cancer and is barely alive, another developed multiple sclerosis, and the third, lost one of her legs. Not all of my so-called friends died due to taking or selling drugs, but three fourths of them did. They were small dealers, but they used enough drugs to cause their own deaths. I believe they died because they sold drugs to children and young people.

All of the names used in my rendering of what happened are fictitious. No hint has been given as to the identity of my friends. I'm not exposing people—I'm exposing the devil and his methods of stealing and killing. Young people need to be made aware of Satan's devices and traps. They must realize just how strong the influence of other people—the wrong people—can be. Parents love your children and stand in the gap for them! The Bible says, "The effectual fervent prayer of a righteous man availeth much" (James 5:16). Don't let the devil destroy your children!

Killed by the Devil

The First One to Die

Joe was an outcast, but he wasn't a wimp, although people called him that and took advantage of him. He dealt drugs in order to be liked, and later, he began to take them himself. We were good friends—not girlfriend and boyfriend—just good buddies. I took up for Joe all the time. In fact, all my life I have taken up for the "underdog," the person no one else likes or accepts. Joe would sit with me at the clubs and help me cover the fact that I was pouring my drinks on the floor when no one was looking.

Night clubs are kept dark—demons like dark places—which made it easier for me to hide what I was doing. Even though my friends couldn't believe that I was downing perhaps fifteen drinks in an evening, they never caught on to my trick. The owner of the club knew, of course, because every night after we had left he would have to clean up the mess I had made.

The week before Joe's death, he looked at me with tears in his eyes and said, "Zona, I wish I had never given you any speed!"

"Anytime you want to give me some, you just go right ahead," I told him. "I can't live without it."

Joe cried and said, "I have done this to you. I have turned you into a speed freak. I'm not going to give you anymore."

"What are you talking about?" I asked. "I'm not a freak. I'm having a good time. Give me some more. I need it for tomorrow." I could always talk Joe into giving me the drugs I wanted. Sometimes, he would even split his drug money with me. Or, if he didn't have any money, I would share with him from the small salary I made at the restaurant.

We had plans to get together the following Friday night. Joe had to work late and then help his mother, but he said he would meet me at the club. That night, I went early to the club, where there was a new band. I later learned that Joe's mother had laid out a brand new shirt and suit that he planned to wear. But when he got home that evening, he decided to lie down for a few minutes.

He tried to call the club and tell me he would be late, but the club owner would not call me to the phone. Meanwhile, I was looking all over the place for Joe. When I called his house, the line was busy. Somehow, I couldn't have a good time that evening; and Joe never showed up.

Early the next morning, when we had planned to have breakfast together, I couldn't eat because Joe was on my mind. I went home and crawled in bed to sleep for awhile. Later that morning, I was awakened by the phone ringing. I was told that that Joe had choked to death on the mucus in his throat, one of the side effects of speed. It was a miracle that the same thing hadn't happened to me. Sometimes my whole body would be pounding when it was time to go to bed, and I would repeatedly have to clear my throat.

I could not believe Joe was dead! The funeral was just awful. His parents knew how close Joe and I had been, and they knew I was a speed freak.

Joe had written me a little note—a gag, really—telling me that he was in jail and asking me to come bail him out. He had also written that he appreciated me because I was his best friend—the only one who had ever been loyal to him. He was going to put the note in my car. Instead, they found it on him when he died. Joe was the first one to die.

The Second One to Die

Gary drank all of the time, as well as took speed. One night, he was stopped by the police for driving while intoxicated. That night in the county jail, he hung himself with his belt. Gary was always getting citations for driving while drunk. So why did he commit suicide after this arrest? I knew he did it because he thought his parents didn't care, that they didn't love him. Gary always talked about his upbringing. There were no restrictions on him. When he was a teenager in high school, his parents didn't care what time he came in at night. They didn't care whether he got his homework done. They didn't care whether he went to school cleaned up or even whether he had anything to eat at noon. Many times, I gave him lunch money or my lunch. That's just the way it was for Gary.

There were several children in the family, and he was in the middle. He said that his parents just didn't have time for him. He called it being "busy." The Department of Human Services would have called it neglect. Parents, you must not only *tell* your children you love them—you also need to *show* them kindness and love. Actions do speak louder than words; and unless you get your actions straightened out, your words alone will not mean a thing. Gary was the second one to die.

The Third One to Die

Steve went to sleep and never woke up. We let him off at his house on our way home from the club one night, and the next morning, his parents found him dead. I heard the announcement on the radio. The coroner couldn't find anything wrong with Steve—he had just died. My friends used to joke and say that he died partying. That would make me so angry, because even in the state I was in, I knew the truth - Steve had died and gone to hell, unless he had repented without telling anyone.

The gang kept after me to go places with them, but they called me a "stick-in-the-mud." When we went to the beach and they started that "he died partying" stuff, as if it were a great compliment to Steve, I would try to get them to stop. When they were drugged up, sometimes they would say, "Let's walk on water!" That also made me angry. Then they would call me "Little Miss Holy Girl" and laugh at me. But even when I was in sin, I couldn't stand for them to joke about anything pertaining to God. Steve was the third one to die.

The Fourth One to Die

Mike also drank and bootlegged liquor. One Saturday night, he went to a nearby town to get some alcohol to bring back and sell. On the way home, he got drunk himself. He had a wife and children, but they had gone somewhere that night. When he got home—they owned an expensive, beautiful house—he was so drunk that he drove right through the garage wall.

Directly behind the wall of the three-car garage were the electrical outlets to the kitchen appliances. On contact with the electric current, his car exploded and burst into flames. The house, and everything around it, burned totally. Mike's body was completely devoured by the flames, except for one gold tooth which was used to identify him. Mike was the fourth one to die.

The Fifth One to Die

Jerry was reared in a godly home, but as he grew older, he decided not to serve God. He became mixed up with a heavy-duty drug crowd and began dealing dope. He sold acid (LSD), coke (cocaine), and anything else he could get his hands on. One night, he was murdered. We believe it was because he knew too much about his drug sources. In the drug world, if you know too much, your life is worth nothing. Jerry was always at the wrong place at the wrong time, and had picked up too much information for his own good. Jerry was the fifth one to die.

The Sixth One to Die

Tim owned a well-known business, and he drank a lot. His wife was absolutely gorgeous. We used to party over at his house—really a mansion—all the time. We thought he was great. He always provided food and everything we needed to have a blast.

One day, he found out that his wife had been involved in an affair. He was so upset that he checked into a local motel. Arranging more than one hundred pictures of her on the ceiling and walls, he lay down to die. A diabetic, Tim purposely did not take his insulin shots. He died surrounded by his wife's pictures.

Tim was always so sweet, but he was in misery. He was a dope fiend and an alcoholic, but we never saw him lose his temper. His wife would be friendly with other guys right in front of him, but he would never show anger. I always felt so sorry for him. This time, her behavior apparently was the last straw. Tim couldn't cope, so he "checked out." Tim was the sixth one to die.

The Seventh One to Die

Jeff was a nice guy. I liked him a lot, but I never knew him extremely well. We were at a nearby lake one night waterskiing. We always had a good time there. But when Jeff went out on the lake, he suddenly disappeared. He went under the water, skis first, and never came up. We found out that he had been pulled under by a whirlpool. His body was never found—*ever*. Talk about blowing your mind. Some of the kids who were drunk sobered up instantly. Jeff was the seventh one to die.

All This Time, My Dad Was Praying

All this time, when I was out partying and "having fun," my Dad was home praying for me—*standing in the gap.* Deep down I knew that one day payment was going to come due. You may think, as I did, that partying is fun, but that kind of fun never lasts. Inside, I was miserable. But Dad kept praying for me, and even when things in my life looked worse and not better, he didn't let up. He kept right on binding Satan from me and lifting me up before God, standing on Scriptures, and believing God for His mercy for me.

If it hadn't been for my dad standing in the gap for me like that—when I was still coming home wired on drugs—even when he didn't have a thing to go on except God's Word, and if it hadn't been for God's mercy, I might have wound up dead like some of my friends. If not for Dad's prayers and God's mercy, I might be in hell right now.

The Long Road Back

I took drugs for three and a half years, and those were three and a half years of hell for me.

For the first two and a half years, I didn't believe anybody loved me. During that time, I didn't even believe in the word *"love."* Everyone, it seemed, had disappointed me, had been untrue, or had walked out on me. For the most part, I hated everybody. I started thinking more and more about my mother and what she had done. I started blaming myself for what had happened. I never thought there was anybody who would stay with me for any period of time. I blamed it on the way I looked, because I wasn't beautiful.

I was always a hard worker; so I thought if I worked real hard, maybe my father would brag on me. I always wanted Dad to be proud of me. And now I was a disgrace to him—he had told me so himself. At the beginning, even though deep down I knew Dad loved me, he would get aggravated with me. He would tell me that the Hayes family didn't do things like go to night clubs and drink and all that.

"You are disgracing me, Zona," Dad would say. "You are a disgrace to our family."

One time he even told me that he wished I was dead. He said that he would rather lose me than have to go through the agony I was causing him. In the beginning, when I was in sin, I tried my best to make that wish come true, because I didn't care whether I lived or died. I thought that Dad was all I had, other than God, and I didn't really think I had God. *My mother has left,* I said to myself, *and my dad will get tired of me and leave, too.* I just thought that everyone would leave me—even God. That's how messed up my thinking was.

Dad was harping on me all the time about the way I was behaving and I would say, "Dad, you're out of town all the time. How does it make you feel to know that you can go and win all those other kids to the Lord and you can't even do anything for your own child? Every time I come home, you're always helping all these other kids. You never have anything for me." What I couldn't see was that he loved me deeply and was trying to get me to do right. He was just going about it the wrong way.

You've Got to Start Loving Her More!

My dad went to the home of Brother and Sister J. R. Goodwin in Pasadena, Texas, to minister in their church. From there he was to go on to Brother and Sister Kenneth E. Hagin's home in Tulsa. While traveling between Texas and Oklahoma, my dad was told by God, "The things you want the most will never come to pass unless you start loving your daughter more. When she comes in at two or three o'clock in the morning, don't start yelling at her. Tell her that you love her. Tell her that I love her. Whatever she says to you, no matter how mean or hateful she is to you, just tell her that you love her and that I love her. Then shut up."

That's exactly what Dad told me the Lord told him. And that's exactly what he started doing.

He would tell me that he was praying for me. If you've ever heard my dad speak, you know that he is very persistent about everything.

He was the same way with me about coming back to God. On Sunday morning he would come into my bedroom and say, "Zona, honey, do you want to come to church with me?"

"I'm not going to church with you," I would tell him. "Those people have talked about me and backstabbed me, and I'm not going."

Later when he prayed at the table, he would say, "Thank You, Lord, for the food and everything You've done for us. And thank You that my daughter is going to church with me. I claim her soul, Lord; and I thank You that I see her raising her hands in church."

He did that all the time! It almost drove me crazy because he did it so much. Every time we sat down to eat, he did it. I told him, "Dad, I'm not going to church with you."

And he would say, "Oh, praise the Lord that my daughter is going to church with me next Sunday. Pass the beans, Zona!"

That's how my dad is. No matter what the situation, he will not take "no" for an answer.

And that's how you have to be with the devil. You can't get down. You can't get discouraged. You can't get depressed. I don't care if your child comes home drunk—love that son or daughter and thank the Lord for his or her deliverance. Then do as Dad did: *bind the devil and claim your child's soul for Jesus Christ.*

As I have said, I always knew deep down (especially after I came back to the Lord) that my dad loved me. Even though at the time I didn't think the love of God was shining through Dad, it really was. After everything I've been through, I think my father is the smartest man in the world.

Lord, Have Your Way with Her!

Bobby still loved me when he filed for divorce. I just wouldn't have anything to do with him. Now he was back in my life and had asked me to marry him again. It was the night before I had to give him my answer. That evening, my dad had begged me not to go out. "Just stay home," he said. "We'll pop popcorn and have a good time here. We'll be together just like a family." (I used to say that to him: "Let's do stuff, Dad, just like a family.") So that night he told me, "You don't have to go with those people, Zona."

"Daddy, I know you love me," I said. "I know you do. And I don't want to go with them."

Then he asked me, "Zona, what's it going to take to bring you back to the Lord?"

"I guess He'll have to knock me down," I answered, "because I'm not going to come back to Him. I don't trust Him. He may do me the way everybody else has done me!"

I was nuts. I just wasn't thinking straight. I thought everybody was out to get me. But I knew my dad loved me because he stood by me. And he had changed. He wasn't yelling at me anymore—he was showing me love. After I left, Dad went into the spare bedroom and put his hands on one of the twin beds. I never slept there unless I came home real, real late and didn't want him to know what time I had come in. He prayed, "Lord, You heard Zona. Whatever You have to do, shake her up! Have Your way with her."

Well, that night I came home about 3:00 a.m, because I had started getting numb all over. I couldn't understand it because I hadn't been drinking or anything. I had already stopped all that. I had just been out partying. So I lay down on the bed and went to sleep. When I woke up a few hours later and turned over, there was a man sitting on the floor with his legs crossed, looking right at me. I couldn't see any farther up his body than his waist—that's how big he was.

The sight of this strange being scared me so bad, I started to scream, but I couldn't get anything out of my throat. I didn't look up because he crossed his right leg over his left and put his right arm to the left side of his body to get up. He stood up and walked out of the room. I pulled the quilt over my head and, peeking out from under it, looked out the door. I saw him walk down the hall. I followed him around the corner and then watched him as he walked right through the wall. I almost fainted right there!

I thought it was a demon and that he was coming after me. I didn't know what to do. So I went to my dad's door and knocked. I tried to call out to him, but I couldn't get anything out but squeaky noises. When Dad opened the door, he asked, "What's wrong with you?"

I said, "Man!... Big!... Big, big man! I don't know...big, big... devil...man!"

The Lord blessed my dad by showing him that the man I had seen was my guardian angel.

That was on Thursday. On the following Saturday, Bobby and I went to the courthouse and were married again. We moved to Alabama, but for six months I could not get away from that vision of my angel. I kept in touch with Dad through letters and he wrote to me about an upcoming service at Faith Memorial Church in Cleveland, Tennessee, where he would be ministering. Brother and

Sister Hagin would be there, too. I knew I wanted to go to that service. I also knew that Bobby would be off work that weekend.

I knelt and said, "Lord, You helped me get off that speed when I went cold turkey for three days." Now I wanted God's help to get Bobby to go to that service with me. Kneeling, I prayed, "Lord, I don't know if You're even going to listen to me because of everything I've done like partying and being mean to my father. I have been hateful, really. But if You'll listen to me, would You please inspire Bobby to go with me to that service?"

It was a miracle I was asking for, because Bobby wasn't going to church either. He wasn't a mean person—he was a good person—but he just didn't go to church. We weren't doing anything wrong, but we were *backsliders*. To my great surprise and joy, Bobby agreed to go to the meeting. When we came into the service, Kenneth Hagin, Jr., had a vision. He saw a dark cloud over Bobby. Later he and Brother Hagin were praying during the altar call, and Dad came back to get me. I had been under conviction for six months, but I didn't return to the Lord and ask Jesus to come back into my heart until that night. I went up front, and my dad went back to get Bobby. Bobby came forward, and we both dedicated our lives to the Lord. Bobby prayed for forty-five minutes in tongues. We began serving the Lord together from that night on.

God Is Faithful to Restore

God is faithful. And I am so appreciative to Him, even to this day. If I let myself, when I think about it, I just weep. He restored my marriage. He brought Bobby and me back together and to Him. He prospered us. He blessed us with a child, even after five different doctors had told me that I could never have a baby. Bobby went into full-time ministry and I went to Bible school. I began teaching full-force, speaking at a couple of meetings a month and today I am the director of New Life Bible College.

I am restored mentally and physically—inside and out. My mind has been healed. My body has been healed. And my mouth has been healed. *(You know, your mouth has to be healed, too.)* I speak no words of doubt. That's what God has shown me—that to seek to know Him with all your heart, you have to pray for the mind of Christ, the heart of Christ, and the mouth of Christ.

It's the same for parents who are praying for their children. They have to desire the total nature of Christ: first the heart of Christ, then the mind of Christ. Next they have to get the mouth of Christ. When they get their words lined up with God's Word, their children will come back into the kingdom of God as I did.

Don't Give Up On God!

Parents, stand in the gap for your children and don't give up on God! Again, the Bible says, "The effectual fervent prayer of a righteous man availeth much" (James 5:16). Stand in the gap! Don't let the devil destroy your children! Bobby and I both came to serve the Lord because my dad stood in the gap and refused to give up, even when it looked as though nothing was happening. If anything, it looked as if my life was getting worse. If your children have never known the Lord, the Bible says that they can come to know Him. Acts 16:31 says, "Believe on the Lord Jesus Christ, and thou shalt be saved, and thy house."

If your child has known the Lord but has fallen away, he or she can come back. Jesus will love your child and accept him or her, just as He did with the prodigal son. He will restore your child's life, just as He has restored mine. In Joel 2:25 and 26, the Scriptures say that God will restore the years that the locusts have eaten, the years that have been stolen from you.

Stand in the gap for your children, just as my father did for me— and don't ever give up!

Parents, I cannot stress too strongly that it is time for you to get down on your knees and get serious about praying for your children. It is time to stop talking to God about your problem and to begin talking to your problem about God. Otherwise, your children may never come into the kingdom of God. Pray and confess the Word of God over your children and over whatever situation they may be in.

Remember that Satan is going to try to make it look as if God doesn't hear you, and that your children won't ever turn to the Lord. But remember that Satan is a liar and a thief. The Bible says that God hears your intercession. (1 John 5:14,15.) It's His will that everyone be saved. (1 Timothy 2:1,4.) Right now, Jesus is pleading your case before the Father. (Hebrews 7:25.)

The Lord is no respecter of persons, according to Acts 10:34; He has a miracle waiting for you just as He did for my dad and me. Stand in the gap. Continue there in faith, no matter how bad the situation may look. Don't waver, and don't give up. *Don't let the devil have your children!*

How You Can Stand in the Gap for Your Children

Norvel shares the following:

In Genesis, chapters 18 and 19, we read the account of how Abraham stood in the gap for Sodom. God was going to destroy

Sodom because the city had turned against Him, but Abraham interceded. He asked God if He would destroy the righteous with the wicked. (Genesis 18:23.) Then he asked that if fifty righteous people could be found, would God spare the city. God said He would. Abraham continued to intercede and reason with God until He agreed to spare Sodom if only ten righteous people could be found. But there weren't ten. There was only one—Abraham's nephew, Lot.

God sent two angels to Lot to tell him to leave the city because it was going to be destroyed. Lot obeyed. Genesis 19:29 tells how God remembered Abraham and spared Lot. Because Abraham stood in the gap, Lot was spared.

We see in Ezekiel 22:30 that God was looking for someone to stand in the gap for Israel. Israel had shed blood, profaned the Sabbath, lived immorally, and turned her back on God. In this case, God could not find anyone who was willing to stand in the gap for Israel, so He poured out His anger upon her (v. 31).

Don't Waver

It is important that you know how to stand in the gap so that you will not waste time. I had stood for two years, thinking I was doing right, and God told me I had been wavering. You must not waver in your faith; wavering faith doesn't please God. To receive from God, you have to please Him with your faith.

"Now faith is the substance of things hoped for, the evidence of things not seen" (Hebrews 11:1). Your faith brings God's power down from heaven to earth no matter what your need. The same faith that brought you salvation brings all the rest of what God has for you, no matter what it is. Don't worry about when or how the manifestation is going to come. If you wonder when or try to reason how, you are in doubt. You are doubting God, and binding His power to bring the manifestation. God doesn't need your worrying; He demands your faith.

Believe God's Word and stand on it—God will do the rest. Just be concerned about your faith and about God's promises. Leave the results to God. Believe that you have it before you get it, before you see any results. Then wait patiently for the manifestation.

Take Control of Your Mouth

Take control of your mouth, because it is your mouth that speaks your faith. Continually and sincerely speak your faith by praising God for the answer—because by faith *it is done*. Remember, "We walk by faith, not by sight" (2 Corinthians 5:7). Stand and speak your faith, no matter what you see.

Love and Not Condemn

Another important thing you must do is love, and not condemn. Don't allow wrong words to slash out at your children. God doesn't like it. He wants you to reach your hands out to your children right in the midst of their sins.

Slashing out at your children—saying things like, "I taught you better than that!"—shows that your spiritual pride has been hurt. I know it's spiritual pride because I've been there. I was there when Zona was running around to the dance halls. You feel like a failure. You feel like all the blood has been drained out of your body. You sit alone in your house while the devil points his finger at you and says,

"See, it doesn't work. Why don't you stop? Why don't you go out and do what you want to do?"

When the devil told me that, I said, "No! I'm not going to do it. I'm going to stand up for God's righteousness no matter what! My daughter is not going to hell! Satan, you're just a thief and a liar! I'm not going to let you have her. I'm going to stand in the gap for her!"

After I had reached out to Zona for six months when she was in the midst of her sin, she finally lost any desire to even go to the dance halls. "I know the people in the dance halls are phonies," she told me. "Don't you think I have sense enough to know that? Besides, it's getting so sweet in this house. I can see the difference between the way people treat me at the dance halls and the way you love me. I don't even want to go to those places anymore."

God's Obligation

Most of God's promises are conditional, and standing in the gap is conditional. If you meet God's conditions for one who can stand in the gap, He has an obligation to perform His Word by reaching out and saving your lost loved ones. Let me explain what God will do when you stand in the gap. If parents will stand in the gap for their children or children will stand in the gap for their parents or all people will stand in the gap for their loved ones, God's power will rule upon the earth and honor their prayers.

If you pray right, God will honor your prayers. If you pray wrong, God won't honor them. God has standards that the human race must go by, and His number one standard is faith. Faith means you believe you have something before you get it—that you are going to trust God.

By the word of the LORD were the heavens made; and all the host of them by the breath of his mouth.

Psalm 33:6

The LORD looketh from heaven; he beholdeth all the sons of men. From the place of his habitation he looketh upon all the inhabitants of the earth.

Psalm 33:13,14

Our soul waiteth for the LORD: he is our help and our shield. For our heart shall rejoice in him, because we have trusted in his holy name.

Psalm 33:20,21

The angel of the LORD encampeth round about them that fear him, and delivereth them. O taste and see that the LORD is good: blessed is the man that trusteth in him.

Psalm 34:7,8

The eyes of the LORD are upon the righteous, and his ears are open unto their cry .... The righteous cry, and the LORD heareth, and delivereth them out of all their troubles.

Psalm 34:15,17

The compassion that God has upon the lonely heart, upon the heart that has been defeated in life, is amazing. When you don't know what to do, just cry out to Him for His mighty power.

The Lord hears the cry of the righteous and delivers them out of all their troubles. Jesus died so you could become righteous. Because you are the righteousness of God in Christ Jesus, you fit into this promise. God will hear your cry and deliver you out of all your troubles. It is amazing how much compassion God has for you. If you get into trouble, all you have to do is cry out to God and He will deliver you.

If you want to go your own way, God will let you and He won't turn against you. He will always be there waiting for you to cry out to Him so that He can perform His Word. God watches over His Word to perform it. (Jeremiah 1:12.) He is obligated to do it. Parents, all you need to do is love, believe God's Word, and stand in the gap by standing in faith on that Word. Let God use you to reach out to your child and show His love to him or her. Your part is to let your light shine and praise God for producing the end result—a born-again, Christian child. God will do the rest. *Let God reach out through you and perform His Word.*

Chapter 12

How to Live and Not Die

"I shall not die, but live, and declare the works of the LORD."

Psalm 118:17

G od doesn't want you to have any diseases. He wants you to receive His miracle-working power and be totally free. In writing this book, Norvel did his best, by God's power, to drive out and to demolish every disease in every person who reads this book. And the same principles taught here regarding disease can be applied to all critical cases—financial, emotional, social, spiritual, or physical.

Good Things Come from God to You

You can receive miracles, and you can have authority over sickness and disease. Know this once and for all: all bad things that come to visit you are from the devil—all bad things! They come from hell— not from heaven. The Bible says all good things come down from the Father of lights to you. "Every good gift and every perfect gift is from above, and cometh down from the Father of lights, in whom is no variableness, neither shadow of turning" (James 1:17).

God sends good and perfect gifts from heaven down to you. Not one heartache has ever come from God. Not one weak day or one defeated moment has ever come to you from heaven. *God knows no defeat or sickness. Heaven knows no pain.* I've been to heaven twice. The air is full of peace. There is no sickness in heaven. There are no worms in the apples in heaven.

The grass is about ten times greener in heaven than it is on earth. Everything in heaven is alive. Everything is full of life, power, and love. It saturates you all the time. Heaven is not a misty place out in the air, where a bunch of little spirits float around, wondering who they are. It's a real world! I'm excited about the good things from heaven that we can enjoy in *this* life. Good gifts, perfect gifts are coming down from heaven, from the Father of lights to you.

First Things First—Worship

Only after you worship and praise God, do you have a right to ask God to heal you or do anything else for you. If you don't know this, it can cost you your life! When I tell people this, some say, "But, Brother Norvel, I love the Lord." That's not good enough! A lawyer came to Jesus one day and asked him, "Master, which is the great commandment in the law?" (Matthew 22:36). Jesus answered, "Thou shalt love the Lord, thy God, with all thy heart, and with all thy soul, and with all thy mind. This is the first and great commandment.(vv. 37,38)

In other words, Jesus was saying not to have any other gods before Him. He's supposed to be number one in your life. And when you worship the Lord, you have made Him number one in your life. You can't love your church more than you love God. You can't love your family, your business, or your money more than you love God. If you do, you're in bad trouble. Learn to worship God first. When you do that, you have a right to ask Him for anything. He'll give you what you ask for.

One of the reasons why so many church people get in trouble with the devil is because they don't worship Jesus. You have to worship God *for yourself.* Just singing a song or two in church is not worship. That doesn't honor God. If you run to church real quick for that, it's a wonder you even find the church. And one of these days you won't, because the devil will attack you so much. Did you know the devil goes to church every Sunday? That's right. He'll help you sing, and he'll help you teach a Sunday school class. He'll sit beside you if you've got cancer and pat you on the back. He'll tell you, "You're a perfect Christian—don't change. You'll just have to die."

But, if you'll put first things first, there's no such thing as the devil killing you. He doesn't have the power to kill you, if you'll worship God. You can know God, have power, and still lose out. Maybe you've been a Christian for twenty years and know God really well. Realize this: the devil knows God, and he knew God real well, too. In fact, the devil had lots of power. He went upon the holy mountain of God and walked up and down the stones of fire.

What iniquity was found in Lucifer, the anointed cherub; that caused his fall from heaven? "How art thou fallen from heaven, O Lucifer, son of the morning! How art thou cut down to the ground..." (Isaiah 14:12). The devil started doing his own thing, going his own way, and that caused his fall. "For thou hast said in thine heart, I will ascend into heaven, I will exalt my throne above the stars of God; I will sit also upon the mount of the congregation, in the sides of the north, I will ascend above the heights of the clouds; I will be like the Most High" (Isaiah 14:13,14).

The devil's downfall can be yours, too. How? You could have been the best Christian in the world for twenty years and won thousands of souls to God. But if you turn your head away a little bit from Matthew, Mark, Luke, and John and start doing your own thing, you'll fall just like the devil did. You could build a church of five thousand people and win one hundred thousand people to Jesus. You could be sharp and strong for twenty years of your life. But if you start getting settled and satisfied and start doing what *you* think needs to be done instead of what God tells you, you've had it!

If you don't watch yourself, even though you're called of God to preach, you'll get to preaching so much you'll just start floating along. One day you'll check up on yourself in your home and discover that you and your family haven't worshipped God in your house for four or five weeks! *You'll get weak and lose your vision.* It's easy for ministers to get that way. I mean, I have to watch myself. You can't afford to get so busy that you don't worship God in your house. From that time forward, you won't go anywhere but down.

You'll lose your desire to pass out tracts. You may say, "What do you mean, 'lose your desire to pass out tracts'? I don't pass out tracts now!" No wonder God has you reading this book! You'd better watch yourself or you'll get weak and lose your vision for getting people in your community saved who are dying and going to hell. You'll lose your vision for getting people healed who have cancer and are dying with nobody to help them. You can't help these people unless you know how. And sometimes if you do know how, you won't have the ambition to go and do it because you've lost your vision. Why? Because you have ceased to worship God every day. So these people in your community just die while you're living right among them with the Holy Ghost in your belly.

Remember what John 7:37-39 tells us: "In the last day, that great day of the feast, Jesus stood and cried saying, If any man thirst, let him come unto me, and drink. He that believeth on me, as the Scripture hath said, out of his belly shall flow rivers of living water.(But this spake he of the Spirit....") He, the Spirit, knows how to get people saved, healed, and set free, and He lives on the inside of you. But, He won't do very much for you or through you unless you worship God.

Obeying nine out of ten commandments won't give you an abundant life if you're not worshipping God. Notice what Jesus told the devil himself. "Get thee hence, Satan: for it is written, Thou shalt worship the Lord, thy God, and him only shalt thou serve" (Matthew 4:10). Verse 11 tells us what happened next: "Then the devil leaveth him, and, behold, angels came and ministered unto him." If you don't obey God by worshipping Him, the devil has a right to come into your house and give you cancer. I'm warning you, the devil has the right to walk in and do anything he wants to do to you, *if* you don't worship God. But, when the devil comes into your house and sees you on the floor worshipping and praising Jesus every day, he can't do what he wants to do. He'll leave you, too, just like he did Jesus. Notice I didn't say *"once a week,"* but *"every day."*

Do you want God to come and hover over your house and stay manifested in each room? When you get up in the morning do you want every day to be exciting? God inhabits the praises of His people. (Psalm 22:3.) When you praise the Lord, you build Him a habitation, a dwelling place. Do you build God a habitation with your praise and worship every day?

Worshipping and praising God is a way of life. "Rejoice in the Lord always (every day): and again I say, Rejoice" (Philippians 4:4, explanation mine). When Paul was getting ready to go to the

Corinthians, they were talking about having power. Paul wrote them and said he didn't know if they had power or not. He was coming and when he got there, he'd let them know if they had God's power. "But I will come to you shortly, if the Lord will, and will know, not the speech of them which are puffed up, but the power" (1 Corinthians 4:19).

You'll have God's power if you'll worship every day. Here's how to start your day off by worshipping God. Bring your hands out from under the covers. If you can't lift them very high, just lift them a little bit. Open up your mouth and say, "Jesus, I love You. I belong to You and I thank You, Lord, that my name is written in heaven. I worship You, Jesus. Thou art great, O God. I worship You, Lord. There are no other gods before You, Jesus. And I just want to thank You, Jesus, because You are my Savior and Healer. Thank You, Lord, for Your divine, healing power. Oh, precious Jesus, Your healing power is flowing through my body right now to drive out every affliction, in Jesus' name. No affliction can stay in my body. I belong to You, Jesus, and I worship You." Remember: put first things first. Only after you worship and praise God, then and only then, do you have a right to ask Him for anything.

God's Will Is Praying

After praise and worship, prayer is a natural step. Heaven doesn't come to earth cheap. It never has! It takes prayer. Prayer is a channel that God has provided so that a man can reach heaven and see the things of heaven done on earth. *God's will is praying, not just thinking about something.* And wondering isn't God's will either! The most important decision you'll ever make isn't whether or not to go to college and get a degree. It's all right to do that—I'm not knocking it. But it's a lot more important for you to learn how to pray.

Prayer isn't limited to anything. If you'll learn how to pray and believe what you read in the Word, you can have anything you want. Glory to God! When Saul of Tarsus was on the road to Damascus, to drag Christians out of their homes and haul them off to prison, God stopped him in his tracks. Then God told Ananias to go to Saul, "… for, behold, he prayeth" (Acts 9:11). God sent Ananias because Saul prayed. You may say, "The Lord would have sent Ananias anyway." No, he wouldn't, because it takes prayer. "If my people, which are called by my name, shall humble themselves, and pray, and seek my face, and turn from their wicked ways; then will I hear from heaven, and will forgive their sin, and will heal their land," 2 Chronicles 7:14.

Get Scriptures to Cover Your Case

To pray in faith for anything, whether it's healing for your body or a financial miracle, you need to know God's will. Then faith can begin. The way to find God's will is to go to the Bible and find a Scripture that covers your case. For example, Jesus paid the price for our redemption and for our healing. First Peter 2:24 says, "…by whose (Jesus') stripes, ye were healed." "Were" is past tense, and that means we are healed. God will manifest Himself to you and your disease will disappear, as soon as you find out from the Word that you're healed. This Scripture covers your case.

Many people are waiting on the Lord to come and heal them *sometime*. They are trying to convince God to heal them. The price has already been paid, but you have to find the Scriptures that cover your case and make them a part of you. Never let them depart from you, regardless of the circumstances. If you don't do this, you're whipped. You will live your whole life without victory. It may even cost you your life.

Suppose you died at an early age from sickness. When you got to heaven, you went to church and heard Jesus preach. After the service you walked up to Him and said, "Jesus, I was a pastor's wife (or this or that), and my husband and I love You and we saw You heal lots of people. But, Jesus, why didn't You heal me?" It will be sad, my friend, when Jesus turns to you, shows you His back, and says, "I did! Why didn't you accept it? Why didn't you take a long, hard look with your natural eyes at the stripes on My back?"

You may say, "Well, Jesus, I didn't see You on earth." And He'll reply, "You saw that verse of Scripture. Why didn't you accept that as truth? It says that by My stripes you were healed!"

Attend to God's Word. Read Proverbs 4:20: "My son, attend to my words; incline thine ear unto my sayings. Let them not depart from thine eyes; keep them in the midst of thine heart. For they are life unto those that find them, and health to all their flesh." Pay close attention to verse 20: "My son...." God is talking to *you*. When He says "son," he means "daughter," too. "My son, attend to my words...."

Attend to them, means that *you're responsible to know what is in the Bible for yourself.* Quit driving around the country, wearing your tires out, looking for someone to pray for you all the time. *You* never walk the floor, *you* don't worship God, or read the Bible very much. That's why *you* want someone to pray for you all the time. Come to God on your own.

You may think you've got to get to a particular person so that he can pray for you. You don't need to get to anybody except the Lord Jesus Christ! That's what you need, and it's *all* you need. Come to God on your own. Recently I was ministering to about 2,000 people in Baltimore, Maryland. I was teaching on the importance of coming to God on your own and asking Him for mercy. While I was speaking, about 200 people got up and ran to the altar, fell down on their knees, and began praising God. And all over the place God began to heal them.

One lady had been pushed to the front in a wheelchair. After being shaken by the power of God for about twenty minutes, she arose from the wheelchair healed! I did not pray for her. She received from God on her own. She came to God and showed great and deep appreciation for Jesus as her Healer. She reminded Him of how much she loved Him and how much she knew He loved her. After God shook her like a tree, she rose up and walked off. Jesus said in Matthew 11:28, "Come unto me, all ye that labour and are heavy laden…." You look up the Scriptures that cover your case, and you claim them boldly in Jesus' name.

Go before the throne of God and remind God of what He said. "For we have not an high priest which cannot be touched with the feeling of our infirmities, but was in all points tempted like as we are, yet without sin. Let us therefore, come boldly unto the throne of grace, that we may obtain mercy, and find grace to help in time of need" (Hebrews 4:15,16). "Put me in remembrance: let us plead together: declare thou, that thou mayest be justified" (Isaiah 43:26). Claim a Scripture for yourself, and the Holy Spirit will absolutely perform it for you.

Put the gospel first and, "all these things shall be added unto you" (Matthew 6:33). Get the Word in your heart. Let's take another look at Proverbs 4:21: "Let them (God's words) not depart from thine eyes; keep them in the midst of thine heart." I want you to learn how important it is for you to know the will of God, how important it is for you to not let the Word of God depart from before your eyes. The victory for you is in the Word, not somewhere else. But you have to get the Word on the inside of your heart, so your mouth can speak it. If the Word gets in your heart, it will come out of your mouth, "…for out of the abundance of the heart the mouth speaketh" (Matthew 12:34).

Do What the Holy Spirit Says

"Submit yourselves, therefore, to God. Resist the devil, and he will flee from you" (James 4:7). *First,* submit yourself to God and obey Him. *Then* resist the devil and he will flee from you. Submitting yourself to God means submitting yourself to the Word. "In the beginning was the Word, and the Word was with God, and the Word was God" (John 1:1). God and His Word are inseparable.

Again, let me remind you of Proverbs 4:20-21: "My son, attend to my words, incline thine ear unto my sayings. Let them not depart from thine eyes…." To effectively resist the devil, you must keep your eyes on victory all of the time. How do you do that? By keeping your eyes on God's Word, because the Word is the book of instructions for victory. It tells you how to fight the enemy. If you don't submit yourself to God's Word, you won't be able to resist the devil. And if you don't resist the devil, then you will be doing your own thing the rest of your life. You won't obey God.

Remember, "as many as are led by the Spirit of God, they are the sons of God" (Romans 8:14). The Spirit of God will lead you according to God's Word. The Word and the Spirit agree (1 John 5:6-8). If you don't know the Word, you won't know if you're being led by the Spirit. You may say, "Brother Norvel, I'm not led by the Spirit of God, but I know God and I'm a son of God." You can be a son of God and a rebel too—a rebel son of God! God has a lot of children who won't obey Him. Often I write about things I've learned from God and done right, but a lot of times I've missed God.

I missed God once in Atlanta, Georgia, at a convention. The first day of the convention I taught on prophecy. When the Spirit of God came upon me, I didn't know what He wanted me to do. Before I got His leading, a man in the back of the congregation began to prophesy. He got me off track.

When I got to the motel room, God let me know in no uncertain terms, "You missed Me!" He told me He had wanted to bestow the gift of prophecy to various ones in the congregation. "I am the Giver of gifts," He said. "And I wanted to give them the gift of prophecy— but you missed Me. You let that fellow prophesy; you let him get you off course, and you missed Me." I said, "I know it, Lord, and I'm sorry. In my next teaching session, I promise You, God, I'll obey You. I don't care what I feel, I'll obey You and I won't miss You anymore. I repent, God, I repent."

The next day, the minister who had prophesied in the previous day's session wrote me a long letter. I read it to the congregation. He said, "Dear Brother Norvel, when I got to my room, the Spirit of God dealt with me. He told me that I shouldn't have prophesied in that meeting, even though the spirit of prophecy was on me. I know I was out of His will by doing that." The Spirit of God had wanted to prophesy in that meeting, but the anointing was on me. This minister had the gift; but sometimes just because you've got the gift and the Spirit of God is on you, that doesn't mean that you should get up and prophesy. Wait and let the fellow up front either prophesy himself, or let him call upon somebody.

You'd better learn to be led by the Spirit of God! *You can't do just anything you want to do in your church.* When the Lord first began to use me in prophecy, He told me, "I want you to prophesy, son. But first of all, I want you to go and ask your pastor if you can prophesy in his church." You don't run your church. You have no right to do just anything you want to, even though you pay your tithes there. You don't have any right to override your pastor. God will not honor that. Your pastor is the head of the church (under Jesus), not someone else. Deacons are fine men. As a deacon, I helped build a church. But do you know what we elders and deacons are supposed to do? We're supposed to sweep the floor and pay the bills. I know that deflates some people a little bit, but it's the truth.

Now, read this carefully. Once you make up your mind that God is a certain way, it's hard for Him to ever help you anymore. Most Christians have made up their minds and have their own approach to God. Almost every church in America, whatever their doctrine, believes their approach is correct. And God just doesn't bother them.

You make the decision about what you believe. God won't *make* you believe anything. You have to make a choice to believe God scripturally. And, of course, when you believe scripturally, there's no defeat. A lot of good Christians who died before their time, believed God and loved God. Yes, they were good Christians, *but they didn't believe God scripturally.* Everybody that is born again believes God. They love God and trust Him. And if somebody asks them a question like, "Do you believe God can do this?" they say, "Oh, yeah. I believe God can do anything."

There's a vast difference between believing in God and believing God scripturally. God's Word is His perfect will. You must know and believe that God's Word is God's perfect will for you. And the

Holy Spirit who lives inside of you will perform the part of His Word that you believe. He will perform it *for you!*

Keep God's Word Before Your Eyes

I want to talk you into memorizing healing Scriptures in the New Testament and confessing that Jesus is your Healer. Don't worry about the whole world: first get things straight for yourself. *Speak God's Word.* The first thing in the morning, I worship God. Then I confess: "Jesus, You're my Healer. You're the One who keeps me strong. You're the One who gives me health in my body. And I will never have any want for anything, Jesus, because You are the best businessman I have ever met. All of my bills are paid, glory to God! And all of my businesses make a profit. Thank You, Lord, for thousands and thousands and thousands of dollars coming in above the bills, in Jesus' blessed, holy name. Thank You, Lord that my Bible school and my children's home have no needs and they have thousands of dollars in their account. And that's the way it will be forever. Thank You, Lord, that because I'm going to give my money to help other people's ministries, men will give back to me again. You said it, Lord, and that's the way it is, in Jesus' name."

This is the Scripture I've found to cover my case: "Give, and it shall be given unto you; good measure, pressed down, and shaken together, and running over, shall men give into your bosom. For with the same measure that ye mete withal it shall be measured to you again" (Luke 6:38). Based on my confession, I believe that I will never have a need in anything that I do or that I touch. I will be successful all the time. My accounts are filled with thousands of dollars, in Jesus' holy name. My accounts don't run short. If I slack up on my confession, my accounts begin to get a little bit low. Then

I grab and shake myself and say, "Get your mouth straightened out, Norvel! This Bible school account has only a few thousand dollars in it. You'd better get your mouth straightened out."

Start confessing total victory in every area of your life, but first you've got to get victory Scriptures on the inside of you! Don't just read—study. The *only* part of the Bible that will ever work for you is the part that you confess and obey. The Bible never works for you by just laying it on the table beside your bed. It won't work for you just because you read it. You must read it and keep it before your eyes until it gets in the midst of your heart, "for they (God's words) are life unto those that *find* them, and health to all their flesh" (Proverbs 4:22, emphasis mine).

Reading God's Word and keeping it before your eyes gets it into your heart. Then, when it comes out of your mouth, you'll have the power of confession on your side, because you believe what you're saying. (Matthew 12:34.) Until you get the Word to this degree, you haven't really *found* it. And the Word that you find, that's the Word that will be life and health to your flesh; that's the Word that you'll actually experience. If you haven't found healing Scriptures, you won't experience healing life and power in your flesh. If you haven't found devil casting-out Scriptures, you won't experience devil-casting-out power in your life.

When I gave my life to Jesus, I put a Bible beside my bed every night. I was going to be real spiritual. I was going to make sure that I prayed every night before I went to bed. I promised God that I was going to read two chapters in the Bible every day, either in the morning or at night. But sometimes at night I would be tired, so I would read my two chapters real fast. I did this for about a year. Then one day God came and grabbed me. (You need to be grabbed by God sometimes.) I had just finished reading my two nightly chapters real fast, and I thought, *Oh, I'm a Bible reader. Boy, am I pleasing the Lord.* God shook me right there in the bed and said, "Son, don't you know it's a lot better to study two verses and know what's in there and confess them, than it is to read two chapters and not know anything?" I stopped reading so fast.

You need to take it easy and *know* what's in the Bible. Study it, like you studied your schoolbooks. *Get rid of pet doctrines.* This may come as a shock to you if you don't pray very much, or go to church or read the Bible very much: Jesus *really* loves you! He loves you so strongly and so much that you can hardly understand it. He wants you to be victorious all the time, but you've got to find this out in His Word. You've got to get Scriptures to cover your case. Jesus wants to heal you and bless you. He wants to save your children. He doesn't want them to go to hell. He wants to bless you financially.

Some people identify financial blessings with God, and some with the devil. The Lord wants you to have everything you can believe Him for. He has provided everything for you. Notice what Jesus said: "I am come that they (talking about you) might have life, and that they might have it more abundantly" (John 10:10, explanation mine). In 2 Peter 1:3, we read, "According as his divine power hath given unto us *all* things that pertain unto *life*...." And 3 John 2 adds, "Beloved, I wish above all things that thou mayest *prosper* and be in *health*, even as thy *soul prospereth*" (emphasis mine).

I have a diamond ring that was made twenty-five years ago. I don't have a lot of money in it, because I bought the diamonds used. They're good diamonds, but used. A while back, I sat in a fellow's office who thought he was real spiritual. A person can get wild when he thinks he's real spiritual and get caught up in pet doctrines. I don't know how some people get these pet doctrines in their heads.

This fellow looked at me while we were talking and said, "Norvel, you know, I used to have a diamond ring like that, but the Lord told me to not wear it." I said, "Well, fine! If you can't stand diamonds, then you should take them off. If my ring gets to damaging me, I'll take it off myself. I'm not hung up on anything!" What in the world is a ring, but a half-ounce of gold? I'm not moved by people who judge me spiritually because of a half ounce of gold.

You may say, "But I want to be just like Jesus." Jesus walks on streets of gold. In heaven you'll be walking on streets of gold like He does. You can't tell me that God doesn't want me to have gold when it says in the Bible that He walks on the stuff. "And he carried me away in the spirit to a great and high mountain, and shewed me the great city, the holy Jerusalem, descending out of heaven from God. And the twelve gates were twelve pearls: every several gate was of one pearl; and the street of the city was pure gold, as it were transparent glass" (Revelation 21:10,21).

I asked that fellow who said that God told him not to wear his diamond ring if he could read. Sometimes I wonder if people can! They wonder if the Holy Spirit will do this or that. *Keep God's Word before your eyes.* The Holy Spirit will do what the Bible says and what you teach concerning the Word of God. Find Scriptures that cover your case, and get them on the inside of your spirit by confessing them. Then the Holy Spirit will keep you strong and the Scriptures will work for you.

If you will confess these Scriptures are yours, this is what will happen. When the devil decides to attack you, weapons will come forth for you to fight him with. He will have no chance to get you, because the Holy Spirit will bring to your remembrance those healing Scriptures, or those on finances, or those on other areas that you have memorized. Jesus calls the Holy Spirit our Teacher and Comforter. "But the Comforter; which is the Holy Ghost, whom the Father will send in my name, he shall teach you all things, and bring all things to your remembrance, whatsoever I have said unto you" (John 14:26). When the Holy Spirit brings to your remembrance what's in your spirit, then it's your responsibility to boldly confess: "It's mine! It's mine! No, you don't, devil. You're not taking anything from me!" Finding a Scripture to cover your case and keeping it before your eyes will bring you victory every time.

It Takes Only One Verse of Scripture

It doesn't take but one Scripture to heal you. Find it. Stick with it. Say, "It's mine, it's mine! I've got it!" You need to get a verse of Scripture on the inside of you.

One night, I was ministering these verses, "Is any sick among you? Let him call for the elders of the church and let them pray over him, anointing him with oil in the name of the Lord; and the prayer of faith shall save the sick, and the Lord shall raise him up; and if he have committed sins, they shall be forgiven him" (James 5:14,15). I told the audience to pray the prayer of faith and to get James 5:14-15 to be a part of them. I told them they must do it.

A man with club feet came forward, and I prayed and anointed him with oil. I didn't feel anything when I prayed and anointed him. And as far as I know, he didn't either. All he needed to know and believe, and say was: "I got anointed with oil tonight in the name of the Lord. The prayer of faith was prayed for me. According to James 5:14-15, I've got new feet; and according to James 5:14-15,

I'm healed. Because it was ministered to me, I've got my healing! I'm accepting it; I'm making it a part of me. Thank You, Lord, for healing me!"

I told him, along with the rest of the congregation, "When you get home, don't start talking with your wife or husband. I mean, don't hold a natural conversation with them. Go to bed and go to sleep saying, 'James 5:14-15 is mine! The prayer of faith was prayed for me and I got it! It's mine!'" The man with club feet went home saying what I told him to say. He went to sleep saying it. When I teach you something from the Word of God, if you'll do it, you can receive your healing and your miracle. If you veer away from it just a little bit, you're not going to receive anything. Get that straight! You either believe Jesus by faith, or you don't believe Him.

The next night in the parking lot of the church, a very distinguished looking businessman came up to me and said, "Brother Norvel, I've got something to tell you! For years I've heard James5:14-15 preached. I've seen people anointed with oil for twenty-some years of my life. But I never received until last night. You pounded it into me; you taught it to me. You kept on teaching it, and I accepted it. You kept on and on giving me instructions in what to do, until I got it! I did exactly what you told me to do, and I began to receive on the inside of me. I went to bed and went to sleep without talking to my wife because you told me not to. This morning when I woke up, I moved the cover back and swung my legs over onto the floor. I wasn't really thinking about anything, but when I looked down at my feet, I saw that they were normal!"

The man's club feet were healed! *Don't live in a world of talk not based on the Scriptures.* It's all right to talk to your wife, but not while you're trying to talk to God. Talk to God first, then to your wife, and you'll make a lot better husband. Don't go around talking to your wife without ever quoting Scriptures. If you do, all you'll do is live in a world of talk, talk, talk. Then you'll say things like this: "I wonder why God doesn't do this. I wonder why God doesn't do that. I wonder why I'm sick. I wonder why I've got club feet. Well, maybe He just doesn't want to heal me, or maybe He's using this for His glory."

Human beings shouldn't get glory for what God does. I was just a teacher who very simply instructed him on two verses of Scripture—that's all I was. But because the man with club feet got those two Scriptures down inside him, God came to him sometime during the night with His healing power. You can get so messed up talking to other people that you don't know what you're doing. If you want to be healed, don't talk to another human being—*talk to God!* Go to bed talking to God. Forget about human beings and go to bed with James 5:14-15, saying, "I've got it, Jesus; it's mine!" Learn it, believe it, do it.

I've been called to be a Bible teacher. I'm a channel for instructions. A teacher obviously *teaches*. For example, an evangelist comes in and holds salvation-type services, but a teacher's calling is to teach you about God. I can walk into a room, open the Bible up, and God will unfold to me exactly what to do for a certain time. For example, He'll show me what to do for a crippled person. I can teach him how to have total deliverance and total freedom.

I walk in the office of a teacher; I teach a verse of Scripture. But *you* have to learn it. You have to learn what it says, and believe what it says, and do what it says. I have to teach people, day after day. It might take me days and days to teach them exactly what to say, and to say it every day. But I can teach them to talk like they're supposed to talk and to call upon Jesus. I've had them calling Jesus their Healer and calling their legs straight. I've had them saying it loud and strong. It might take two years, but it doesn't make any difference. God will come to them one of these nights, and they'll wake up totally normal. The man who had club feet believed James 5:14-15 and did what it said. He doesn't have club feet anymore. God gave him two brand-new feet. He had never run in his life. When you've got goofed up feet, you have to walk. But when he looked down and saw two normal feet, he got so excited that he jumped up, pulled his trousers on, and ran a mile. Thank the Lord!

I thought of Elijah, who outran the chariots and horses of King Ahab. (1 Kings 18:46.) I told this man that the power of the Lord had to have been with him, or he would have had a heart attack. He gave his testimony to the church that night. He pulled up his pants legs and showed the people his normal feet. The whole church laughed. Did you know that most churches don't even know that Jesus will come to you and heal you and give you two new feet if you need them? But He will. All it takes is getting one verse of Scripture on the inside of you and sticking with it!

Quit Talking After You've Said What God Says

A lady who attended a Nazarene church stood on one verse of Scripture and saw her twisted, deformed daughter made completely whole and become a worldwide evangelist. This Nazarene woman read in the Word that Jesus said, "If thou canst believe, all things are possible to him that believeth" (Mark 9:23). So she said with her mouth, "Jesus, You said all things are possible to him that believes. I love You, Jesus, and I believe for You to come to my house and make my daughter normal." Then she never wavered!

The reason God doesn't come and visit some people more is because they don't quit talking after they've said what God says. The Lord was saying *only believe.* This Nazarene mother believed all the time; she stood on this one verse of Scripture. Every person you know who is facing death before their time needs only one verse of Scripture to bring them total health. You don't have to memorize a chapter in the Bible to be healed. You only have to know one verse. It can bring you a total miracle.

This Nazarene lady knew more about the Bible, but it was one verse that brought her a miracle: "all things are possible to him that believeth." Many churches don't believe that a handicapped baby can be made completely normal while in your hands. They don't a bit more believe that than they believe Castro is on the moon dancing with a pink apron on. The average church in America would say, "Well, yes, I know God could do it if He wanted to. Oh, yes, I believe God can do anything!" Why, they don't either! If they did, they would stand on the Scriptures *all the time* and would *never* waver. They would totally refuse to waver!

The Nazarene mother went on and on. Every day, every week, every month, every year, she said, "Jesus, I believe! I believe for You, Jesus, to come to my house and make my daughter normal." Her daughter was so twisted and crippled when she came forth out of the womb that she had to be fed through her veins. Everything about her was deformed. Still the mother said, "I believe for you to come to my house and make my daughter normal." How long did she say it? How long did she believe it? *She believed it and said it for fourteen years.* If you get tired at twelve years, it won't work. Just don't ever get tired.

In the fourteenth year, Jesus said, "Your faith has pleased Me, and I'm going to come to your house and heal your daughter." That's exactly what Jesus told her. Coming from her house, her faith had welled up before the throne of God for fourteen years. Jesus *heard* it. He *saw* it. For fourteen years, He was pleased. The Word of God will get Jesus to manifest Himself by the power of the Holy Spirit.

So on the day Jesus told this mother He was going to come, a little white cloud began to form in the living room. The wind began to blow around the house, and the cloud got bigger and bigger in the living room. All of a sudden, Jesus appeared and stepped out of the cloud. He walked over to the wheelchair and laid His hands upon the deformed girl. Her jawbone began to pop and crack. It became normal and straight and smooth. All of her bones began to pop and jerk. The little girl was made totally normal. She leaped out of the wheelchair and began to run and jump with her totally healed body. Her back had been so twisted and knotted that the doctors at Mayo Clinic said it was impossible for her to ever be normal. Every knot on her back disappeared and her backbone was totally healed. All this happened because a mother confessed and believed one verse of Scripture for fourteen years and didn't give up.

Talk Right

God's power is released the moment God stamps your confession approved. The power will come and give you what you've been confessing. If it's a blessing for finances, your body, mind, or your children, it will come. If you're confessing for your children, God will come to them. "What do you mean, 'God will come to them'? My children won't listen to anybody, Brother Norvel." My daughter wouldn't listen to anybody either; but God sent an angel into her room about as big as two men and scared all the devils out of her! But, I confessed right regarding her. Let me teach you how to talk. If you'll let me do that, you'll be able to teach your relatives and friends who need the Lord Jesus to do something for them.

The Holy Spirit will perform the scriptural words of anyone who says them and obeys them. God is a Spirit and God performs words. Your whole world is made out of your words. You put yourself in the kind of world you're living in today—rich, poor, healthy, sickly, or whatever—with your mouth. I didn't say someone else's mouth; *your mouth* put you there. Always remember this: you are your own worst enemy—not someone else, you. You don't have to pay any attention to flaky people who will get you all messed up.

You have a right to walk with God yourself. You have a right to claim the Scriptures, the riches of heaven, yourself. And if you will do it yourself, God will come and visit you. "What will He bring with Him, Brother Norvel?" Everything that you can believe Him for and everything that you've been confessing. God always brings to your house and to your life gifts from heaven. Every gift that you've ever claimed (really claimed) from heaven, you've gotten it! "Well, I haven't claimed anything, Brother Norvel." That's the reason you're a total wreck. You just sit around and don't claim anything.

The Lord Jesus Christ has paid the price and given His name and His power over to the New Testament Church. The New Testament is a better covenant than the Old Testament. "But now hath he (Jesus) obtained a more excellent ministry, by how much also he is the mediator of a better covenant, which was established upon better promises" (Hebrews 8:6). The better covenant is enjoyed by people who learn how to talk right. I mentioned earlier that whatever state you're in today, your own mouth put you there.

Your mouth or your tongue is like the steering wheel of a car. The car goes whichever way you turn the steering wheel. It's like the helm of a ship. "Behold, we put bits in the horses' mouths, that they may obey us; and we turn about their whole body. Behold also the ships, which though they are so great, and are driven by fierce winds, yet are they turned about with a very small helm, whithersoever the governor listeth. Even so the tongue is a little member, and boasteth great things" (James 3:3-5).

The way you confess every day is the kind of life you will have. "Death and life are in the power of the tongue: and they that love it shall eat the fruit thereof" (Proverbs 18:21). Thank God, I begin my day by walking the floor and worshipping God. Thank God, I've already started my day, today, speaking right things. You've got to stir up the gift that's within you and get your mind functioning right. (2 Timothy 1:6.)

A tremendously successful minister in our world today said one of the worst things about Americans is that they haven't learned how to live yet. They just do whatever they want. They get up every morning and just float along and let whatever happens, happen. And whatever doesn't happen, well, they think that just wasn't for me. Nothing *just happens* to you, unless you let it happen! When something bad begins to happen, bind it in Jesus' name and throw it out!

God doesn't believe in your having sad days. He doesn't have any. God doesn't even know the meaning of blue Mondays, because He talks right and confesses right *all the time*. I mean, if God wants a world, He says, "World, I speak to you, come into being." And all of a sudden, there is a world. "In the beginning God created the heaven and the earth. And God said, Let there be light: and there was light. And God said, Let there be a firmament in the midst of the waters….And God said, Let the waters under the heaven be gathered together.... And God said, Let the earth bring forth grass, the herb yielding seed, and the fruit tree yielding fruit....And God saw every thing that he had made, and behold, it was very good" (Genesis 1:1,3,6,9,11,31).

The world was formed by words from the mouth of God. "Through faith we understand that the worlds were framed by the word of God..." (Hebrews 11:3). Your body was formed and made by the words of God. "And God *said*, Let us make man in our image..." (Genesis 1:26, emphasis mine). All of the good things that you see here—the lakes and the mountains—were formed by words out of the mouth of God. And the same kind of thing happens to you all of the time. Your whole world is formed out of the words *your* mouth speaks—out of *your* confession.

There's all kinds of power in confession! "What kind of power, Brother Norvel?" Any kind of power you want, just name it. Anybody in the world can be successful, if they learn how to talk—anybody can. You can have anything you want from God, if you'll learn how to talk! "What do you mean talk?" I don't mean the natural kind of talking; almost anyone can hold a conversation. I'm talking about looking up Scriptures that apply to your life, Scriptures that you really need, Scriptures that cover your case, and getting them on the inside of you, so you can talk right.

Confession Brings You Possession

Once I was in Canada speaking at a small church, and the Lord started dealing with me to teach the people how to talk. I had no earthly idea that learning how to talk could be so powerful and so important. Jesus thought it was very important to talk right. In

Matthew 21:21, He said, "...if ye shall say unto this mountain, Be thou removed, and be thou cast into the sea, it shall be done." That day I used this Scripture and taught *Confession Brings You Possession.* After I spoke, I gave an altar call that dealt along the same line. The Spirit of God was working pretty strong. So when I gave the invitation, about forty or fifty people came forward.

Someone pushed a man in a wheelchair down the aisle. I'd never heard any minister in the world tell someone what the Holy Spirit was about to have me tell this man in the wheelchair. And I'd never seen anyone minister to someone like I was about to minister to him. (It's amazing how much smarter God is than you or me. If you just listen to yourself, you'll think you have a lot of sense, especially if you've been preaching or reading the Bible for a long time. Let me pass this on to you: you'll never know just how dumb you are until you get to heaven! And the same goes for me, too.)

As the man came rolling down the aisle, I yelled, "Confession brings you possession!" As I said this, the word of the Lord came unto me saying, "What you taught will work for him, *if* he will obey it! Now, son, I want you to point out that there are *if's* in there. Turn in your Bible to Matthew 21 and point out the *if's* to the people. Point out the *if's*, so they can see for themselves." I'd never heard anything like that in my life at any gospel service. So I said, "Is that right? Glory to God! It will work for him, if he will obey it."

In verse 21, Jesus tells us what the if's are: "Verily I say unto you, If ye *(talking about you)* have faith, and doubt not" God doesn't want you to doubt. He works with your faith. God is a faith God. *If you're ashamed, you don't believe.*

"If ye have faith, and doubt not, ye *(not somebody else for you)* shall not only do this which is done to the fig tree, but also if…" (Matthew 21:21). Also *"if"* means believe and doubt not. Realize this: You don't believe if you're ashamed to run a big ad in your hometown newspaper in bold letters, saying, "We are going to have a healing service on Sunday night and Jesus is going to heal people in our church. Bring the sick and the demon-possessed so Jesus can heal them."

If you're the pastor and you're ashamed to put your church name and your name in this ad, that means you don't believe! You only think you believe. And you'll never be able to believe God to do things for you, until you get rid of some of those religious ideas of yours or your relatives. The Bible says, "If the Son, therefore, shall make you free, ye shall be free indeed" (John 8:36). Jesus has paid the price for you to be free. He wants you to open your mind, your spirit, and your entire being to God and believe God for anything. Believe God boldly! "But, Brother Norvel, I don't have very many friends who believe like that!" Who cares what your friends believe? God says for you to get delivered from your friends and your relatives.

If you can believe it, God will do great things for you. It's amazing what He will do for you, but you need to have faith. Anything you're holding back and making excuses for, that's doubt and unbelief and God won't work through it. You say, "Well, don't you believe that God would still do such-and-such in these conditions and this-and-that in those conditions?" If that's what you think, you're a doubter! An unbeliever! "Oh, I'm not an unbeliever. I love the Lord and I believe the Bible." Do you believe it all? "Oh, yes!"

Do you believe in speaking in tongues?

"Well, Brother Norvel, yes, I believe it's for some people, but not necessarily for me."

Well, thank God that you're trying to believe, even though you don't yet. So just keep on and on. The teaching in this book could help you a lot if you'd let it. Tell God, "Anything that I can read in the New Testament, I'm going to boldly believe it's mine." God will say, "Good! Show Me!" And when you start showing Him, He will start manifesting Himself to you. And He will give you anything that you want.

Talk to the Mountains

Jesus tells you how to overcome mountains in Matthew, chapter 21. In verse 21, Jesus said, "…if you shall say unto this mountain…." You need to talk to mountains. Use your *mouth*. What's a mountain? *Mountain* could mean a thousand and one things. It could and does mean, for example, disease. Jesus said to me, "Son, you have to teach the people to talk to the mountains and to the devils. 'Mountains' or problems are caused by devils, so talk to the mountains and the devils and tell them to get out. Pull them out."

Verse 21 continues, "…if ye shall say unto this mountain, Be thou removed, and be thou cast into the sea; it shall be done!" Jesus said it! "It shall be done!" And it will disappear in the bottom of the sea of forgetfulness. God won't remember that dumb mountain anymore. It will be gone.

In verse 22 Jesus said, "And all things, whatsoever ye shall ask in prayer, believing, ye shall receive." This was the Scripture I used for my text *Confession Brings You Possession* in the small Canadian church. If you make up your mind to believe God, you will see great things happen all the time. It's amazing what you will see, while the whole church world is sitting around wondering if it's going to happen or not.

To the man in the wheelchair, I said, "Mister, the word of the Lord came unto me saying that what I taught this morning would work for you, if you would obey it! If you would obey it! I taught confession brings you possession. You know, talk to your mountains. Look at your crooked legs and call them straight. Talk to them. Tell them what you mean. You can have what you say. Your confession brings possession. Don't say your legs are crooked. Call them straight! Romans 4:17 says that God calls those things which be not as though they were. So, call your crooked legs straight. You do it. Call your crooked legs straight."

He looked at me like he was offended. But I don't pay any attention to offenses when it comes to God's work. That's usually the devil anyhow. I only thought, *God said that confession would bring possession to him, and I'm going to get it into him. I'm going to bombard his mind.* You see, people's problems are usually with their minds— they don't think straight. I was determined to get this man's thinking straightened out. So I just held on and pulled myself over to him and put my mouth real close to his ear. I said, "Confession brings you possession. Mister, Jesus said, 'Call your crooked legs straight.'" I repeated this several times. "Call your crooked legs straight."

I guess I said that seventy-five to a hundred times. This old human breath wants to give out, but you have to keep on and not let go. I had to blast this man's goofed up mind away from him. Finally, the man in the wheelchair opened up on the inside and said, "I call my legs straight!" I said, "Well, thank God for that! Glory to God!" I almost wore myself out for him. You see, some people's minds are so goofed up, you will wear yourself out trying to get the Word of God on the inside of them. After I got the man in the wheelchair to call his legs straight, I kept encouraging him. "That's right, now you're pleasing the Lord. Keep on saying that."

It was hard for him to get it out, but he kept on. When I had him continually confessing, I backed off. After about five minutes of confessing that his legs were straight, the Spirit of the Lord came and overshadowed him. He will do that for *everyone* who confesses the Bible and claims it for themselves. He'll do it for you, too! The man began to cry. And, you know, I had gotten confession brings you possession so deep into him, that in the midst of his crying he was still confessing. The Spirit of God was blessing him so much. He kept confessing. "I call my legs straight."

I stood there and watched him. He arose from his wheelchair and walked across the front of the church and then walked back. The pastor said, "He hasn't ever done anything like this before." I said, "Do you know why? You've never talked to his crooked legs before. But he talked to them today. He called them straight, they became straight, and he received strength from God."

I told his pastor to keep encouraging him. The Holy Spirit gave this man strength because He heard him say the Word. The Holy Spirit listens to you. He listens to every word that you say. And when you start quoting the Bible, the Holy Spirit starts working for you at that moment. The precious gospel of Jesus Christ doesn't work just for the man in Canada. If *you* will *say* to the mountain, it shall be done for *you!* Jesus said in Matthew 21:21, "If ye have faith, and doubt not…if ye shall say unto this mountain…it shall be done."*Get rid of goofed up thinking*. If you believe that God won't get you out of a wheelchair or that God might not choose to heal you, your thinking is goofed up. You need to have your mind blasted. It's a wonder you even found the church building with that kind of intelligence.

Most Christians would believe the Bible a lot more if their dumb heads didn't get them in trouble. Some people will say, "It sounds good, Brother Norvel. I enjoyed your message, but I'm not going to obey it! I don't have to believe the Lord the same way you do. I have a right to believe my own version of God." No, you don't. You don't have any rights, you dummy, except to believe Matthew, Mark, Luke, and John, just like they're written. You can't dream up a gospel of your own. You don't have any gospel if you have one besides Matthew, Mark, Luke, and John. What you've got is sick! Totally sick!

God Will Send You on Missions for Him

If you don't keep the Word of God before your eyes, then it won't be kept in the midst of your heart. (Proverbs 4:21.) When you allow this to happen, then God's Word won't work for you. It absolutely will not! The power of confession has to be released from your mouth, and your mouth will always speak out what's in your heart. If you have the Word of God in the midst of your heart, and if you know how to talk, God will send you on missions to do things for Him to cause people to live and not die.

You need to get Luke 9:1 in your heart. If you don't, you might not be able to recognize what God wants you to do. He won't give you a revelation to send you on a mission. "Then he called his twelve disciples together and gave them power and authority over all devils, and to cure diseases" (Luke 9:1). You have authority over all devils and to cure diseases. You do! Where do you get the power and the authority? You get it from the Lord Jesus. He gave it to you; you've got it in you, now! But if you don't know this, you'll float along. And being a Christian will never help you.

You need to know it so you will talk right. "What do you mean, 'talk right'?" You have power and authority over all devils, but the power is in the confession part—talking right. Jesus gave you this authority. This Scripture proves it: "And these signs shall follow them that believe, In my name shall they cast out devils..." (Mark 16:17). Remember, the devil is always the one who causes harm and damage to human beings. If I had allowed Luke 9:1 to depart from before my eyes, the Lord wouldn't have sent me on the mission that I'm going to tell you about.

If the sixteenth chapter of Mark which says, "In my name shall they cast out devils," hadn't been in my heart, I wouldn't have been sent either. I don't know if God ever does this to you, but it's just wonderful when He comes on me and tells me the very address where I'm to go. He doesn't usually tell me what for; He just tells me to go.

One day I was in a Chattanooga, Tennessee, shopping center. The Lord came on me boldly and told me to go to a certain address. He sent me to a boy whose mind had snapped. There was no one who could help him. He didn't even know his own name. He just sat there in a stupor. It's important to know God and have God's Word on the inside of you. If you'll study and memorize Scriptures and keep yourself available, God will send you to human beings in need.

God sends only people who are available on missions. You have to know that. You have to *make* yourself available. You need to pray like I do: 'Lord, I'm available. Send me where You want to send me. Lord, let my life be a blessing to somebody. Make my life a blessing."

When you study the Scriptures and get them on the inside of you, then you will know how to do something. You will know the power in Jesus' name. You will know you have power and authority *yourself.*

I prayed for the boy in Chattanooga, but first I said, "I'll pray for him if everyone else will go out of the room and leave me alone here." I did that because I had talked to the people and knew that they loved the Lord and were Christians, but they didn't believe right. With a case like this, I couldn't have any unbelief in the room at all or healing wouldn't come. Jesus did something similar to this when He raised Jairus's daughter from the dead. "And he cometh to the house of the ruler of the synagogue (Jairus), and seeth the tumult, and them that wept and wailed greatly. And when he was come in, he saith unto them, 'Why make ye this ado, and weep? The damsel is not dead, but sleepeth.' And they laughed him to scorn. But when he had put them all out.......he took the damsel by the hand, and said unto her, Talitha cumi; which is, being interpreted, Damsel, I say unto thee, arise. And straightway the damsel arose..." (Mark 5:38-42).

Everyone stayed out of the boy's room and I prayed for him *all night.* When I say I prayed for him, I don't mean I just prayed. At first I prayed for him, then I confessed total victory in Jesus' name. I used the power of confession. I said, "Jesus is stronger than the devil, and in Jesus' name I command this boy's mind to come back to him. Satan, you cannot have this boy. I'm not going to let you have him. I'm not going to turn his mind over to you. The Lord sent me here and I've come to get his mind back for him. In Jesus' name, I command you to come out of him! I command you to let his mind go free! I command, in Jesus' name, his normal mind to come back to him!"

I said it! That's the difference between victory and defeat, between knowing and not knowing. Make up your mind to get God's Word before your eyes and into your heart, until you *talk* right. Make up your mind there's victory in Jesus' name and that you'll not accept defeat. Make up your mind that your confession won't get weak. Remember, once the devil begins to detect a weakness in your confession, he'll keep bombarding you until you're whipped.

You'll finally say, "Oh, well," and just walk off.

For eight hours I confessed that boy had a new mind, in Jesus' name. *A new mind!* I wouldn't accept anything else. At four o'clock in the morning, I was stronger than I was when I started. This was a desperate case. And besides that, it was a case where the Spirit of God specifically directed me to go and bring victory. When God tells you to go to a place and bring victory, you'd better go! After eight hours of confessing, at four o'clock in the morning, white foam began to bubble up out of the boy's mouth. Saliva began to run out of his mouth and onto the floor. And then his mind began to snap back into him!

Now, I didn't get victory that quickly for my own daughter. A few years later, she needed help and well-known and respected ministers came to talk with her. This one would come and that one would come. But she wouldn't listen to anybody. She kept on with her dope, and I kept on confessing. After three years of prayer and confession, she got victory. You might say, "That's not the way I do it. I just pray for people one minute, and poof, there it is!" Sure, but I've got news for you—that kind of ministry works for headaches—not for people in mental institutions.

I'd like to take you up to a mental institution, turn you loose and let you see how much these one-minute prayers work. Yes, they'll laugh right in your face. You have to *break* the power of the devil and *confess* total victory in Jesus' name. You have to stick with it until Satan leaves. I could take any person who was totally possessed of the devil, crippled or anything else, to my home and pray for them every day, and God's power would come and make them totally normal. I would wrap myself around them, and put my hands on them in Jesus' name, and talk victory all the time until the miracle manifested. I would stick with it, no matter how long it took. And I guarantee you God's power would make them normal *every time.*

You Take Authority Over the Devil

God wants you to learn to take authority over anything the devil tries to put on you; over anything that's not right. Learn to take authority over things that buffet or oppress you from the outside the very moment you detect them. If the devil has come to visit you in the form of disease, you can take authority over him (if you're born again by the Spirit of God). You can pray and believe for your own healing. Don't put your faith in somebody else; put your faith in the Jesus you read about in the Gospels—Matthew, Mark, Luke, and John—and be healed.

Be mindful of the fact that you've got power and authority over the devil. Jesus gave it to us when we got saved: "Behold, I give unto you power to head on serpents and scorpions, and over all the power of the enemy; and nothing shall by any means hurt you" (Luke 10:19). "Then he (Jesus) called his twelve disciples together, and gave them power and authority over all devils, and to cure diseases" (Luke 9:1). I'm going to teach you how I stop cancer (or anything else that comes from the devil) dead in its tracks and how you can stop it, too! "Oh, you mean how God stops cancer," you may say. No, I mean how *you* and *I* stop it in Jesus' name. God doesn't have cancer; He doesn't have any diseases. People get cancers and diseases, and God has given born-again people the power to stop them. It's up to us to tell crippled legs, bad hearts, sick bodies, and empty pocketbooks to straighten out!

When Jesus gave His disciples the Great Commission of Mark 16:15-18, He mentioned different signs that would follow the believers. In verse 17, the first sign He spoke of was, "In my name shall they cast out devils." I don't know why that scared people so. Some pastors say, "I don't know about this. I don't know how to deal with devils. I don't want to get my people mixed up."

Casting out devils is a doctrine of the New Testament Church. People who ask, "Why do I have to resist the devil? Why do I have to cast out devils?" are people who've gotten over into their own realm of thinking. They've left the Abraham-kind of faith (see Romans 4:16-21), and they've left the Jesus-kind of authority. In 1 Timothy 4:1, the Holy Spirit says: "Now the Spirit speaketh expressly, that in the latter times some shall depart from the faith, giving heed to seducing spirits, and doctrines of devils." This verse plainly shows that some people will depart from the faith and won't cast out devils like Jesus commissioned.

It's a seducing spirit that talks you into not having anything to do with casting out devils. If a devil-possessed person comes to your door and asks you to pray for him, are you ready and willing to say, "Devil, you turn this person loose. I command you in Jesus' name to come out of him"? Are you willing to let this be a way of life for you? It's a part of my lifestyle. I do it all the time, nearly every day. And I know if I don't get the devil out of the person, it will kill them. Don't forget, the devil comes to steal, kill, and destroy (John 10:10). You've got to make up your mind that you're going to be a Bible believer!

If you are a pastor and your congregation has never seen you cast out devils, they're as confused as you are. All some churches have is a confused congregation. They float in on Sunday morning, then they float out being nice. I've got news for you: *Jesus isn't nice to the devil.* And He doesn't want you to be nice to him either. He said to use His name and throw the devil out of the Church!

"Are you kidding, Brother Norvel?" you may say. "Every person in the Church is a victor. They're all victors all the time." That isn't true. There's total victory in the Church only as long as you don't let religious spirits, devils, and your goofed-up friends invade the place. God doesn't want His Church to be invaded by the religious ideas of men. He wants you to stand boldly and throw the devil out. Take authority over the devil, cast him out, and get people healed.

Let Jesus Be Like He Is in the Gospels

On my way to Honolulu several months ago, the Lord said to me, "Son, start teaching the Word only. Forget about everything else. Forget it and get it out of your mind. Be free from everything else." He told me to be free from what my friends or what other church members believed. Some people have an image of Jesus being like their church service. Realize this: Jesus doesn't go by church services! The services of every church in America are supposed to go by Him. Jesus is the Head of the Church. Jesus is the Great Shepherd. We're supposed to listen to Jesus and not try to change Him.

Jesus, today, is exactly what He is in Matthew, Mark, Luke, and John. He has never changed, and He's not going to change. If you'll make up your mind once and for all that the life is in the Word, you won't have to suffer any longer. The light of God shines down through the Word of God. God doesn't have any shadows. The light is in the Word. What you do with the Word is up to you.

Learn to put the gospel first and stop putting your own or other people's image of Jesus first.

Quit trying to create your own ideas about Jesus, or listening to your friends' ideas about Him. Always remember this: Jesus is a personal Savior, and *personal* means *you!* And if I can convince you not to change Him, He'll show Himself to you personally.

You don't need all of Los Angeles, California, to get God to come to you. Get alone in your living room and He'll come. In fact, the Holy Spirit will bring Jesus on the inside of you, just like He is in Matthew, Mark, Luke, and John. And if you'll accept this, He'll come into your living room and operate on you. He's the best surgeon in the world. He'll come into your living room, stretch your crooked legs out, and make them normal. And I don't *think* that He'll do it; *I know He will!* He'll free anybody!

Devils Are Where Problems Are

In the New Testament, you're given the right to use Jesus' name to keep *all* devils under your feet. Devils are where you have a lot of problems. The devil himself is a destroyer. He's come to do three things: to steal, kill, and destroy. (John 10:10.) *He's your enemy.* You and I are in battle. We're trying to get to heaven, but the devil means to stop us. He was thrown out of heaven, and he's mad about it.

The devil especially wants to attack human beings because they're created in the image of God, and he's mad at God. (Genesis 1:26.)

The devil wants to turn you into an abnormal creature. It doesn't matter to him what kind. He wants your body eaten up with cancer. He wants to make you a drunk or a dope addict. He'd like to make you step out on your mate and live with somebody else. The devil doesn't want you to be true to your mate. He doesn't want you to have sex with just your mate—he wants you to have it with two, three, four, or five different people. He'll tell you how good it feels.

Some people walk by their feelings. That will get you into trouble. They say, "But my body wants, my body needs, my body likes...." Your body lies! You can't live by what your body wants. If you start doing that, you'll stay in trouble.

One day the Lord told me to stop smoking, so I did. That's when I realized how strongly my body controlled my life. I had smoked for twenty years and I didn't see anything wrong with it. At church they had a smoking break between Sunday school and the main service. All my relatives smoked. I thought everyone did. Why should I think it was wrong?

I said, "Okay, Jesus. I didn't know You wanted me to stop smoking. So if You do, I will, Lord." I pulled out my cigarettes, slapped them down on the table, and said, "Thank You, Lord. For You, I'll do it." That was fine, and it sounded nice when I said it; but when you've been used to smoking a pack a day for twenty years, after three or four hours go by, that dumb body of yours will have different ideas. In a few hours, my jaws began to ache and I heard a little voice talking to me. I knew it wasn't God because it was from my body. My body rose up and said, "I want a cigarette." I said, "No, you can't have a cigarette." I mean I wanted one so bad I could taste it. But I said, "No! I've quit smoking!"

It doesn't make any difference to your body what you've decided to do. Your body is only a house that you live in. It's separate, and it has its own goofed up desires. For example, every time my body sees a coconut cream pie, it wants three pieces—especially when it's homemade coconut cream pie. But I always tell my body, "No, you can't have three pieces, you dummy." When your body likes something, it says, "I want it, I want it, I want it, I want it!" You have to say, "You desire for pie (or cigarettes or whatever), go from me!" I said, "You desire for cigarettes, come out, in Jesus' name. Go from me!"

I had to make the dumb thing leave. Your body doesn't care what God tells you. It will rise up and demand what it's craving. You have to tell your body to shut up! I thought I'd put my strong faith to work and make it just fine. But I found out my faith wasn't quite as strong as I thought it was. I had some growing to do. After eight hours, things got desperate! Walking along, I'd meet people who were smoking. My body would say, "Turn around," hoping that a puff might come through the wind, and I would at least be able to smell it.

I'll never forget the second day. My body was desperate. It started screaming. It didn't stay nice like the first day when it would just say, "I want a cigarette." The second day, it screamed, "I want a cigarette! And I want one right now!" I would have given a hundred dollars for a cigarette, but I wouldn't let myself have one. After some tough times, I finally won. But I had to resist my body and its desires, just as I have to resist Satan and his suggestions.

I learned that the only way I could gain control over my body was to deny it, to make it serve me rather than for me to be a slave to it. That's what you must do. You must learn to say "No" to disease just as you say "No" to your body. Remember, don't go by what your body says. When a disease tries to rest in your body, resist the disease and say, "No, disease, I take authority over you, in Jesus' name. Come out of me!"

You Must Say "No" to the Devil

The greatest word in the world that you'll ever say to the devil is "no". It's a real short word, but as long as you say "no" to the devil, he can't do anything to you. Even if you're an unsaved sinner and the devil tries to tempt you to commit a sin, say, "No! No! I won't do that." He can't make you do it. Did you know that the devil can't make you do anything? You have to yield yourself to him. "Know ye not, that to whom ye yield yourselves servants to obey, his servants ye are to whom ye obey, whether of sin unto death, or of obedience unto righteousness?" (Romans 6:16).

Always remember: You have to say "yes" to the devil before he can do anything to you. If you start participating with a lying spirit, you will start lying. You have obeyed the devil and the spirit that's tempting you. And you've become what the spirit is. Watch the company you keep. Be selective about what you let yourself hear, read, or see—on TV for example. The Psalmist David said in Psalm 101:3: "I will set no wicked thing before mine eyes: I hate the work of them that turn aside; it shall not cleave to me."

Good instruction is given in Psalm 1:1 also, "Blessed is the man that walketh not in the counsel of the ungodly, nor standeth in the way of sinners, nor sitteth in the seat of the scornful." Watch where and with whom you walk, stand, or sit. You must say *no* to the devil.

Don't participate with him in any form or fashion. If he has already attacked you, *you must bind him*. Understand this: if the devil has come to you with a disease, bind him first. Then you can effectively resist him. Concerning the Church, Jesus said, "...the gates of hell shall not prevail against it" (Matthew 16:18)." You have to bind the devil!" In Matthew 12:29, Jesus said, "...else how can one enter into a strong man's house, and spoil his goods, except he first bind the strong man? And then he will spoil his house."

If you want to spoil the devil's efforts, you must first bind him. Recognize that God *and* the devil exist! The devil isn't dead. As long as you resist evil—like lying, cheating, and diseases—then the devil's hands will be tied and he won't be able to harm you. But you have to resist him in Jesus' name. James 4:7 makes it very clear, "Submit yourselves therefore to God. *Resist the devil*, and he *will* flee from you" (emphasis mine).

Anything that attacks you from the world of darkness—like confusion, heartaches, or pain—is from the devil. Take authority over it *right then*, and in the name of Jesus say, "No, you don't. Not to me you don't, devil, no, no, no!" Both you and I have power and authority. Any devil I can cast out in Jesus' name, you can, too. Any person I can get healed in Jesus' name, you can, too. *You* can! God doesn't have any pets or superstars. God has believers!

God doesn't let the gospel work for just a few people; it works for everybody. And if you'll believe the Bible, the Bible will work for you. If I believe the Bible, it works for me. If I don't believe it, then it doesn't work for me. Because my name is Norvel Hayes and I have authored several books and I have a Bible school, campus ministries, and numerous tape series, that doesn't mean "fifteen cents worth of nothing." The gospel works for everybody and it works the same.

I have to say "no" to aches and pains that try to visit my body, "no" to temptation, "no" to the devil just like you do. Here's how I do it. I say, "In Jesus' name, no, you don't. I won't accept this pain in my side. I bind you, Satan, in Jesus' name. Go from me!" Then I lay my hand on myself and continue, "In Jesus' name, no, I won't accept this. I break your power, Satan, and I command you to take your hands off. My body belongs to God. In Jesus' name, pain, stop! In Jesus' name, get off of me. I claim the healing power of God. No, you don't; not to me you don't. You can't, Satan. I know you want to, but you can't! When I say you can't, you can't!"

How long do I say this? *Until the affliction leaves!* "But, what if it takes three days, Brother Norvel?" you say. Big deal! Let it take three days. It probably won't. But if it does, I *keep on.* God doesn't promise that you'll see things happen the very moment you pray. He says, "What things soever ye desire, when ye pray, believe that ye receive them, and ye shall have them" (Mark 11:24). When you pray, believe that you receive, and you shall have what things soever you desire. You can have them today, but it may be next week or next month until you have them. But you *shall* have them, if you believe.

Never Change, Never Waver, Never Get Nervous

Once I start resisting the devil, the first morning I wake up the pain may be worse. That's all right—that's a sign I'm getting better. When you resist the devil, he gets all shook up, and he's going to attack you stronger, because you're resisting him. He means to show us he's stronger than we are, so the next day the pain may be worse. If it is, I do the same thing I did the first day. *Never change, never waver, never get nervous.* Just lay your hand on your side, if that's where the pain is, and say, "In Jesus' name, no, you don't. I resist you.

I've claimed a healing. The healing power of God is in me now. I resist you, Satan, in Jesus' name. Go from me! I command my body to be free from you, Satan!"

When you walk back and forth in your own living room, and you do what I've just told you to do, don't let your confession weaken. Do this every day, even if it takes four or five days. Your confession must get stronger every day, not weaker. If the devil sees one speck of weakness coming out of you, you've had it! If weakness or doubt comes, he'll dog your tracks right into the hospital. He'll dog you with pain. He'll dog your tracks into the grave, if he possibly can. The devil doesn't intend to stop or give up. Just show him some weakness and he'll ride you on and on and on. But show him strength and power and you'll stop him!

If you've been binding and resisting the devil and sometimes it hasn't been working, you haven't been doing it right. You haven't been listening to God. You've been listening to yourself. Often, there's a foundation of God that needs to be laid in your life before the victory comes. James 4:7 first tells you to "submit yourself to God," then it says to "resist the devil, and he will flee."

Be the Head of Your House

Whatever happens at my house and on my property is my fault. I can't blame the devil, neighbors, or friends. It's my fault. This truth became clear to me years ago when my daughter had over thirty growths on her body. At that time, I didn't know that God would remove all those growths. I didn't know that He would put new skin on my daughter right in my own house. Man didn't teach me about this kind of God with this kind of love and power. I learned that from no man. In fact, I don't know very many men who know it and believe it; but I've found the truth.

One Sunday night I was praying for my daughter, asking God to heal her of those growths. While I was praying, Jesus came and got me—He pulled me out of my body. I left it there in the living room. I went up into His holy presence. All of a sudden, I was in paradise. Is that Scripture? If it hadn't been, I wouldn't have gone. It was *His* Scripture. As quickly as you can bat your eyes, God can pull you out of your body and take you to paradise with Him. The Apostle Paul spoke of an experience along this line, "I knew a man in Christ above fourteen years ago (whether in the body, I cannot tell, or whether out of the body, I cannot tell: God knoweth,) such an one caught up to the third heaven. And I knew such a man, (whether in the body, or out of the body, I cannot tell: God knoweth) How that he was caught up into paradise, and heard unspeakable words, which it is not lawful for a man to utter" (2 Corinthians 12:2-4).

After Jesus pulled me out of my body and into His presence, He started talking to me. He looked at me and asked, "How long are you going to put up with the growths on your daughter's body?"

"What do you mean me, Lord?" I asked. *(Saying something like that doesn't go over very well in heaven!)*

He said, "You're the head of your house! Be the head of your house!" (Now I know how the money changers must have felt when Jesus ran them out of the temple in Matthew 21:12-13.)

I answered, "I am!" This is when I got the inside revelation from God, that whatever happened at my house and on my property is my fault. But how was I supposed to make those growths leave my daughter's body? In the church I came from, I was never taught how to make growths leave.

Jesus said, "You are the head of your house! If you will curse those growths in My name, they will die! They will disappear! If you will believe and not doubt, they will die like the fig tree did that I cursed."

When I came back into my body, I did exactly what the Lord told me to do. For three years, I had prayed and those growths were still there. But when Jesus gave me the authority to use His name, and told me what to do and how to do it, I got results! I went to my daughter and I cursed the roots of those growths on her body. I told them, "In Jesus' name, you must die! You're in my house, and you must die!" After saying this for thirty days, nothing happened; in fact, the growths looked worse. But I kept on and on.

Finally, after forty days, God's power came into my house and swept over my daughter's body. That afternoon, my daughter had come home from high school and walked into her bedroom. All of a sudden, I heard a noise like the dresser falling over. She came running out of her room and down the hallway, screaming, "Daddy, Daddy, this is spooky. This scares me, Daddy. It scares me! Look at me. Look! Look at my legs. Look at my arms. All of the growths are gone! I have new skin on me."

After three years, as quickly as you could bat your eyes, all of the growths disappeared from her body. Jesus put new skin all over her. It looked like baby's skin. *That's the way God does business.* I don't have to go around wondering what this church believes, or what that church believes. I never wonder whether God will heal club feet, or if He will remove growths and give a person new skin.

This is why: If you expect a glass of water from God, He will provide it for you! If you expect a healing from God, He will provide it for you. God will do for your child what He did for mine. After forty days and forty nights of believing, it was all over! It was just that quick. All the knots were gone and new skin came on my daughter's body. Jesus came along and replaced the ugly, broken, bleeding places on her hands with new skin.

If you think Jesus won't heal you, you're wrong. He'll do anything for you! He'll do anything scriptural for you and for your family. Be the head of your house and pray for yourself and your family. Don't take *no* for an answer. You can obey the Bible for your children and God will work on their behalf. When they grow up, your faith won't work as well for them. It will only work in part. Until your children are about sixteen, you can get healings and things for them by using your faith and your confession. But after that, your confession and your faith will only work in part for them.

When you're married, *you can get a healing for your husband or wife* because the two of you are one. God is merciful, and if you obey the Bible for your mate, God will move on their behalf. Awhile back, a young man was in the hospital unconscious and given up to die. I was the guest speaker at his home church, so they asked me to go to the hospital and pray for him. His wife was by his bedside. I prayed for him then I turned to leave.

On my way out, the Lord spoke to me and said, "Mark 11:23 would heal him, if it was obeyed." When the Lord said that to me, I turned around real quick and went back over to the man's wife and said, "Young lady, the Lord spoke to me and told me that Mark 11:23 would heal your husband. Now the way to get the Holy Spirit to perform Mark 11:23 is to quote it. It says you can have what you say: 'For verily I say unto you, that whosoever shall say unto this mountain, be thou removed, and be thou cast into the sea; and shall not doubt in his heart, but shall believe that those things which he saith shall come to pass; he shall have whatsoever he saith'" (Mark 11:23).

"Sit here and obey it. Look at your husband straight and say, 'My husband will live and not die, in Jesus' name. My husband will live and not die, in Jesus' name.' Say it strongly all the time. You may have to say it thousands of times, day in and day out, but don't stop saying it, and he will live and not die." I got her saying it then I had to leave. I knew the young man would live and not die, *if his wife kept her confession strong.* Now if she had said it only a hundred times and quit, because she got tired of saying it, he would have died. You had better never get tired of talking the Bible if the case is desperate and you want the Holy Spirit to move.

You might say, "Now, Brother Norvel, you don't have to say it so much. You can just believe it by faith." Why should you mind saying it? Remember, faith has works (James 2:17). But I know you can believe God for something and express it once, then thank Him for it. I'm not talking about that. I'm talking about a desperate situation where the Lord told me specifically how to get victory.

Six months later I went back to this young man's area. Before the pastor introduced me to speak, he said, "There's a young man who wants to give a testimony before Brother Norvel teaches tonight."

A young man came forward and walked up to the pulpit. He said, "Several months ago I was in the hospital dying. The doctors had told my wife there was no hope. Your speaker tonight, Mr. Norvel Hayes, was holding a meeting here in the church. Our pastor brought him to my room in intensive care. He taught my wife how to confess a verse of Scripture. She sat by my bed and confessed it, and the Holy Spirit healed me."

After he sat down, I asked his wife some questions for the benefit of the congregation concerning his healing. (I wanted to hear her answers, too. I like to hear the way God does things.) I asked her if she kept making the confession I gave her. She said, "Oh, yes, thousands of times, hours and hours, days and nights. I did exactly what you said."

That's what I call attending to God's Word and not letting it depart from your eyes. (Proverbs 4:20-22.) God warns you to do this. Keep His Word in the midst of your heart, and *then* your mouth will confess it. When you confess God's Word, it will be performed by the Holy Spirit. I asked the wife, "How long did you confess that your husband would live and not die before you saw any improvement? When I left you that day, he wasn't breathing very regularly." She said she made her confession two hours before there was any improvement in his breathing. After that, it sped up a little bit. This was a good sign, because for two days and two nights he had only been taking a breath every once in a while. The doctors wouldn't even give him any medicine. They'd say, "Don't get your hopes up. Every breath could be the last. He'll draw one last breath and then stop. And that will be it."

But she kept her confession going, all day and all night. Two days and thousands of confessions later, his breathing returned to normal. She said, "I said it until I got tired. Then, I'd rest for a minute or two and start again. I said exactly what you told me to say: 'My husband will live and not die. In Jesus' name, my husband will live and not die.'" Jesus said you can have whatever you say. The power of confession is in *saying* words. Jesus said in Mark 11:23 that you can have, that means "possess" or "own," whatever you say! The young woman said, "My husband will live and not die!"

Stick Close to the Blessings

My heart goes out to some people because I know where they are. Jesus knows where they are, too. Many people have never been taught what to do to receive from God, or that they even *can* receive from God. Many have never been taught to worship God, to take authority over the devil, or to stand on a verse of Scripture. But it's all in the Bible.

Jesus told me one day, Son, always remember this: people only believe what they have been taught! In 1 Corinthians 12:2, we read, "Ye know that ye were Gentiles, carried away unto these dumb idols, even as ye were led." *As ye were led,* not as you were forced or driven. You've got to watch whom you let lead or teach you.

My mother died from cancer at the age of thirty-seven. When I asked Jesus why, I prayed for three days before I got an answer. He told me she died because of the church she went to. I told Jesus that the church she went to loved Him. Just because you love Jesus is no sign that He's going to heal you. You have to be unashamed of Jesus and confess Him daily as your Healer. You have to make Jesus your living Healer, *if* you want Him to heal you.

I have no problems being a good businessman, because I confess Jesus over my business *all the time.* I confess this: "Jesus, You're the best businessman I've ever met. You show me how to invest my money in deals You want me to make. I'm not gullible, Jesus. I don't ever have to have another business deal the rest of my life. I'm going to take the Bible and the Holy Ghost and do what You want me to do. But, I do confess that You're the best businessman I've ever met. And anytime You want me to invest money in something, it will make a good profit at no extra effort. I want that kind of investment.

Go before me and get me good investments, ones that I don't even have to work at, because I'm too busy winning souls. Jesus, You're the best businessman I've ever met." By confessing this way, I make a lot more money than I ever did as a slave to my corporation. And as long as I keep thinking that way, that Jesus is the best businessman I ever met, He becomes that to me.

If you confess Jesus as your Healer, He becomes that to you. If you confess Him as your miracle worker, He becomes that to you. He is to you, right now, what you confess Him to be. Whatever situation you're in, it's your own fault. It isn't God's fault, my fault, your friend's fault, or even the devil's. It's yours! You've been at the wrong place at the wrong time. You'd better learn to be at the right place at the right time!

When a certain young lady started traveling with me as a singer, she said, "Now Brother Norvel, I don't want you to give me any money. I'll buy my own plane ticket." I told her, "Now, honey, I'm going to tell you something right now, if you're going to make that kind of dedication to the ministry of the Lord, the blessings of heaven will fall upon you. And if you dedicate yourself to this ministry and you stay the way you are, the blessings of heaven will fall upon you." If you don't stick close, you can't get the blessings. They won't be there. Elisha stuck close to Elijah and you see what he got—a double portion of Elijah's anointing. (2 Kings 2.) Proverbs 13:20 says, "He that walketh with wise men shall be wise: but a companion of fools shall be destroyed."

Stick Close to the Gifts of the Spirit

There are several ways a person can be healed. One way is through the gifts of the Spirit: the gifts of healing and the working of miracles, in particular. God has given these gifts to be manifested only as the

Spirit wills to the church. "Now there are diversities of gifts....But the manifestation of the Spirit is given to every man to profit withal. For to one is given by the Spirit...the gifts of healing....But all these worketh that one and the selfsame Spirit, dividing to every man severally as he wills," (1 Corinthians 12:4,7-9,11).

If you talk about and teach the gifts of the Spirit, the Holy Spirit will manifest the gifts supernaturally, because His Word has been presented. If you've never talked about the gifts of the Spirit, you won't be getting very much from heaven. You need to know that the gifts of the Spirit are the weapons of your warfare. They should be counted as the most precious things in this world to you. Without the gifts, your relationship and experience with God will remain a natural thing. It will be bound to church programs, deacons, hymns, and choir specials. You'll listen to messages preached by Dr. Confused. He's confused, because he goes by man's instructions.

You're just like me, a little human being living on the earth. Even though you have a great power living on the inside of you, you're never going to tell God anything. You aren't the boss of anything. You're to follow instructions, God's instructions. That's all you're to do. God is the boss and you'd better make Jesus the Lord of your life. You'd better make Jesus the Great Shepherd of all the churches. And you'd better follow His instructions, because if you don't, you're in trouble already. "Trouble?" you may say, "Things are going pretty good, Brother Norvel. I might not be in as much trouble as you think I am."

I'm not talking about just any kind of trouble. The kind I'm talking about is when heaven isn't coming down to your sanctuary and blessing it. Things may be going pretty good in the natural, but souls with twisted legs are coming to your sanctuary and they're leaving the same way. This isn't God's will for them. Jesus loves those precious people. He wants His power to go into them and mold them and give them a miracle. It's available to them.

If you're born again, and especially if you've been baptized in the Holy Spirit, you know it's available for them. You know Jesus wants to do it! It's not God's will that any man should perish. (2 Peter 3:9.) It's not God's will that any man should stay sick. God's will, according to 3 John 2 is this, "Beloved, I wish above all things that thou mayest prosper and be in health, even as thy soul prospereth." And according to Acts 10:38, "Jesus...went about doing good, and healing all that were oppressed of the devil; for God was with him."

I have a Southern Baptist friend down in Baton Rouge, Louisiana, who began to teach on the gifts of the Spirit. He prayed for the sick, too. He had a missionary conference of 2,500 people and invited me to come and speak. I usually go to his church about once or twice a year. It's one of my favorite places in the whole world because he's such a precious pastor.

One night, while I was speaking, some people stood up about halfway back in the large sanctuary. I said, "What's going on back there?" They said, "A crippled girl stood up!" I said, "Blessed be His holy name! Jesus likes for crippled girls to stand up. Just tell her to come up here. Come on, little darling." She came walking down the aisle. She looked like she was about fourteen years old. The fellow walking beside her looked about sixteen. The young boy walking beside her said, "This is my crippled sister. I helped her get in here. I take her everywhere. Oh, God, I helped her get in here."

The girl was crying as she walked forward, just as normal as anybody else would walk. Her brother could hardly believe it! By the time he got down front, everybody knew she used to be his crippled sister. I asked the little girl to tell the people what happened. She said, "I don't know! I was just sitting there with my brother, listening while you were teaching. All of a sudden my legs began to turn warm. After they had turned warm for a few seconds, they began to turn hot. And I felt some kind of strength come into them. I reached down and pushed myself up. I stood up. And when I did, both of my legs went completely normal!"

Blessed be God forever! This healing illustrates the gift of the working of miracles. It's a gift to the Church. You don't have to pray for it. The gifts are all free for you! All you have to do is believe, and the Holy Ghost will come and do it! You may think that the Spirit of God always manifests Himself to agree with you and your church. No. He doesn't agree with you or your church. He agrees with Matthew, Mark, Luke, and John. He agrees with the rest of the New Testament. He agrees with all of God's Word. The Holy Ghost can't stand ignorance! He hates it because it keeps Him from manifesting Himself to you.

We are told in Hosea 4:6, "My people (God's people) are destroyed for lack of knowledge…" (emphasis mine). "Don't you think, Brother Norvel that somewhere in the world, there might be a case where it's not the Lord's will to heal?" No! And neither does God! First Corinthians 12:7 says, "But the manifestation of the Spirit is given to every man to profit." It doesn't say, "Every man, except you." Every man means *you*. Jesus wants to heal *you* right away.

Stick Close to the Laying on of Hands

Another way to receive healing is through the laying on of hands. In my opinion, this is the lowest form of faith. The highest type of faith receives healing by believing God's Word on your own. The gifts of healing, which are supernatural manifestations of God, heal any affliction. They manifest when they are taught and preached. The laying on of hands is God's way to heal so that nobody is left out. And that means *you*. It's a doctrine of the Church. The last words that Jesus spoke before He went to heaven are found in the sixteenth chapter of Mark: "...they shall lay hands on the sick, and they shall recover" (v 18).

In another portion of Scripture in the book of Acts, Jesus is instructing Ananias to go lay hands on Saul of Tarsus that he might receive his sight. "And there was a certain disciple of Damascus, named Ananias; and to him said the Lord in a vision, Ananias. And he said, Behold, I am here, Lord. And the Lord said unto him, Arise, and go into the street which is called Straight, and inquire in the house of Judas for one called Saul, of Tarsus: for, behold, he prayeth, And hath seen in a vision a man named Ananias coming in and putting his hand on him, that he might receive his sight. Then Ananias answered, Lord, I have heard by many of this man, how much evil he hath done to thy saints at Jerusalem; And here he hath authority from the chief priests to bind all that call on thy name" (Acts 9:10-14).

Sometimes people make fun of healing services with the laying on of hands. They're really making fun of things Jesus told the Church to do in His name. The story continues, "But the Lord said unto him (Ananias), Go thy way: for he is a chosen vessel unto me, to bear my name before the Gentiles, and kings, and the children of Israel: For I will spew him how great things he must suffer for my name's sake. And Ananias went his way, and entered into the house; and putting his hands on him said, Brother Saul, the Lord, even Jesus, that appeared unto thee in the way as thou camest, hath sent me, that thou mightest receive thy sight, and be filled with the Holy Ghost. And immediately there fell from his eyes as it had been scales: and he received sight forthwith, and arose, and was baptized." (Acts 9:15-18). Thank God for the ministry of the laying on of hands! Blessed be the name of the Lord!

Put the Gospel First

Once while I was sitting around at my mission in Florida, the Lord told me, "This coming Easter I want you to go to Fort Lauderdale and pass out tracts to the college students. There will be thousands of students there who are lost and going to hell, and I want you to pass out tracts." I had planned to buy a new suit and go to church with my relatives on Sunday morning. Then we were going to go out to dinner and would probably sit around and talk for hours. I hadn't seen my relatives for a long time. But when God told me to go to Fort Lauderdale, Florida, on Easter and pass out tracts, I just said, "Lord, I'll go! I'm available. Glory to God!"

This may shock you, but God doesn't have any big shots. All God wants are human beings who will take orders. "Brother Norvel, if I had four Cadillac cars, eleven businesses, a live-in maid, three homes, three condominiums, and enough money to last the rest of my life, I'd be beyond passing out tracts in Florida. Do you understand that?" Yes, I understand that's the way most Christians are. And that's the reason many of them get in trouble, because they won't obey God.

I didn't say that Jesus told you to go to Florida and pass out tracts or do something else. You might not be available. Jesus usually tells you to do only things that you're available to do. You have to *make yourself available.* And you have to make yourself available *for anything.* Then Jesus will give you missions to go on to get people set free! I just love for God to give me little things to do. When I pray, I ask God to send me anywhere He wants me to go. You'd be surprised to what extremes God goes just to have me bring a blessing to someone.

But don't get under condemnation and do things just because Brother Norvel told you to. I'm not leading you; the Holy Spirit is leading you. Those who are led by the Spirit of God, they are the sons of God. (Romans 8:14.) Make yourself available to God for anything that He wants you to do and be *willing* to do it. Then God will come and deal with you personally and tell you exactly what to do. The Holy Spirit may wake you up at six o'clock in the morning and tell you to go tell people about Jesus on the city block four streets down. What will your reaction be? Will you say, "I'm not going to do it. I kind of feel like I should, but I just don't want to"? If that's your reaction, the Holy Ghost will say, "If you won't go for me, that's okay." Jesus will give you a few more chances. He'll say, "I want you to do this for Me over here. Would you go over and do this for Me?'

Would you answer, "No, I won't do that?"

I went to Fort Lauderdale and passed out tracts all week long. I thought I would be the only one there obeying God, but I found out that God has other people besides me. Jesus had sent young Christian boys and girls from all over the country to pass out tracts. Many of them recognized me and said, "Oh, Brother Norvel, what are you doing down here?" I told them I was passing out tracts, too.

They begged me to teach them. Since I was going to be there all week, I had lots of time. So I went over to the Garden Building, where they had a room that would seat a hundred people, and I spoke there at night. During those nights, the anointing of God would come upon me stronger, I believe, than ever before in my life. During the day, these Christian young people would go out on the beaches and bring in those who were strung out on dope and just about ready to go over the edge. They thought their dope was really cool stuff.

I instructed my go-getters to reach out and love those beach kids and tell them the truth. All you have to do is just preach the gospel. If you would learn this, you could get God to do a lot of things for you. Always tell people what Jesus can do for them and how much He loves them. I would say to those kids, "The Lord is the best heart surgeon there is. He's the best physician I've ever met. I'm telling you, He has the love, power, and compassion to drive out all craving for dope and make you free!" When you're teaching like that, God will come in and knock people out on the floor. You'll watch each one fall like a sack of potatoes. And that's just what happened.

I stood up there being nice and told the Holy Ghost, "Get 'em!" You might say, "Brother Norvel, you sure have an unusual way of spreading the gospel." I know it, but it works! I've never been to seminary or any Bible school; I just let the Holy Ghost tell me what to do. The Holy Ghost told me He wanted to train me, and He did. That's the reason I'm so wild, because sometimes the Holy Ghost is wild! He'll do anything to help and bless people.

Face to Face with Total Victory

I have a friend who has a good-sized business. One day he told me that one of his secretaries had cancer. He said, "She's eaten up with cancer and has been operated on twice. She's lost weight until she's just skin and bones and all of her hair has fallen out. The doctors say she's so far gone they can't help her. They sent her home to die." Then my friend asked me, "Does she have to die?" I told him, "No, God will heal her." He asked if I would minister to her. I told him, "*Sure.*" So he called her.

That night his secretary came over to his home. I took my Bible and went into the living room to talk to her. I said, "Now, honey, it's my understanding that you know your surgeons have sent you home to die. I probably wouldn't have mentioned it otherwise, unless the Lord led me."

"Yes, they've sent me home to die," she told me. "'No hope for you,' is what they said."

Now pay close attention to what I told her. One of these days, by and by, when the devil tries to destroy you, you'll need to know this. And remember, the devil always comes. Nobody is too spiritual for him to try and attack. However, the outcome of his attack will depend on what you do.

I told this secretary, "You don't have to die! Get that straight! You can live and not die! But unless you do what Jesus said to do, you will die." The doctors weren't crazy. They were telling the woman the truth. From the natural standpoint, if she left the cancer alone she would die. But, if she obeyed the instructions of the Lord, she could live. I don't care what church you go to, if you accept the doctor's diagnosis and leave cancer alone, it will kill you. I told my friend's secretary, "I'm going to teach you what Jesus says. You are born again, right?"

"Oh, yes!" she said.

"Now, I'm just an instructor—I don't have any power apart from God. But I'm going to teach you how to live."

This will work for you, too. Here's what I told her: Jesus said in Matthew 21:21 to talk to the mountain. (And that's the way you have to do things—not your way, but God's way.) Now "mountain" means problem. In her case, it was cancer. According to verse 21, first you must have faith and doubt not. Then "…if ye shall say unto this mountain, Be thou removed, and be thou cast into the sea; it shall be done." Obeying the Scripture, I said, "In the name of Jesus, I'm going to curse that cancer. In Jesus' name, I'm going to command it to stop tonight. Right where it's at, it's going to stop, now!" Notice I didn't say I was going to heal her. I said, "In Jesus' name, I claim my rights and I'm going to stop it."

The reason I can do this is because it's Bible. Jesus is the Healer, but He told us, "…Whatsoever ye shall bind on earth shall be bound in heaven…" (Matthew 18:18). *You* bind on earth, and it's done in heaven. That's why you can bind cancer and stop it in its tracks. Understand this: it's the Spirit of God who does the work. And you get Him to do the work because you claim the written Word of God, in Jesus' name. If you're dying like this woman was, how can you get the Holy Spirit to work for you?

First of all, either you (yes, you can!) or someone else, bind the disease and say, "No, you can't kill or destroy this person (or me) in Jesus' name." Remember this: when you say, "No, you can't," then the devil can't. I'm telling you, he can't! Face facts. Just like I told my friend's dying secretary: You're going to have some responsibility in getting healed or getting any mountain out of your life. This is where your *mouth* comes in and begins to work. Jesus said, "…if ye shall say unto this mountain." You're going to have to talk to it. Stop dreaming about it. Dreaming doesn't work.

Now open up your understanding to God's Word. Get *every* word. You can't listen to part of what Jesus says then do your own thing. If you'll listen to what Jesus is saying to you, you can receive whatever you want from God. Jesus doesn't stutter. His Word is plain. His words are for your benefit to give you perfect instructions on how to receive. You receive by talking to mountains. This is what Jesus said. When I first taught this sick, dying woman to confess her healing, she would confess a little weakly, "Cancer, you can't kill me." I said, "Honey, that won't work. Say it strong."

When the Apostle Paul was administering healing to the cripple at Lystra, Paul said, with a loud voice, "…Stand upright on thy feet…" (Acts 14:10). You may have to walk the floor every day, saying loudly, "In Jesus' name, cancer (or whatever other mountain there is in your life), you'll never kill me. I'm talking to you, and I'm telling you now, get out of my body, my life. Disappear now! Get totally out! You'll have no part of me because Jesus is my Healer." Remember you have to *confess* Jesus as your Healer. And don't let the devil talk you out of it! Always confess it *boldly,* and He will become your Healer.

That's what Jesus always does—every day of your life—Jesus becomes to you what you say He is. He's the Alpha and the Omega, the beginning and the end. (Revelation 1:8.) He's like that from the beginning until you draw your last breath. *If* you will confess Him as victory in your life, He becomes that to you. Jesus is your Savior. He's your Healer. He's your miracle worker, your surgeon, your love-giver. He's everything good to you. He's the beginning and the end of your life. He's paid the price for everything you ought to receive. Understand that He becomes everything to you that you confess and believe the moment you say it! Keep this in your heart. Jesus watches your faith.

Remember what Jesus said: "…If ye have faith, and doubt not… if ye say unto this mountain, Be thou removed…it shall be done" (Matthew 21:21). It *shall* be done all the time. I worked and taught the secretary all these things that I've written here. Like a broken record, I went over it again and again. I had to make sure she got it. I told her, "I'm not going to let you die, honey. You're too willing to die, and there's no use in it. So just give me your hand, and let's walk and confess."

We confessed and confessed. I made her promise me that she would do what Jesus said. I warned her, "If you don't do what Jesus said, you're going to die. Do you understand?" She said, "I understand." And she confessed and confessed. *She lived!* The Lord created meat on those long, bony arms! God manifested cancer-curing power in her, and she lived! Later the lady testified at one of my meetings. After I told the congregation basically what had happened, she came forward. The congregation went wild with rejoicing.

A totally healed woman walked on stage. Her body, that had been skin and bones, now had meat on it. Her bald head was now full of hair. A human being that had been beaten down by the devil and given up to die was alive! This woman is a testimony to the glory of God! She said that she followed what I taught her. Every day, almost twenty-four hours a day, over and over, she told cancer it would be uprooted and removed to the very seed according to what Mark 11:23 says.

She read the Gospels again and again. She wrote down all the Scriptures that pertained to healing. She clung to God's Word confessing that it was sure and that it would stand forever. (Isaiah 40:8.) All this time, she was a mess. And the devil would hound her all the time, saying, "You're a dying lady, scrawny and bald." But do you know what she told him? "Devil, Jesus has come to give me life and life more abundantly according to John 10:10. According to 1 Peter 2:24, Jesus took my infirmities and bore my diseases!"

You can live and not die! The Lord, the Holy Ghost, will manifest what you say. Confess Jesus as your Healer *every day*. Confess that disease can't kill you. Every day walk the floor confessing victory and that the Holy Spirit will begin manifesting Himself. He has all kinds of power and all kinds of personalities. Whatever power you need to overcome your mountain, He will deliver that to you.

Devils hate me because I won't let them snuff people's lives out. I take Jesus and the Word of God and rescue them. A lot of times when I'm ministering to people, the devils rear up. They scream, they fall on the floor, and often they look at me and say, *"I hate you."* Things like that happen all the time. It's like drinking a glass of water. After a while, you don't pay any attention to it. A well-known minister's son asked his dad once, "Daddy, Brother Norvel and I were at a meeting in Illinois when suddenly a young fellow rose up and began to scream. That's happened before, too. People would rise up, scream, and throw a fit. Why does that happen in his meetings?"

His dad told him I was a threat to the devils in those people. The devils know it, and it makes them nervous. If you're dying from some disease right now, the spirit that caused you to get that way is a nervous wreck because you're reading this book! Do you know why? *You're about to come face to face with total victory!* Glory be to God forevermore!

Jesus Wants to Heal You Now

Jesus loves you and wants to heal you *now*. But more important to Jesus than your healing is the condition of your soul. This must come first. "For what shall it profit a man, if he shall gain the whole world, and lose his own soul?" (Mark 8:36). "…for it is profitable for thee that one of thy members should perish, and not that thy whole body should be cast into hell" (Matthew 5:30). The fact of the matter is that Jesus wants your members (body) to be whole *and* for you to go to heaven, too. But, you must be born again. (John 3:5.) Your soul comes first and your healing is second. John says it like this: "Beloved, I wish above all things that thou mayest prosper and be in health, even as thy soul prospereth" (3 John 2).

Be in health *even as thy soul prospereth!* The Psalmist David made reference to the Lord first as the One "who forgiveth all thine iniquities," then as the One "who healeth all thy diseases" (Psalm 103:3). Isaiah said of Jesus, "But he was wounded for our transgressions, he was bruised for our iniquities, the chastisement of our peace was upon him; and with his stripes we are healed" (Isaiah 53:5). If you don't know Jesus as the One who has washed your sins away and made you a new creature, then come to know Him today. (2 Corinthians 5:17.) Right now! "…if thou shalt confess with thy mouth the Lord Jesus, and shalt believe in thine heart that God hath raised him from the dead, thou shalt be saved" (Romans 10:9).

Pray this prayer: "Jesus, I ask You into my heart as Lord and Savior of my life. Thank You for forgiving me of all my sins. I'm a new creature in You on the authority of Your Word. You're faithful to do what You said You would do if I would come to You and ask. Thank You, Jesus!" Now that you're a child of God, if you need healing, you can come to the Father in Jesus' name and claim your healing. *You* can live and not die! *You* can talk to mountains. *You* can live a completely victorious life in Christ Jesus!

PART FOUR

Norvel's Present-Day Ministry

Chapter 13

Present-Day Ministry

God's Explanation to Me About My Mother's Death

After I got into the business world, I was very successful and my business grew. At the end of the month I liked to see credits instead of debits on my profit and loss statement. The same thing applies to the spiritual realm. I couldn't find any place in the New Testament where God put diseases on His children. If I hired an employee and he was a good one, I promoted him. God does the same thing with His children. If we stay in line with His Word, we'll enjoy the benefits thereof.

So as I was seeking the Lord in prayer for some answers about my mother's death. I said,

> *Jesus, I don't want to pray wrong, so if I'm out of line, forgive me. Being a businessman who likes credits instead of debits, it really makes no sense to me why You killed my mother. To You, one soul was worth more than the whole world, and my mother was winning souls for the kingdom. But You killed her when she was only thirty-seven. If You had let her live to sixty-five or seventy-five, she would have won a lot more souls.*

I don't want You to get angry with me, Jesus; but it doesn't make sense to me why You took my mother and brother. I just don't understand. Please tell me why You did it.

On my third day of prayer, the Lord began talking to me about it. Very plainly, God said, "Son, I didn't kill your mother; I didn't have anything to do with it."

That statement was a shock to me. "Well, if You didn't have anything to do with my mother's death, then why did You let her die? She didn't want to die. She loved You; she was a Christian."

The Lord said this: "I tell you in My Word that death is My enemy. I don't go around putting sicknesses and diseases in people's bodies; the devil does that. I didn't put those tumors in your mother's body; the devil attacked her. Those tumors killed her, but they didn't come from heaven. There's no sickness here to be given out.

"I tell you in My Word that all good things come down from heaven. Your mother could not receive divine healing for her body because she didn't know how to receive it. Remember, Son, people can't believe something they haven't been taught."

"That's right, Lord. People can't believe something they haven't been taught."

Jesus told me why my mother wasn't healed. It was because of where she went to church. He said, "Your mother could not receive My divine healing power because her church did not teach the people how to receive their healing. People only receive what they are taught how to receive."

My mother didn't know how to receive God's healing power for her body. She had never been taught how to receive it. She had never been taught to obey the healing verses in the New Testament.

Those promises don't work automatically; they come through faith in God's Word. God *is* the Word, God *was* the Word, and God will *always* be the Word. God and His Word are the same.

In God's Word we find out that Jesus—the Word made flesh—is the indisputable Victor: "And having spoiled principalities and powers, he made a shew of them openly, triumphing over them in it" (Colossians 2:15). "Death is swallowed up in victory" (1 Corinthians 15:54.) To believers, He said: "Because I live, ye shall live also" (John 14:19); and, "Behold, I give unto you power to tread on serpents and scorpions, and over all the power of the enemy: and nothing shall by any means hurt you" (Luke 10:19). "All the power of the enemy" includes power over sickness and disease, over sin and over the enemy of our soul—the devil. This authority has been given to *every* believer, without reservation.

Hosea 4:6 says: "My people are destroyed for lack of knowledge." God didn't put this Scripture in this chapter for just a few people. This verse means that for the lack of knowledge of what God's Word actually and literally says, people are destroyed. If people don't have the knowledge that it is God's will to heal them (through going to a church that teaches the Bible or through reading and studying God's Word themselves), the devil can kill them with sickness and disease. God wants us to be informed so that we can live an abundant life!

I had told Jesus that the church my mother went to loved Him. But just because you love Jesus is no sign that He's going to heal you. You have to be unashamed of Jesus and confess Him daily as your Healer. You have to make Jesus your living Healer, if you want Him to heal you. Whatever situation you're in, it's your own fault. It isn't God's fault, my fault, your friend's fault, or even the devil's. *It's yours!* You've been at the wrong place at the wrong time. You'd better learn to be at the right place at the right time—and with the right people, including the right church!

You have to stick close to where the blessings of God are. If you don't stick close, you can't get the blessings. They won't be there. Elisha stuck close to Elijah; and you see what he got—a double portion of Elijah's anointing. (2 Kings 2.) Proverbs 13:20 says, "He that walketh with wise men shall be wise: but a companion of fools shall be destroyed."

The kind of religious training I had received growing up hadn't left me with much sense. However, God let me know that He had some. I still don't claim to have much sense. But God, the One who lives on the inside of me, knows how to do everything. He knows exactly how to save precious souls and heal crippled legs. He knows how to give you a new body. I don't know how. I'm not that smart. But Jesus is. All it takes is the Word of God, and Jesus is the Word. (John 1:14.) Stick close to ministries that aren't ashamed of all that Jesus teaches and represents. If you do, you'll be blessed.

Conclusion

orvel Hayes is a successful businessman, Bible-school founder, and Bible teacher. Always bold, always simple, not bound by precedent, and sometimes, for the religiously-possessed, peculiar, strange, and even outlandish, Norvel has stripped people of their illusions, that they need experts to explain and interpret the Bible. He has made sense of God's Word to the people. When he gets through speaking, nothing fuzzy remains. The enigmatic and illusive have vanished away. He says, "As long as you wonder, it won't work. God hasn't called you to a life of wondering—including wondering prayers—wondering if He will do this and wondering if He will do that."

Norvel Hayes' original, novel, relevant, starkly honest, non-religious, and fresh approach to sharing the gospel has been infectious among the hundreds and hundreds of Bible school students who have passed through New Life Bible College since 1977, and among the thousands upon thousands who have sat under his ministry in seminars and conferences across the nation and even overseas. Imitated...*yes*; but duplicated...*no!* Only Norvel Hayes has been dubbed as "God's Boot Camp Commander"— *and rightfully so.*

Norvel Hayes, through four decades of ministry, has been and continues to be faithful. Multitudes of others, who had no real understanding of what praise and worship were about, have become worshippers of God as Norvel has instructed, demonstrated, and modeled putting first things first. He has taught others, and even more — *he has trained them to do the work of the ministry.*

He has been God's Boot Camp Commander. He has been a forward-thrusting tackler of the less glamorous aspects of the ministry — turning meek, shy, quiet Christians into bold, confident, unashamed, highly-motivated, disciplined, and basically trained soldiers for God.

He is especially recognized for his role in dealing with the Enemy, including casting out devils, for training the body of Christ to do the same.

He has gotten people to listen, to *really* listen, to the message of the Bible. He has also gotten them to read the Bible. Norvel emphatically states, "God will confirm your words, as long as they're lined up with the Word of God, with signs following—just as much as He will for any big-time preacher.

"There are many different versions and opinions about God; and, more often than not, people just believe what they want to believe. The reason the Christian world is so weak and half-flaky is because they think they know something when they don't. You have to watch yourself in the work of the Lord , so that you try not to have your own thing. I don't care how powerful you get, you can't have your own thing. You have to have God's thing going. And God's thing is Jesus—just like you find Him in Matthew, Mark, Luke, and John.

"God doesn't go by what you think. And God doesn't go by what your church thinks—if it's unscriptural. Churches will give you tradition. But tradition has never saved anyone. In fact, it has kept many people out of the kingdom of God. You need to check up on what your family, friends, and church believe. Some or most of them may be far out. Your friends may not be half as smart as you think they are. Believing that 'the gospel is for some people'— is the dumbest thing I've ever heard a human say! I'd tell the Pope the same thing. Some people have an image of Jesus being like their church service. Realize this: Jesus doesn't go by church services! The services of every church in America are supposed to go by Him. Jesus is the Head of the Church. We're supposed to listen to Jesus and not try to change Him. He has never changed, and He's not going to change."

Norvel Hayes—the man, the ministry, the style—has been a welcomed pill to the Body of Christ. Norvel asserts that the devil loves to beat up on sweet, nice Christians who have their own version of the gospel. The devil does not listen to weak Christians. He beats them to the ground in spite of the authority Jesus has given them. Having authority and exercising it are two different things. "But, Brother Norvel," someone may say, "I go to church." Rats and mice go to church, too!

The apostle Paul states, "For I am not ashamed of the gospel of Christ" (Romans 1:16). The Norvel Hayes' rendition of this verse is: "You are responsible to God, not to men. Do not apologize for the Word!" These words of Norvel Hayes' haven't been cheap, but have been unmistakably backed up by both his life and ministry.

Epilogue by Zona Hayes-Morrow

I have always considered my father one of God's generals because he has always spoken the uncompromised Word of God, but he didn't start out that way. He was just a normal man who worked hard. He never had above an elementary school education. He was raised by a godly mother who died at a young age. He started working when he was young, picking cotton. He didn't have a fancy upbringing or education. He just used what he had and worked hard at everything he did in order to be successful. And he became very successful in business.

He was married to a beautiful woman, they were part of society, lived in a nice house in Indianapolis and everything seemed to be perfect. The only thing missing was God. After God got a hold of my father, our life was never the same. He knew that his priorities would have to change. He wanted my mother to change with him, but she was more concerned with social status than following God so she chose to leave. She left when I was 8 ½ years old and I never saw her again after I was 10 years old.

It seems like it has always been me and my dad and that's it. I was with my dad before he totally sold out to God. I've seen and been through the natural things that children go through and the frustrations that he would go through when I lived with my aunts. He was so hurt when my mother left, so he buried himself in his businesses because he was so hurt. He was 100% sold out to his business and he traveled quite a bit because that was all he knew. He thought his life had stopped. He knew that God had more for him but he didn't know where to start. So I lived with my aunt for several years. He would come over there at night when he was in town. At one time he owned seven restaurants, the Atlanta Auto Auction, the Yellow Cab Company in town and Varsity Engravers which was a manufacturing company that manufactured invitations, stationary and various other items for fraternities and sororities in major colleges all around the United States. He had 42 salesmen and he was a very busy man. Then he met a pastor by the name of Brother Littlefield and everything changed.

My dad finally found the first steps to stepping into the ministry that God had for him. We began attending Brother Littlefield's church and this was where we were first introduced to the Holy Spirit with the evidence of speaking in tongues as well as feeding the poor. I received the baptism of the Holy Spirit first and my dad's family thought my dad had lost all of his good sense and had joined a cult. He became introduced to ministers like Kenneth Hagin, Lester Sumrall, John Osteen, and Phineas Dake. But he stuck with it and learned anything and everything that he could. And he was able to get a strong foundation in the Word of God.

I have watched Dad all of my life and he is like a living example of Jesus and has influenced my life so much. My dad has always been a good moral man. He's never drank and I've never heard him use a swear word…not even when he was angry. My father has never told me a lie and he has always been there for me. My dad, as well as my two aunts and my two uncles, were always an example to me. Every night when we would stay with my aunt, if my dad was there I would lay his pajamas out and then I would open the Bible up and lay it on the bed. I didn't know that I was laying the Bible out for my dad to study and read it. I didn't know that he was going to be a world-renowned teacher, but I would open the Word for him to read. God was just putting the Word inside of him.

My dad tells the story of wanting to be really spiritual and he was going to read two chapters in the Bible every day. He would be tired often when he would get in so he would read two chapters really fast. Then one night God literally shook him in his bed. God said, "Son, it's better to read two verses and know what's in them and study and meditate on them rather than read two chapters really fast and not get anything out of them."

My dad has always been there for me, even when I said one time after I backslid that I would never serve the Lord again. But the Lord used two very renowned people that were in Brother Hagin's life, Brother & Sister Goodwin. God used them to reach my dad and show him how to stand in the gap for me. You need to understand that at that time in my life, I didn't think that anyone loved me and my dad was losing patience with me. He would scream and holler at me and he would tell me what a disgrace I was, but he didn't know any other way to react than that. Because I was a disgrace to the family…I was backslidden.

Then the Lord said to my dad through Brother & Sister Goodwin, "The thing that you want most in the world will never happen. Zona has gone too far out into darkness. She'll never come back on her own. When she comes in at 3 or 4 o'clock in the morning, you tell her that you love her and you tell her that I love her, then you need to shut up and not say anything else because she doesn't believe anybody loves her."

My dad did that for six months. Every night when I came home, he would call me into his room. He would say, "Little Zona, come here." I would march into his room and smart off. He would say, "Jesus loves you and I love you."

I would say, "Is that all?" And he would have to bite his tongue to keep from saying anything else, but he did it. Then about the sixth month, I was getting ready to go out and I called him in to the living room and I asked him to sit down that I wanted to talk to him. I said, "Dad, I know that you love me. And those people that I run with, they don't love me. They don't even love themselves, how could they love me? But I know that you love me and I don't really want to go with them tonight."

My dad said, "Oh little Zona, you don't have to go with them. You can stay here with me. We'll pop popcorn and we'll watch TV or do something together." About that time, the car horn beeped. I told him, "They're here. I've got to go. I love you Daddy."

He said me, "I love you, little Zona. What is God going to have to do to bring you back to him?"

I told him, "Well He's going to have to knock me in the head because I'm not going back to Him." As soon as I left and pulled out of the driveway, he put his hand out toward me as I was going down the street with the people that I ran with. He said, "Devil, you can't have my daughter. I bind you off of my daughter in Jesus' name. In Jesus' name I see my daughter saved and going to church with me." My dad walked in the house and went to the guest bedroom and laid his hands on the bed and said "God, you heard her. Shake her up. Do whatever you have to do, just shake her up." My dad got on the floor and he paid the price.

He paid the price every day by praying for me. If my dad had not paid the price by praying for me, then I never would have come back to the Lord. I had already made my mind up. I would have rather gone to hell than be around all of the two-faced Christians I had met that had used my dad for his money or because of his influence. Other ministers would try to use his influence in an attempt to get their ministry built. I saw it all. But my dad kept a calm spirit with those people and he just loved people. No matter what they did to him, he loved them. He may not have anything to do with them but he loved them.

About three o'clock in the morning, I came in and I laid down on the guest bedroom bed and went to sleep. About five o'clock in the morning, I turned over and as I opened my eyes, there was a belt-buckle staring me in the face. There was a man sitting on the floor of the guest room. He got up then he stood there and looked at me. I'm telling you that it scared me so bad! He walked out of the room and down the hall. I got up out of the bed and walked down the hall to the back door. I turned the corner and he was standing there waiting for me. He turned back towards the door and he walked right through the wall.

I ran back to my dad's room and started knocking on his door. He was getting ready to go out of town. I asked him, "What am I supposed to do? I can't stay here in the house!"

He said, "Well you'll have to go down to the motel." That was back when he had a motel near downtown. It's now our lodge where the students stay.

I said, "Well I can't stay by myself. I don't know what that was!"

He said, "That was your angel."

I said, "I don't want him, he's too big."

He said, "It takes a big one for you, you're so flaky." But it shook me up. It wasn't long until I stopped running with those people.

I consider it an honor to be Brother Norvel's daughter, but I didn't always feel this way. A lot of my mistakes were in his books and he has used them in his sermons. I always tell him that he built his ministry on all of my mistakes. Life with my dad was certainly not like the average American family and it still isn't. We didn't go on vacations. He wasn't always in town for holidays like Thanksgiving and Christmas or even birthdays. But it isn't all about celebrating Thanksgiving, Christmas and birthdays…it's all about souls. And that's what I learned. My life was not normal but then of course, Brother Norvel is not normal.

Brother Hagin would say that about my dad. He always said, "There's nothing normal about Norvel Hayes." I often listen to my dad discuss things that would happen in his services. God would guide him in supernatural ways. He totally lived by faith in his businesses, as well as in his personal life. I was very jealous of the ministry and of his businesses for a while. But when I grew up, I saw that he had to pay the price to live a life of celibacy for over thirty years.

Even though I never did understand why my mother left and why I never had a relationship with her, God in His infinite wisdom sent us a wonderful woman named Margarita (Maggie) Garza. I always say that she loved me first before she loved my dad. She has been nothing but a blessing in this family. She takes care of my dad every single day. My father is 84 years old now and I don't know what we would do in this family without Maggie. My dad is her first ministry and it shows. She has a lot of character and integrity. My dad was single for so many years and he is asked all the time, "How is Zona accepting your marriage with Maggie?" Well it was all my idea. My dad called me and he said, "What do you think about me marrying Maggie?"

I said, "I think you need to do it today!" So I planned their wedding from a dialysis chair in the latter part of 1996 and they got married in January of 1997. It is as though she is my mother and I love her with all of my heart, and my father loves her with all of his heart. But my dad was faithful to God and didn't marry again until God brought him the right one.

My dad takes the Word of God very seriously and the Lord has really used my father to help thousands and thousands of people. He has taught people to walk by faith. He has taught prayer and true worship. There are so many people who have accepted Jesus through my dad's ministry. So many people have learned to walk by faith. So many people have learned prosperity the Bible way. So many people have learned to worship God. So many people have learned that confession brings possession. So many people have learned how to cast out devils. So many have learned how to make the devil leave them alone. His books and tapes have been translated in many different languages and spread all over the world. They bring truth because they teach and preach the uncompromised Word of God. He teaches the truth of Jesus and those truths will never change. These truths can transform people in their hearts and in their minds and in their whole body. There are so many people who have my father's books especially, *How to Live and Not Die*. Thousands of people with cancer and other diseases of all kinds have been healed through the teaching in that book. But you have to follow it to the "T", you can't just read it one time.

My dad not only teaches faith, but he's trained me and I follow in his footsteps. I know that God has a ministry for me. I know that God has used me in my own ministry, but I want to be as pure in my spirit as my father is. He has such a pure heart. He doesn't have any hidden agendas. He's not in this for money, fame or fortune.

There's one thing I have learned from my dad that I will need as I carry on this ministry, it is to have a humble heart and be a servant. That's why God dealt with us to have a soup kitchen where we serve a hot meal every day…seven days a week. My dad has always told me not to forget the little churches. He said, "When I go to heaven, you can go speak to the big churches but don't forget to go to the little churches…the ones with only 20 or 30 people in them. You might have 50 people or you might have 500 people but don't forget the little churches."

Norvel Hayes Ministries is grounded and rooted in the Word and it will be carried on. New Life Bible Church is in Cleveland, Tennessee and I am the senior pastor of the church and the administrator of Norvel Hayes Ministries. We will continue the legacy of faith and giving that my dad established in these ministries.

My dad doesn't come in the office very much now because he's older and he's due a rest, but he still teaches the Word of God on the weekends and he comes to teach in the Bible College and church anytime that he can. Anytime my father can teach the Word of God, he does. The effectiveness of this ministry is enduring because of the values that we have, the truth that we share and the uncompromising faith that my father lives and we live. We are rooted and grounded in winning souls, feeding the poor, saving little babies in our unwed mother's home, and training Bible College students.

How do I carry on the legacy of this ministry and of a man whose shoes cannot be filled? I'm going to be like Joel Osteen, I'm going to get my dad's shoes and I'm going to stand in them behind the pulpit when my father goes to heaven. I love the Lord and I am blood of my dad's blood and bone of his bone. I believe with all my heart that the Lord has given me the same spirit and the Lord is alive in me and I want to teach people how to walk by faith. I want to teach people to feed the poor. I want to teach people how to worship God and how to cast out devils. I'll continue to allow Jesus' love and life to be expressed to people through me. I'm committed just like my father told me, "Zona, stay committed. It's not your ministry and it's not your church, it's God's church."

My father was a simple and real man who taught a simple and uncompromising Gospel. He always believed and taught that it isn't about who does or doesn't lay hands on you, it's about getting ahold of God for yourself and believing Him with all that you have. You have the same Bible…you serve the same God…so let's take Him at His Word and do something about it!

PRAYER OF SALVATION

God loves you—no matter who you are, no matter what your past. God loves you so much that He gave His one and only begotten Son for you. The Bible tells us that "...whoever believes in him shall not perish but have eternal life" (John 3:16 NIV). Jesus laid down His life and rose again so that we could spend eternity with Him in heaven and experience His absolute best on earth. If you would like to receive Jesus into your life, say the following prayer out loud and mean it from your heart.

Heavenly Father, I come to You admitting that I am a sinner. Right now, I choose to turn away from sin, and I ask You to cleanse me of all unrighteousness. I believe that Your Son, Jesus, died on the cross to take away my sins. I also believe that He rose again from the dead so that I might be forgiven of my sins and made righteous through faith in Him. I call upon the name of Jesus Christ to be the Savior and Lord of my life. Jesus, I choose to follow You and ask that You fill me with the power of the Holy Spirit. I declare that right now I am a child of God. I am free from sin and full of the right-eousness of God. I am saved in Jesus' name. Amen.

If you prayed this prayer to receive Jesus Christ as your Savior for the first time, please contact us on the Web at **www.harrisonhouse.com** to receive a free book.

Or you may write to us at
Harrison House • P.O. Box 35035 • Tulsa, Oklahoma 74153

A landmark biographical collection that highlights the founding leaders of the Word of Faith and Charismatic movements.

Legacy of Faith

collection

T.L. OSBORN

PIONEER OF MASS MIRACLE EVANGELISM

$22.99 Hardback
336 Pages
ISBN: 978-1-60683-029-1

The Legacy of Faith Collection is a biographical collection that highlights the founding fathers of the Word of Faith and Charismatic movements. Each volume includes a summary of the most notable teachings and signature messages from each of these ministers and underscores the contribution of each to the modern day movement. This volume includes the ongoing legacy, teachings and extraordinary life of T.L. Osborn, the "Pioneer of Mass Miracle Evangelism." It includes candid interviews, stories, teachings and photographs that document the miracles and ministry of this world renowned author and evangelist as he has traveled to the farthest corners of the world to share the Gospel of Christ to all that would hear.

To Order, Call (800) 888-4126
or Visit www.HarrisonHouse.com

Harrison House

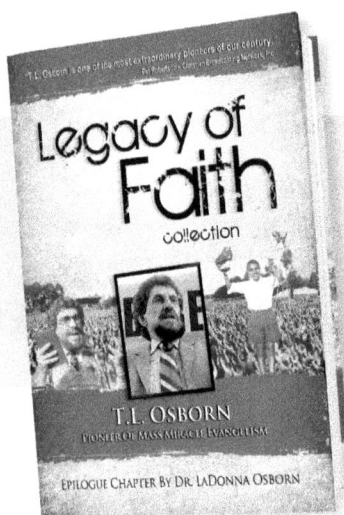

A landmark biographical collection that highlights the founding leaders of the Word of Faith and Charismatic movements.

Legacy of Faith

collection

MARILYN HICKEY

TRAILBLAZER OF WORLDWIDE MISSIONS

$22.99 Hardback
368 Pages
ISBN: 978-1-60683-028-4

The Legacy of Faith Collection is a biographical collection that highlights the founding leaders of the Word of Faith and Charismatic movements. Each volume includes a summary of the most notable teachings and signature messages from each of these ministers and underscores the contribution of each to the modern day movement. This volume includes the ongoing legacy, teachings and impact that Marilyn Hickey has had on the body of Christ. Known for her insightful teaching and worldwide missions emphasis, Marilyn Hickey has reached millions of people through radio, print, television and through her travels internationally.

To Order, Call (800) 888-4126
or Visit www.HarrisonHouse.com

Harrison House

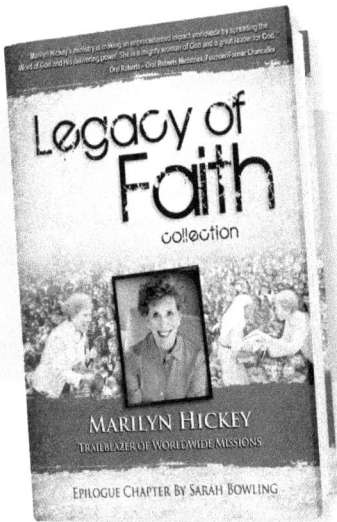

Fast. Easy. Convenient.

harrisonhouse.com

For the latest Harrison House product information and author news, look no further than your computer. All the details on our powerful, life-changing products are just a click away. New releases, E-mail subscriptions, testimonies, monthly specials—find it all in one place. Visit harrisonhouse.com today!

harrisonhouse

The Harrison House Vision

Proclaiming the truth and the power

Of the Gospel of Jesus Christ

With excellence;

Challenging Christians to

Live victoriously,

Grow spiritually,

Know God intimately.

www.ingramcontent.com/pod-product-compliance
Lightning Source LLC
Chambersburg PA
CBHW062151080426
42734CB00010B/1641